W9-BSI-591

The People Look at
EDUCATIONAL TELEVISION

The People Look at
EDUCATIONA

A REPORT OF NINE REPRESENTATIVE ETV STATIO

GREENWOOD PRESS, PUBLISHERS
WESTPORT, CONNECTICUT

TELEVISION

Wilbur Schramm, Jack Lyle, and Ithiel de Sola Pool

TH ASSISTANCE, DURING THE FIELD STUDY, FROM BARBARA ADLER,
WARD ROWLAND, MERRILL SAMUELSON, HOWARD MARTIN,
ARTHUR CULLMAN, AND GRAYDON AUSMUS

Library of Congress Cataloging in Publication Data

Schramm, Wilbur Lang, 1907-
The people look at educational television.

Reprint of the ed. published by Stanford University Press, Stanford.
Bibliography: p.
Includes index.
1. Television in education. I. Lyle, Jack, joint author. II. Pool, Ithiel de Sola, 1917- joint author. III. Title.
[LB1044.7.S28 1977] 371.33'58 77-1923
ISBN 0-8371-9507-1

Originally published in 1963 by Stanford University Press, Stanford, California

Reprinted with the permission of Stanford University Press

Reprinted in 1977 by Greenwood Press, Inc.

Library of Congress Catalog Card Number 77-1923

ISBN 0-8371-9507-1

Printed in the United States of America

Acknowledgment

The more than 30,000 interviews and the extensive analysis reported in this book were made possible by research support from the United States Office of Education, under the National Defense Education Act. A grant was made directly to the Center for International Studies, Massachusetts Institute of Technology, and a contract was made with the National Educational Television and Radio Center, which asked the Institute for Communication Research, at Stanford University, to carry out the research for them. NETRC, however, has been more than a middleman in this activity: it has been an adviser, when asked, and has made available a great deal of useful material; nevertheless, it has made no effort to impose its viewpoint or its interests on the interpretation of the research results. To the officials of the Educational Media Branch of the Office of Education, to the chief officers of NETRC, to the staffs of each of the nine ETV stations we studied, to the M.I.T. Computation Center, to the Western Data Processing Center of the University of California at Los Angeles, to the scholars named on the title page who were our field supervisors, and to the several hundred persons who, as interviewers, research assistants, and clerical assistants, participated in this research, we express a deep sense of gratitude.

WILBUR SCHRAMM
JACK LYLE
ITHIEL DE SOLA POOL

Contents

1 Educational Television—What It Is 1
2 Measuring the Audiences of ETV 18
3 The Nine Stations and Their Programs 31
4 How Big Is the Audience? 46
5 Who Is in the Audience? 59
6 What Programs Do They View? 91
7 Why Do They View? 110
8 What They Think of ETV 134
9 The Potential Audience of Educational Television 151
10 The Significance of These Results 164
Appendixes
A. Noncommercial Television Stations, March 1963 177
B. The Interview Samples 180
C. Tables from the Stanford Studies 182
D. Tables from the Boston Study 196
Bibliography 205
Index 207

The People Look at

EDUCATIONAL TELEVISION

I

Educational Television—What It Is

Educational television is something of a paradox. Part of the greatest sales medium ever developed, it sells nothing. Part of a medium with unequaled ability to attract people to it, it programs for minority audiences. Part of a highly expensive medium which needs the support of more than a billion dollars of advertising money annually, it gets no advertising support and exists on Spartan budgets and a rickety financial structure of gifts and school money. Part of a great entertainment medium, it invites its audience to come not for entertainment, but rather for work. It invites them, not to relax, but rather to stretch their minds in order to capture new ideas and information.

Part of the paradox is in the nature of television itself, which is not only a great entertainment device, but also a great educational medium. Some of the people who first experimented with it were educators.[1] But it was the entertainment side that drew audiences and support. There were already 200 commercial stations, supported by advertising, and specializing in entertainment, before the first noncommercial educational station went on the air. The fact that it went on the air at all was a tribute to the farsightedness and toughness of a small group of educators who resolved that the teaching qualities of television should not be lost sight of in the great success of its entertainment qualities. They rallied educational interest and public support, got some channels re-

[1] Experimental telecasts were made at the University of Iowa as early as 1932.

served, raised money here and there, and slowly, haltingly, with all the mistakes of beginners, idealists, and inadequately financed operators, got the sound and sight of education on the air.

In this book we shall call it educational television, but what we are really talking about is *noncommercial* educational television. There is some magnificent educational material on commercial stations, although it bulks small in their total offerings. A national political convention is an educational experience as well as an absorbing, entertaining spectacle. The Kennedy-Nixon debates on the commercial networks had educational as well as persuasive effects. The best of the documentary programs and press conferences on commercial television stretch their viewers' minds. An occasional fine music or dramatic program on commercial television is presented with skill and talent hardly equaled elsewhere. All these are educational television. And some commercial stations even broadcast formal education; for example, the "Continental Classroom," broadcast on a network, for several years was able to get half a million listeners out of bed at 6:00 A.M. to hear lectures on mathematics, physics, chemistry, and political science. No informed person would ever imply that there is no education in commercial television, but merely that it is a very small part of commercial television, and usually buried in the hours when few people are listening (like the 6:00 A.M. lectures, or the Sunday afternoon press conferences). In this book, however, we are concerning ourselves not with this small segment of commercial television, but with the stations which are devoted *wholly* to educational purposes, which are not permitted to accept advertising or operate commercially, and which are licensed to nonprofit educational or civic organizations in order to serve the educational needs of their communities.

Ten years ago there was no such station. The first noncommercial educational station went on the air May 12, 1953. At the time of the research described in the following pages, there were 56 educational stations. As we write, there are 63 (see Appendix A). By the time this is published—so fast are the stations growing —there will be more than 75. Approximately one out of every ten stations in the United States is a noncommercial educational station, and the proportion is growing.

How ETV came to be

It is worth recalling how this movement started. Educational institutions and educators had used radio and films for a long time before television arrived. Nearly 200 schools, colleges, and universities had constructed radio stations in the 1920's. The University of Wisconsin had built and put on the air, beginning in 1917, one of the half-dozen stations that hold some claim to be called the "first" regularly programed voice radio station in America—station 9XM, later relicensed as WHA. The year 1929 was not kind to these educational radio stations, but 35 of them still stood, even after that storm. Most of these were maintained by the land-grant colleges and universities, and were used to help fulfill the obligation of these institutions to agricultural extension and off-campus education. The number of educational radio stations grew slowly through the 1930's and 1940's. As television came nearer to reality, there was much talk about the possibility of being able to transmit the kind of educational experience offered by a talking film over the kind of carrier wave provided by radio. The Iowa State College (now Iowa State University) actually built and licensed a television station, supported by commercial advertising but offering a large amount of educational material along with selected programs from the networks.[2]

That was the situation in September 1948 when the Federal Communications Commission imposed a "freeze" on all further television construction permits. At that time there were 108 television stations on the air in the United States, of which only one (the Iowa State station) was licensed to an educational institution. There were no noncommercial television stations. But already there was a new stampede into TV. The Federal Communications Commission was swamped by applications for channels and construction permits. The signals of existing stations were beginning to interfere with each other. It was perfectly clear that 500 or

[2] For a more complete account of the early history of educational television by one of the pioneers in the movement, see the chapter by Richard B. Hull, "A Note on the History Behind ETV," in *Educational Television*, pp. 334–45. As this is written, a new book on the history of ETV has just become available, *Channels of Learning*, by John W. Powell.

more television stations were going to be built in the United States, and if channels were not allocated in such a way as to avoid interference, no viewer would be able to get anything except distorted pictures and fading sound. Furthermore, if applications were granted without reference to location, some parts of the country would be oversupplied with television and other parts would not be served at all. The pattern became all the more difficult to design because it had to be made, so far as possible, to include the competitive U.S. networks, rather than the single services which were being supplied to most of the other countries in the world. There wcrc simply not enough channels available to provide very-high-frequency channels in every community for every network. Therefore, the networks proposed different plans designed to serve their respective competitive positions as well as possible. Overstuffed with applications, undersupplied with channels, the FCC had a monumental headache, and suspended all further station permits while it pondered how to allocate the air space it controlled.

During this period, of course, the Commission received advice and persuasion from all sides. Amidst these powerful voices, the voice of education was, by comparison, at first a mere whisper. One of the first prominent people to speak out in favor of channels for education was Frieda Hennock, who had recently become one of the FCC Commissioners. Through the succeeding developments she was education's friend at court, a rather unpopular position in view of the strong pressures to cut the pie entirely for commercial consumption. This may perhaps have had something to do with the fact that Miss Hennock was not reappointed to the Commission when her term expired. It was her friendly interest, more than anything else, that encouraged educators and civic organizations to act.

A group representing educational institutions and organizations filed a petition, several times revised and supplemented, asking that channels be reserved for educational use. At first it was "nonprofit" educational use, on the theory that sparsely settled sections of the country might not be able to afford educational service unless it could be provided as a part of commercially supported television. Later, however, and not without strong objection, the application was changed to "noncommercial" educational television, meaning not only that educational stations would be restrained from making profits, but also that they would be restrained from selling advertising time.

In some respects it was a blessing to educational television that the Commission froze allocations for two years. This provided time to alert the educators and civic organizations to the opportunity television offered. Education moves slowly. Although faculties and researchers are sometimes accused of living in the future, or of being devoted to change, academic administrators are traditionally cautious and often conservative, restrained by boards and trustees and public opinion from rash or unfamiliar moves. To educators, educational television looked like a very large sum of money, a diversion of resources and talents to a peripheral part of education, and additional public relations problems. To many of them, the potential of television for teaching was not at all apparent in 1950, nor was it clear how a community, a school, or a college could ever meet the financial requirements even if educational television would do all that some people said it would.

But during the period of the Great Freeze, education did succeed in arousing support and consolidating behind a petition to reserve channels. It will be of interest to mention here some of the leaders in this movement, even at the cost of neglecting to mention others. There were I. Keith Tyler and former President Howard Bevis, of Ohio State University. There was Richard B. Hull, director of the Iowa State ("commercial educational") television station already mentioned. There were George Probst, director of the Chicago Roundtable (now president of the Thomas Alva Edison Foundation), and Seymour Siegel, director of the Municipal Broadcasting System of New York. There was Franklin Dunham (now deceased), of the United States Office of Education. There was Robert B. Hudson, once of CBS, at that time Director of Broadcasting for the University of Illinois, now vice president of NETRC. There were Dr. Arthur Adams (now retired), president of the American Council on Education, and Dr. George Stoddard, then president of the University of Illinois (now chancellor of New York University). There was Telford Taylor, who had been a counselor at the Nuremberg trials and who brought his great prestige and skill to the task of representing education as attorney before the FCC. There were C. M. Jansky, the designer of pioneer educational radio station 9XM, whose firm of Jansky and Bailey did much of the engineering work, and Melvin Marks, of Cohn and Marks, who had long been the chief attorney for educational radio, and who did much of the work that went into the petition for educational frequencies. And there were others. They found a strong and wise supporter in C. Scott Fletcher, president of the Fund for Adult Education (founded by the Ford Foundation), who supplied both advice and financial help, then and later. With this support, the Joint Council on Educational Television was founded, representing the American Association of School Administrators, the American Council on Education, the Council of Chief State School Officers, the National Association of Educational Broadcasters, the National Education Association, and the State Universities Association. Thus a substantial group of citizens, and an impressive number of educational organizations, rallied to represent education in its quest for channels. And when the FCC terminated the freeze with its Sixth Report and Order, in 1952, there were 80 VHF and 162 UHF[3] channels reserved for noncommercial educational stations.

In the excitement of the campaign for channels, some brave things had been said and some assumptions had been made about the speed at which education would take up its new channels. In the cold light of the morning after the Sixth Report and Order,

[3] The abbreviations VHF and UHF may not be familiar to all readers of this book. VHF (very high frequency) refers to the group of 12 channels that most television stations in the United States now use. Television began with VHF, and most receiving sets currently in use are made to receive only VHF channels. UHF (ultrahigh frequency) refers to a somewhat larger group of channels at a higher frequency. Ultimately, most television may be in the UHF band. But an educational station assigned to a UHF channel, as many of them have been, has faced two handicaps: (1) dependable signals of the same power do not carry as far on UHF as on VHF, and (2) in order to receive UHF a viewer has to buy a special set or a converter for his present set. An educational station on a UHF channel would thus be at a great disadvantage in competing for an audience with commercial stations on VHF. The reservation of 162 channels, in 1952, was therefore less impressive than it sounded, for only UHF channels were available for educational television in many of the largest cities of the country, including New York, Los Angeles, Philadelphia, Detroit, Baltimore, Cleveland, and Washington. However, the recently passed bill requiring sets in the future to be able to receive UHF bands should make a difference for the better in the situation of UHF stations.

education had to face up to the realities of television. To build and equip a station would cost from a quarter-million to a million dollars. To program a station on anything like an adequate basis would cost from a quarter-million dollars up, per year. There was no commercial income to cover these costs. There was no network to furnish the majority of the programs. Television required special skills, which were in short supply. It is not surprising that there was no rush to make use of the educational channels. John W. Powell says in his recent book, *Channels of Learning*:[4]

> The motives that inspired the scores of groups that sought to establish community ETV stations . . . were too various for easy generalization.
>
> The "normal" path of development starts from one of two sources: a formal but unhurried committee of educational and civic officials, or an inspired amateur lifting the torch of ETV for others to catch its light. Early leadership then moves into the hands of a recognized group of public-spirited men and women who still do not have command status. Finally, a powerful figure from the inner circle of influence is persuaded to take charge. . . . The word "normal," however, is in quotation marks because there are so many important deviations from this pattern.
>
> It is clearly the business community that commands the destinies of the community station. . . . The motives appear to be dual. These are the "public's" stations; but where the business community furnishes the principal leadership and financing it is—partly, at least—in order to keep the station from falling under State or municipal control. The reasons here appear to be mixed: In some degree, it is distrust of "politicians" who might use TV for propaganda leverage; in some, it is disapproval of public ownership as such. In Boston and Chicago, these were explicit elements in the business appeal. In Philadelphia, where it was complicated by the fear of "socialists," the issue of City and School Board control was the source of the conflict that almost wrecked the station. In Denver, on the other hand, it was chiefly the assurance that the schools would run the station *without* public appeals that brought the Chamber of Commerce to abandon its opposition.
>
> . . .
>
> The evidence remains fairly strong that it takes the lay civic and business community to put the educators on the air: over all, a tremendous tribute to the abiding American faith in Education—in the *idea* of education, even among people who don't watch the station themselves.

The community stations had to get the support of business and community leaders, and leadership in the station campaign often came from this leader group. The university station, the

[4] Pp. 144–45, 163.

state station or network, each had to win over a board of trustees, or a school board, or a legislature. In these cases, leadership was crucial. It usually came from an inspired advocate "raising the torch." In a state university the leader was often the director of the radio station, or of extension. In a school system it was usually the superintendent, or one of his top staff. In a state network it was usually a member of the legislature. Somehow this leader won over his opposition, got approval, got a budget, got equipment. And without precedent, without example, without experience, often without any reserve of cash, stations began going on the air.

The Fund for Adult Education was again of great help, with grants of money to buy part of the equipment stations needed. The first noncommercial educational station went on the air in the spring of 1953. It was owned and operated by the University of Houston, which used it to teach some of its large classes (rather than teaching them in great lecture halls), to extend its teaching beyond the campus, and to furnish public service programs to the city and the surrounding portions of Texas. A second station also went on the air in 1953—station KTHE in Los Angeles, occupying a UHF channel—and this is the only educational station that has ever failed and gone off the air.[5] One failure in 64 stations is not a bad record for an operation that is on such shaky financial ground as educational television. See Figure 1.

In 1954, eight new stations began to broadcast. Four of these were university-owned, as in Houston, by the universities of Nebraska, Washington, Wisconsin, and Michigan State. The other four represented a different pattern. They were licensed to community groups, a group of citizens or organizations calling themselves a Television Association or Television Foundation, raising money from a variety of community sources. These new community stations were in Pittsburgh, San Francisco, St. Louis, and Cincinnati.

In 1955, eight more educational stations went on the air, and

[5] KTHE received most of its support from a single donor. When he withdrew, in 1954, there was insufficient base of support to keep the station going. It should be added, for the sake of accuracy, that a Michigan State University UHF station also went off the air, but it was replaced by a Michigan State VHF station, owned by the University but shared with a commercial operator using a separate license.

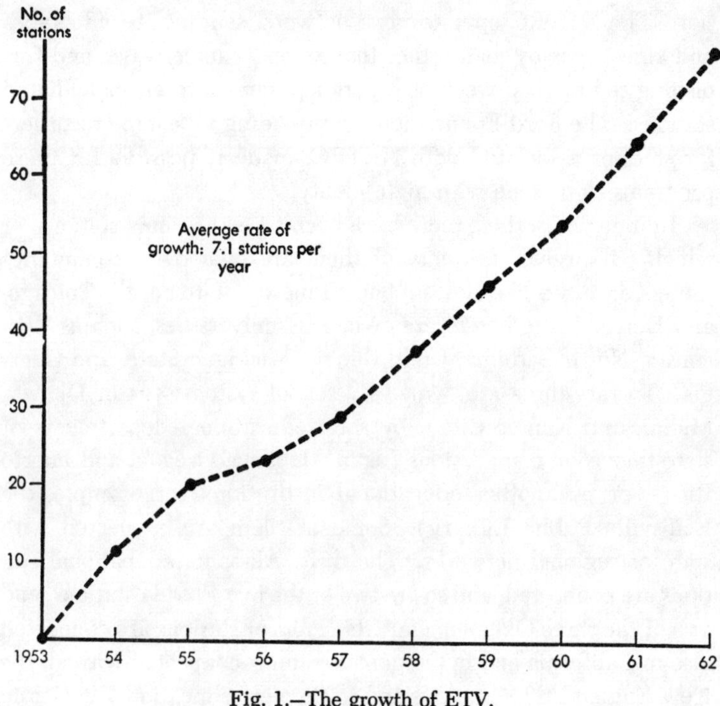

Fig. 1.—The growth of ETV.

among these were still other patterns of ownership and support. The State of Alabama, operating on a grant of funds from the Legislature and under the supervision of a commission appointed by the Legislature, put into operation the first two of three stations intended to serve as a state educational network. And the first school-board station, WTHS, in Miami, Florida, licensed to the Dade County Board of Public Instruction, went on the air to serve the schools by day and the public by night.

Five more stations in 1956, six in 1957, eight in 1958, ten in 1959, seven in 1960, ten in 1961, 13 in 1962—this is the rising curve of educational television's growth. One of the most important chapters in that growth (unfortunately too long a chapter to recount here) was the formation of the National Educational Television and Radio Center, founded and supported during its first years by the Fund for Adult Education, after that by the Ford Foundation. The NETRC operates as a network, sending its videotapes and kinescopes by mail rather than wires or microwave, and furnishing ten hours a week of superior programs to all its affiliated stations. The Ford Foundation, by providing videotape recorders for stations associated with NETRC, made it possible for these programs to be seen with high fidelity.

In nine years, then, there have been 64 educational stations, of which 63 survive.[6] Twenty of them are owned by community groups, in cities like Boston, San Francisco, Pittsburgh, Chicago, and Detroit. Another 20 are owned by universities, such as Wisconsin, North Carolina, Utah, Illinois, Michigan State, and Georgia. Twenty-three are owned by school systems (as in Denver, Miami, and Kansas City), by state educational departments of state television commissions (as in Alabama, Oregon, and Puerto Rico), or by another educational institution (for example, the Louisville Public Library). Some of them are connected with state or regional networks. The three Alabama educational stations are connected, and so are two of the five Florida stations, and two of the three Oklahoma outlets. Pairs of stations are connected also in California and in Oregon. Boston is connected with all the New England ETV stations and to the new educational station in New York. These are the stations we are talking about when we speak of noncommercial educational television.

The money behind ETV

In order to see what it means to a station to be *noncommercial* and educational, we must look at educational television's financial reports.

In the last nine years it cost about $30 million to build and equip those 63 educational stations. At present their annual budget is in the neighborhood of $18 million. Inasmuch as the

[6] To complete the picture, it should be added that there are between 300 and 400 closed-circuit educational television operations in the United States, serving chiefly school systems and universities. Their capital costs are estimated at roughly $15 million, their annual operating costs at about half that. There is also the Midwest Program on Airborne Television Instruction (MPATI, or Airborne, as it is more commonly called), which maintains two airplanes flying over northern Indiana and broadcasting instructional television over a radius of 200 miles. The capital costs of this project have been between $3 and $4 million, and the budget is a little over $8 million.

National Educational Television and Radio Center, their "network headquarters," spends about $3.5 million a year, it appears that the total annual cost of educational television stations is between $20 and $25 million.

By commercial television standards, this is dirt cheap. The income of the three networks and the approximately 550 commercial stations in the last year for which at this writing we have figures was around $1.2 billion. Per station, therefore, it cost about five times as much to bring us commercial as educational television.

We are not implying that commercial television squanders its money. It broadcasts more hours a day, pays higher-priced talent, operates from live networks, does more with remote coverage of events. The educational television broadcaster would love to do all those things if he had the money to pay for them. He doesn't. Educational television has been a lean and hungry operation from the start. To understand that is to understand many of the things that will be reported in the remainder of this book.

Program cost has had to be low. Told recently that an educational station was estimating $1,200 as the cost of each of a series of filmed programs for circulation around the network, a commercial network vice-president remarked that his network could hardly afford to open a big studio for that. On the other hand, another educational television director smiled approvingly at the $1,200 figure and pointed to some of the programs he had done with budgets of $100 and $200.

The educational station is in a squeeze. It cannot afford a live network and thus cannot depend on the network, as the commercial station does, for a large proportion of its programs. Therefore, although short on money for talent and production, it is nevertheless compelled to produce a higher proportion of its own programs than a commercial station does. Thus, both the financial system and some of the equipment of an educational station may appear to be held together by bandages and bailing wire. In the community stations, especially, one sees frequently the odd combination of low finances and high morale. The station may be about to run out of cash, but many of the staff are there because they love the job and believe in ETV. In fact, one of the most prominent of the educational station managers has said wryly that the morale of his station goes down whenever the financial situation improves, and rises again when hard times return to demand sacrifices, Spartan administration, and ingenuity at stretching funds.

The ability of the educational station to call forth loyalty from its employees and its viewers is a very important factor in community response to a station. Station KQED in San Francisco is one station that has been remarkably successful in gaining support from many individuals in the community. KQED has upwards of 15,000 subscriber members, paying $10 to $100 each. Every spring, friends of KQED donate articles of all kinds, from automobiles to pet kittens, to be auctioned off for the benefit of the station, and then compete with each other to buy the articles. In 1962 this auction brought KQED about $107,000. Viewers who thus involve themselves in the task of supporting the station are likely to be loyal audiences.

It is only fair, however, to say that no other educational station has ever been quite so successful as KQED in this respect, although the quick and generous response of the Boston community in raising $1,200,000 when educational station WGBH burned down indicated a similar station loyalty. But the educational stations as a whole draw only a small part of their income from contributions by individuals. About three-fifths of the income of the stations as a whole comes from public schools, boards of education, and state, county, or city appropriations. This money pays most of the cost of the university and school-board stations, and a substantial part of the cost of community stations. But a large part of this public money is given to pay for school broadcasts, leaving the station to dig up where it can the substantial moneys required for a broad adult educational program.

Whereas $30 million in capital costs, annual budgets totaling about $18 million, and a $3.5 million "network" would have seemed astronomic in size to the educators who reviewed what they could do with television just after the "freeze" ended, still it seems very small and constricting to the educational producers who have to put together a year of programs and to the station managers who each week must scrape up money to meet the payroll. The truth is that ETV from the start has been a shoestring operation, long on imagination, but short on cash; high on ideals, but low on salaries; strong on program standards, but weak in money for talent and equipment.

ETV programs

What kind of programs come out of this lean and hungry operation? How does educational television look on the air?

At this writing, the educational stations are broadcasting a total of about 2,500 hours a week. This is probably less than 5 per cent of the total hours of television broadcasts in the United States, but it makes a distinct difference in the program resources of the communities where educational television can be seen, especially where it can be seen on a VHF channel. The typical educational station broadcasts five days a week, eight hours or a little more per day. Some ETV stations are on the air six, and some seven, days a week, but the majority of them broadcast Monday through Friday. From 9:00 A.M. until 3:00 or 4:00 P.M., they carry school broadcasts—programs produced by teachers for wide use in classrooms of the neighboring school districts.[7] They usually go off the air during the noon hour, and often for an hour or so in the afternoon. At 4:00 or 5:00 P.M. they can come back on the air with children's programs; they follow these with an evening of thoroughly adult programs of an educational and informative nature.

Let us follow through a day of programs as offered by an educational station. On this typical day, the station comes on the air at 9:30 A.M. with a class in mathematics. Taught by a master teacher, planned by a group of teachers and school administrators from the surrounding area, this class is intended to "enrich" the mathematics offerings of the area schools, and, incidentally, to help the schools introduce some of the concepts of the "newer" mathematics. At 10:00 A.M., the station has another mathematics class, this one on problem solving. At 10:30 there is a class in elementary school science, taught by a well-known scientist from

[7] Almost exactly one-third of the 2,500 hours of ETV each week are school broadcasts.

a local college. At 11:00 there is another science class—this time, space science. After this talk, the station goes off the air until 1:00 P.M. Then come three language classes, two in Spanish, one in French. The French class is the well-known "Parlons Français," produced and recorded in Boston and exchanged among some of the educational stations. These three hours of school broadcasting are less than the daily average of educational stations, but they nevertheless enter into the school experience of more than 150,000 children in the station's coverage area. They do not in any sense replace the classroom teacher, but do provide a change of pace for the pupils, share expert teaching and excellent classroom demonstrations, and sometimes fill in parts of the curriculum where local schools are less well equipped than they might be. For example, television classes have made it possible for hundreds of thousands of children throughout the country to begin to learn a foreign language in elementary school. Not many elementary schoolteachers were equipped to teach foreign language at fourth- or fifth-grade level. Television gave them the help they needed, both to develop their own competence and to enable their students to hear the language spoken by experts in a realistic situation.[8]

For an hour and a half in the afternoon, the station is dark. It comes back on at 4:00 P.M. At this time there is a half-hour on some of the problems of growing up. This week it is a frank discussion of how children use television: do they spend too much time with it? do they look for the best programs? and so forth. (The next time it may be a discussion of the problems of dating: when should a child begin to date? what do children do on a date? what shouldn't they do? and so on.)

At 5:00 there is a kind of "variety" program for younger children. Children take a walk down a woodland trail, and are shown some things to look for that they might not otherwise notice. There is an answer to one of a series of questions on "How it began." This time it is on money, and viewers are shown wampum and

[8] ETV school broadcasts are by no means restricted to elementary and high schools. Many universities put some of their classes on television. The City of Chicago offers an entire junior college curriculum by television. Memphis teaches literacy to adults by television, under the direction of Frank C. Laubach.

other types of primitive money, and are told how it developed into our own type of currency. Then there is a discussion of the human body; the topic on this sample day is human endurance. What are some of the remarkable feats of strength and endurance humans have accomplished, and what are the limits of human endurance which one should not try to exceed? There follows a half-hour when children are invited to join a well-known singer-guitarist in singing folk songs. Then comes a preview of children's television for the following day. This brings the station to 6:30 P.M. At this time, supposing that some families are at the dinner table and would rather have a background of good music than of pictures, the station simply focuses a camera on the record album of a Benjamin Britten symphony, and plays the record.

At 7:00 there is a lively program on ethnic folk dancing. This evening is concerned with the dancing of Trinidad. Geoffrey Holder, who was born in Trinidad and played in the Broadway musical production "House of Flowers," and his wife, Carmen de Lavallade, formerly with the Metropolitan Opera ballet, are the chief performers. They demonstrate Trinidad dancing and, in discussion with a Smith College professor, explain how each dance is done and what it means.

At 7:30 comes a science reporter program. Under the guidance of an M.I.T. professor, viewers are shown an atomic reactor. They are told how the various parts work and how the machine is used.

At 8:00 the station manager has half an hour. He gives a brief weekly report to the viewers on what is happening at the station, on new programs, on increases in station memberships, and on other items of importance. He then spends 20 to 25 minutes interviewing, with real skill, a guest. This evening his guest is Walter Van Tilburg Clark, author of *The Ox-Bow Incident.*

At 8:30 there is a program about the harpsichord. A well-known concert artist, who is also a university professor, shows how the instrument operates, talks about its history, and plays a selection by Bach and another by Chopin.

At 9:00 comes an hour-long panel discussion, moderated by Mrs. Eleanor Roosevelt. Following up the afternoon talk on children's use of television, this panel now digs more deeply into the problem. On the panel are Newton N. Minow, chairman of the

Federal Communications Commission, who has to defend his "wasteland" speech against the questions and comments of Marya Mannes, the salty critic of the *Reporter* magazine; John F. White, president of the National Educational Television and Radio Center; and Irving Gitlin, the well-known network television producer. This is prime time on educational stations. Most of the programs at this time of day are furnished by NET, Mr. White's organization, which acts as network-by-mail for the educational stations.[9]

When the discussion on television is over, about 10:00, there is a repeat of a previous program, showing how one scene from the opera "La Bohème" is developed from rehearsal into performance. Educational stations often show a program more than once. They can afford to be less concerned about the size of audience at any particular time than about the convenience of their interested viewers. Thus on educational television a program is not necessarily dead after one showing; viewers often have two or three chances to see it. Those who like it well enough can see it twice, and those who are busy at one showing can see another one.

At 10:30 comes a 15-minute news analysis. This is not the typical television newscast, presenting a series of short bulletins with accompanying pictures. It is presented by the telegraph editor of one of the local papers, who reviews thoughtfully some of the leading news happenings, trying in each case to point out the significance of the news and to make it more understandable.

Finally, at 10:45 comes another repeat. This time it is an hour-long program designed to bring local problems out of the level of rumor and private conversation to the level of open discussion. The moderator of this program is a respected lawyer and former state assemblyman. Each week he brings to this program men who know most about the facts involved in the problem, and men who

[9] On Wednesday nights it furnishes special programs on "significant persons," on Friday nights a "festival of the arts." The Friday evening special this week will be a theater presentation of Julius Caesar. The "significant person" will be the Welsh portrait painter Augustus Johns and authors Nathan Asch and Alvah Bessie. On Tuesday at this same time, the station will broadcast "Open End," with David Susskind leading the discussion. On Thursday evening, prime time will feature a hard look at the various arguments on nuclear war.

represent opposing points of view concerning it. The station is not afraid to prod sore points or cause controversy.[10]

At about 11:45, after approximately ten and one-half hours of broadcasting, the station signs off.

How typical of educational broadcasting is this day? No two stations are exactly alike, of course. The one we have described is a community station, therefore by its nature somewhat different from a school or university-owned station. The school station will probably broadcast more classes; the university station may deal with extension materials, less with civic problems. The station we described is well established, and therefore will broadcast more hours a day than a recently established station which is still feeling its way and practicing its skills. This station is well run and skillfully programed, but there is a lot of talent throughout the educational stations. The day we chose to describe was a random day, neither more nor less impressive than most other days on the station. Whereas the programs will not be precisely the same, one station to another, and day to day, the tone of the programing will be the same wherever there is noncommercial educational television. A little rarified, perhaps; a little tense, certainly not relaxing; a bit serious and solemn; short in humor, long in problems; long in ideas and short in entertainment—it is nevertheless a kind of programing that is bound to make a difference wherever it is available. Even though this sort of programing *is* only 5 per cent of all U.S. television, remember that it is presented at choice hours and its best programs are frequently repeated. It is the kind of programing we might expect to make itself heard even above the hoof beats, gunshots, and persuasive silken voices of the other 95 per cent of American television.

But the question is, *will* it make itself heard? How many viewers, what kind of audience, will it attract? To what extent, and by what portions of the public, will it be welcomed as a supplement to American commercial television? These are the questions the remainder of this book tries to answer.

[10] Among the topics recently discussed in this particular program have been homosexuality, "big government," alcoholism in the area, segregation in the area (facing up frankly to the fact that the North has a segregation problem too), campaign costs, and the radical right wing in politics.

2

Measuring the Audiences of ETV

The preceding chapter described an exercise in idealism. Only idealists would have launched educational television into the expensive and competitive world of the commercial networks and stations. Only idealists would dare to offer the American people, who have been busy proving by the millions that they want to relax and be entertained in front of the television set, a television alternative of lofty ideas, fine art, and pressing problems. This is something like inviting American children to give up their summer vacation from school. And only idealists would be willing to operate these stations as many of them have to be operated—with their eyes on immortal concepts and the finer things of life, and only enough cash in sight to run the station for ten days more!

It is often embarrassing to study idealism. One feels sometimes that the important thing is the idealistic act, and perhaps it is better not to look too closely at how much good it did to anybody other than the doer. But educational television is expensive idealism. Its financial costs we have already noted, and nothing more about them need be said here, except that they will be much larger if the medium develops along the curve projected for it by educators.[1] But ETV is also costly in broadcast resources. For example, it is occupying now some extremely valuable channel assignments which entrepreneurs would like to have for commercial stations. And no less than $6.2 million was paid recently to buy ETV a

[1] For example, see the report of a high-level advisory panel to the U.S. Office of Education (in *Educational Television,* pp. 1–13), which urges that steps be taken to assure "every American the opportunity to receive ETV signals."

channel in New York City. Comparable expenses will probably have to be incurred if ETV is to be seen on VHF in Los Angeles, Detroit, Philadelphia, and certain other large cities. Educational television is costly and demanding also in human resources. Many people have sacrificed time and energy, imagination and talent, to it. It would be a waste of precious commodities if all this expenditure and devotion were seen to be ineffective. Therefore, even at the cost of embarrassing idealists, it is important to have a reading on what educational television is accomplishing, and most particularly on what audiences it has and what the viewers think of it.

The research problem

But examining the audiences of educational television is not so easy as it might seem. There are no audience ratings for ETV—nothing comparable to the regular Nielsen, Pulse, Trendex, Hooper, American Research Bureau, and other such figures for commercial television. No television interviewers call up a list of numbers every quarter-hour to inquire about ETV, "Do you have a television set? It it turned on? Do you recall what channel you are tuned to?" and so forth. No diaries are kept regularly, or recording audimeters placed in receiving sets, for the special information of ETV. This is because ETV has no advertisers, and hence no one to pay the rather large costs involved in collecting audience figures regularly. It would be difficult and expensive to do so anyway, because educational stations are scattered widely through the country, and because their total audiences are small compared with the audiences of commercial programs. The commercial network programs, whose audiences are the ones chiefly measured by the rating services, are heard all over the country. A random sample of only a few thousand calls will therefore give a reliable national figure for the audience of any of these programs. And even in individual communities, it can be assumed that everyone with a receiving set views commercial television, whereas only a minority are likely to view educational television regularly. In studying ETV audiences, one is faced with the problem that bedevils the students of most minority behavior not of a public nature—to find the minority.

That is one problem. A second problem has to do with the

need for home interviews. Research on the audience and effectiveness of educational television can hardly be conducted on the basis of short telephone interviews only. Interviews of that kind are all right for arriving at gross figures of audience size, but we want to know a great deal more than that about how people react to ETV. Therefore, it is necessary to talk to people face to face, so that they can reflect at leisure on the questions asked, can be shown documents or materials to which they can be asked to react, and can be asked a number of searching questions that would not be feasible in the five to ten minutes that are usually the limits of a telephonc interview. The cost of home interviews is principally the cost of getting the interviewer to the front door of the right home at a time when the person to be interviewed is able or willing to talk. If interviewers go to homes on a random basis and find that only a few of the homes contain the kind of people they are seeking—that is, regular viewers of educational television—then the interviewing is going to cost a great amount of money before a sample of sufficient size is obtained. So here again, before investing money in home interviews it is important to find the minority that one wants to interview.

There is still another problem in planning research on the audiences of educational television. We have not been sure that ETV is homogeneous. The differences between types of stations may reflect spectacularly in the audiences. For example, do community stations and school or university stations attract the same kinds and numbers of viewers? Does a state ETV network look much different to an audience than a community ETV station? What differences does a UHF channel assignment make to an educational station? These questions are at least as interesting as, and probably more important than, questions about the size of educational TV audience nationwide, or about the characteristics of ETV viewers as a class. At least these questions about the differences between audiences of different types of stations must be answered before national figures will be very meaningful. If unlimited amounts of money were available, of course, one could study the audiences of *all* the ETV stations and collect the individual figures along with the national ones. In our case, there was not enough money to do this, and it was necessary to decide whether to sample in such a way as to get a reliable national figure, or to get figures on the differences between kinds of station audience.

The research strategy

We approached these problems from two different directions:

1. *The M.I.T. study examined in detail the audience of one educational station, WGBH in Boston.* By obtaining 9,140 telephone interviews (8,666 with owners of television receivers) and 511 home interviews in the communities served by the station, Ithiel Pool was able to answer certain questions about the composition of the WGBH audience—their program choices, attitudes toward WGBH and commercial TV, and leisure-time patterns—and especially the *potential* audience for ETV—the kinds of people who might be attracted to it and how far good programing can go toward winning some of them over.

2. *The Stanford studies examined, in somewhat less detail, the audiences of eight educational stations chosen to represent, as nearly as possible, all the main types of stations, all sections of the continental United States, and both VHF and UHF channels.* They included:

a) Two VHF community stations, WQED in Pittsburgh and KQED in San Francisco;

b) Two university stations, KUON in Lincoln, Nebraska, which is on a VHF channel, and WOSU in Columbus, Ohio, which is on a UHF channel in a community where all the commercial stations are VHF;

c) One school-board station, KRMA, in Denver;

d) Three VHF stations, interconnected by microwave, owned by the State of Alabama, and operated as a state network—WBIQ, WCIQ, and WDIQ.

In the coverage areas of these stations we completed approximately 22,000 telephone interviews (19,267 of them with owners of television receivers), and 1,611 home interviews.

Thus we had a detailed study of one station audience, and comparative studies which permitted us to say something about the representativeness of the audience we had studied in detail, about different kinds and sizes of audience attracted by different kinds of educational station, and about the size of the national audience for ETV. The Boston study was undertaken initially quite independently of the other studies and under a different grant. It and the Stanford studies ultimately so closely converged that we decided to bring them together in one book. That happened partly because we were concerned with the same problems and partly because as individuals we had influenced each other.

How the research was done

In general, the research strategy was to locate the ETV audience by telephone and to find out its general size and composition, before trying to study it in depth. Therefore, in each test community a very large number of telephone interviews were held in order to identify and estimate the number of ETV viewers. Afterwards, home interviews were conducted with a subsample of the viewers and nonviewers identified by the telephone method. (See Appendix B.)

More specifically, the procedure in the Stanford eight-station study was this:

a) In each of the test communities, probability samples were drawn from the telephone books within the coverage area. A probability sample is one that gives every name in the total list an equal chance of being selected. Therefore, if we interview enough of the persons selected we can be reasonably confident that we have talked to a representative number of people in that area (or rather of the 90 per cent or so who have telephones).

b) Girls trained as telephone interviewers completed an interview (by phone) lasting five to ten minutes with every name on the sample they could reach. By calling back no more than three times when a line was busy or a phone did not answer, they actually managed to complete between 21,000 and 22,000 interviews, almost 90 per cent of the entire sample.[2] Of these, as we have said, 19,267 proved to have television receivers in their homes.

c) From the persons interviewed by telephone, subsamples

[2] A sample was taken of the persons who could not be reached by telephone. These were interviewed personally in their homes to see in what respects, if any, they were different from the people who were reached. No significant differences were found.

were then drawn in each community. These contained roughly three viewers to one nonviewer, because we were deeply interested in some things the viewers could tell us, and wanted the nonviewers chiefly for a series of comparisons which did not require large numbers. Interviewers were trained, and completed home interviews lasting approximately 40 minutes with about 87 per cent of the sample as drawn. These totaled 1,611. Three call-backs was the rule, as in the telephone interviews.

d) Interviews were coded, punched on IBM cards, run, tabulated, and given necessary statistical treatment.

e) While this was going on, the program schedule and structure of each of the stations were also analyzed.

Interviewing was accomplished between January 20 and May 28, 1962.

The design of the Boston study was the same as that used in the other eight communities. From November 10 through December 17, 1959, and January 10 through February 24, 1960, 9,140 telephone interviews were completed between the hours of 5:00 and 10:00 on weekday evenings, and between 11:30 and 6:30 on Sundays, the hours during which WGBH-TV broadcast. Each interview lasted about 14 minutes. Then a year later, from September 1960 through February 1961, some of the same people were approached for personal interviews lasting somewhat over an hour each.

Like the other studies, the M.I.T. study was most interested in ETV viewers, so 222 of our 511 interviews were devoted to them although they are only one-fifth of the population. Eighty-three other interviews were with fuzzy cases, for which, in the Stanford studies, we used the term "occasional viewers," but which, as defined in the M.I.T. study, might better be called marginal cases. One hundred thirty-seven interviews were with a representative sample of nonviewers. By weighting and then combining these three samples totaling 442 cases it was possible to get a picture of a cross section of Boston metropolitan area adults.

There was one further feature to the design of the Boston study, namely, interviews with matched samples of viewers and nonviewers. Comparisons of ETV viewers and nonviewers are tricky. Let us illustrate the problem with an example. Thirty-one per cent of WGBH viewers have completed college while only 9 per cent of the nonviewers have gone that far with their education.[3] Now we find that 40 per cent of nonviewers of ETV admit that they sometimes watch TV because they started on one show and "got stuck for the rest of the evening," while only 30 per cent of ETV viewers admit that this happens to them. Is that a difference in TV habits characterizing ETV viewers as such, or is it just a difference in television viewing habits between better educated people and less educated people?

To answer such questions the M.I.T. study undertook certain matching procedures to compare the viewers of ETV not just with nonviewers, but with nonviewers of the same social and educational character. What about two men of identical age, education, size of family, and suburban or urban residence, of whom one watches WGBH and one does not? Would they differ in susceptibility to lead-in, or would they be the same?

To answer that question and questions like it, it was necessary to interview nonviewers who in social characteristics matched the viewers. Such people do not fall into a sample naturally in any large number. For example, the nonviewers produced by a small probability sample will not include many people of high educational level. So from the large pool of telephone respondents in the Boston study, each member of a representative sample of WGBH viewers was matched with a nonviewer who was like him in major social respects.[4] These people were then also interviewed

[3] The gremlins that bias even a carefully drawn probability sample are illustrated by the fact that in our face-to-face interviews with nonviewers, refusals and moved persons took away more persons of low education. Thus our telephone sample of nonviewers contains 13 per cent persons with only grade-school education, but these were only 8 per cent of the face-to-face nonviewer respondents. Persons with some college education were but 14 per cent of nonviewers originally, but were 20 per cent of those who had face-to-face interviews. This is important, for it tends to reduce the differences between interview results with nonviewers and viewers below what they really are. Some of our findings in this study may therefore be overly conservative.

[4] Nonviewers were matched with viewers with respect to sex, age, size of household, urban or suburban residence, education, and family income. However, even in so large a population as that sampled in the telephone interviews, every nonviewer could not be matched with a viewer like him in all these social characteristics. In some cases one and in a few instances more of the criteria were dropped in the following order: family income, size of family, education.

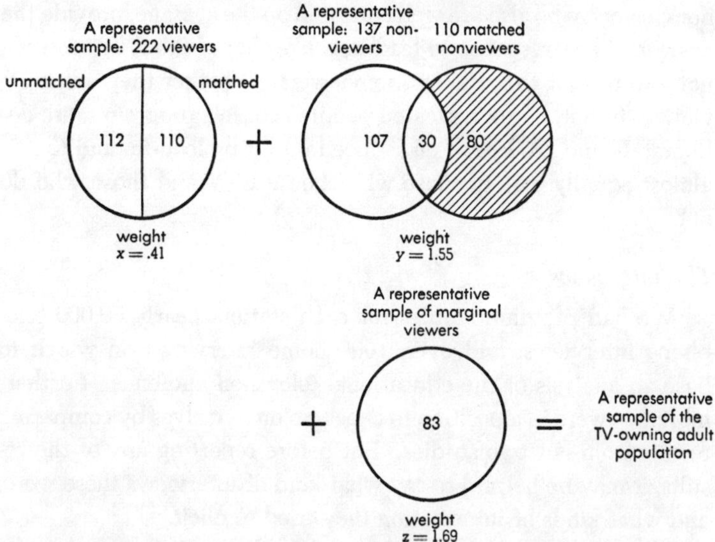

Fig. 2.—A representative sample of the TV-owning adult population, Station WGBH, Boston. (The shaded portion was not included in the weighted sample.)

in person. Some of the results reported in the following pages thus consist of a comparison of 110 ETV viewers and 110 individually matched nonviewers.[5] Other results compare 222 representative viewers with 137 representative nonviewers.

The Boston sample may be diagramed as shown in Figure 2.

The usefulness of this design is illustrated by the question about lead-in, which we posed before. ETV viewers were less likely to be captured by lead-in than were the nonviewers. See Figure 3.

0 M N 100
V=30 32 40

Fig. 3.—Per cent of viewers, nonviewers, and matched nonviewers who sometimes watch because of lead-in.

But, we asked, is that a characteristic of ETV viewers as such or does it simply reflect their higher educational status? The matched

[5] Normally we compare the 110 matched nonviewers with all 222 viewers (not just the matched ones) to take advantage of the greater stability of the larger number. The 110 matched viewers were tabulated only to check that they did not differ from the larger population, of which they are one-half.

nonviewers, who also are well educated on the average, provide the answer. Their response to lead-in is like that of the ETV viewers, not like that of their fellow nonviewers. Whether they are ETV viewers or not, better educated people choose a program more deliberately and are less often seduced into it by lead-in, and that is almost equally true of those who choose ETV and those who do not.

The interviews

We had program studies for each station, nearly 30,000 telephone interviews, and over 2,000 home interviews on which to base an analysis of the educational television audience. Furthermore, we were in a position to check up on ourselves by comparing results from our two studies. But before reporting any of the results, it may be helpful to say what kind of interviews these were, and what kinds of information they tried to elicit.

The telephone interview began like the ordinary commercial rating interview (the so-called "telephone coincidental" survey) by finding out whether the family had a television set, whether it was turned on, and if so to what channel. If the channel was not the educational one, then the respondent on the phone was asked whether he ever viewed channel so-and-so, the local educational station, and if so whether he had watched it in the last week or the last month or when. If he said he had viewed it in the last week, or "viewed every week," then he was asked to name a program he had seen in the last week, or to tell us something about the program if he could not remember the name. The person who had viewed at least one program in the last week, and could prove it with some information about the program, we called a *regular* viewer. The person who could not pass that test, but still said he viewed the station, we called an *occasional* viewer. Everybody else was a *nonviewer*.[6]

[6] The Boston study defined a viewer as someone who asserted he watched WGBH, said the last time he did so was less than four weeks before, and was able to describe what he had seen on WGBH in a convincing fashion. A nonviewer was someone who said he did not watch WGBH. The remaining cases, whether the persons asserted that they watched but could not prove it, whether they watched but too long ago, or whether they said someone else in the household watched but they did not, we have called marginal cases. One type of

Then the interviewer tried to find out as much as possible about the differences between these regular, occasional, and nonviewers. Previous studies had advanced some hypotheses concerning the differences; for example, the viewers were thought to be better educated and culturally more active. So the interview was designed to test those differences and many more. The respondent was asked about his education, his age, his occupation, whether he had children, and if so how many and what ages. He was asked how many books he could remember reading since last summer, how many magazines he read regularly, how many concerts, how many lectures, how many discussion groups or evening courses, how many civic meetings he could remember attending in the last two months. He was asked to think back over the last week (if he was a regular viewer) and try to remember how many programs he had seen, or how much time he had spent, on ETV. He was asked what other members of his family viewed ETV, and how often.

The girls became quite expert at this telephone interviewing, and found a quick and relatively painless way of getting a lot of information in a short time. The Boston interview was fundamentally similar to the Stanford one.

The information derived from the telephone interview was, of course, rather gross. We wanted to be able to make finer distinctions, to learn to know the viewers better, to give respondents a chance to be more relaxed and thoughtful in some of their answers, and to get their reactions to some statements and materials we could not show them in a phone interview. Therefore, we planned home interviews that lasted from 40 minutes to well over an hour each.

The Boston home interviews were not just like the eight-station-study interviews, although both covered much of the same ground.

---

respondent who in the Stanford study would have been called a nonviewer was in Boston called marginal. This was the person who responded that he did not view ETV, but someone else in his household did. On the other hand, the Boston study called a person a regular viewer if he had viewed ETV in the past four weeks; the Stanford study, if he had watched in the past one week or every week. On the basis of the figures available, we estimate that the marginal-case category in the Pool study is 2 or 3 per cent larger than it would be if it were computed as Schramm and Lyle computed their occasional viewers.

Pool concentrated on finding out as much as he could about these viewers, and particularly about how educational television fitted into their leisure time and into their use of other media. Schramm and Lyle, on the other hand, given their sample of different stations, tried to find out whether these stations had different kinds of viewers, what programs they viewed, what they were seeking, and what opinions they held of the different stations as well as of educational television in general.

The Boston interview was presented to the respondents as a study of leisure. It covered the full range of leisure-time activities. How much spare time did the respondent have? How much did he participate in sports, games, music (either by playing instruments or playing records), clubs or organizations, discussion groups, adult classes, hobbies, church, and political activities? In the context of leisure-time activity, the interview moved into the respondent's use of mass media. How much did he listen to radio, and what did he get from it? How many newspaper did he read, what did he turn to first, and what kinds of news most interested him? What were his favorite magazines? What books had he read recently? How often did he see movies, and what kind of movies?

Questions about television were treated in the same way as other questions about leisure. While the more subtle among the respondents may well have guessed that TV was our major interest, that was not obvious. The personal interview was not identified with the phone interview a year earlier. The respondent was asked how much time he spent on television—both commercial and educational television. How did he describe and characterize the different TV channels in Boston? He was given a list of words, such as fun, dull, serious, "my sort of station," entertaining, and relaxing, and was asked to say which words best described each channel. He was asked questions designed to allow him to express some of the reasons why he watched television. He was also asked his opinions of television, and how often he discussed television, with whom, and what he discussed.

Turning to channel 2, the educational station, the interviewer inquired who in the family, if anyone, watched ETV, who selected the programs? What were his favorite ETV programs? How many programs per week did he watch on the educational station? Did he watch programs by series, or select a single program?

Finally, the person being interviewed was asked to respond to a number of questions which fitted together into scales to describe his opinions on several very important dimensions.

The eight-station interview gathered some material on leisure time and on use of the other mass media, but concentrated on other matters. It was important to get some information on what were the most popular programs on ETV—not to get a program rating for them, but at least to put them in relation to other programs. So the home interviewer, among other things, went over with the respondent a schedule of the local ETV station for the past week, and checked the programs he had seen.

Another intention was to see how ETV was evaluated in comparison with other mass media. Therefore, questions were asked about which medium the respondent would keep if he could keep only one, about which media he found most useful for what purposes, which ones he depended on for what kind of information or entertainment, and how much time he habitually spent on the different media.

There have been some claims that the viewer of ETV tends to be an influential person. This, of course, is not easily determined, but nevertheless the questions that have been used in other studies to identify influential persons were included. So were questions about social class and class norms. Several scholars have found that "serious" commercial television and educational television use (as contrasted to entertainment television) seems to be much more popular with the middle class than the lower class. It has been suggested that this is somehow related to the common middle-class *work* or *self-betterment* norm. To test this, we gave the respondent certain statements on which, by stating agreement or disagreement, he could tell us how he felt about this norm.

Other questions were designed to find out how long the individual viewer had been making use of educational TV and, if he could remember, what first attracted him to it. This was obviously better for recent converts than for old-timers. We also tried to find out whether he had favorite programs and whether there were any programs he found too difficult.

Some questions and statements then tried to find out something about the rationale for viewing ETV. The respondent was asked why his friends did or did not view, as he understood it. He was given some statements of such a nature that by reacting to them he could give us a good idea of his attitudes toward ETV. He was asked what he thought ETV was doing well, and what poorly, and was asked to compare it in these respects with commercial television.

Finally he was given semantic differential blanks to fill out. The "semantic differential" is a highly ingenious test developed by Dr. Charles Osgood, of the University of Illinois. It is very easy to administer or use, and measures with a great deal of validity and reliability what a given something "means" to a person, and some of his attitudes toward it. These respondents were asked to fill out semantic differentials on *educational television* and *commercial television*, and on *viewers of ETV* and *nonviewers of ETV*. From this part of the interview it was possible to tell, for example, how much "fun" and how "interesting" viewers thought ETV was as compared with CTV, and to compare the judgments of ETV made by regular viewers with those made by nonviewers. It was also possible to get judgments of the kind of people viewers and nonviewers thought ETV viewers were and to get projective judgments of the reasons they thought people viewed ETV. The semantic differential data were very rich.

Of course, many of these questions were not asked of nonviewers. The interviews with nonviewers averaged 15 to 20 minutes shorter than those with viewers.

This was the kind of information the interviews tried to obtain, and the kind of material we had for a portrait of the educational television audience.

3

The Nine Stations and Their Programs

What kinds of station were the nine we chose to study? This chapter will describe them briefly, and say something about the programs they put on the air.

The stations

Boston. Station WGBH (channel 2) has the advantage of being in a city with a long heritage of culture. The Boston Symphony and the Boston Museum of Fine Arts are known around the world. Harvard and the Massachusetts Institute of Technology help make Cambridge symbolic of education in the United States. Metropolitan Boston, reaching up and down the Atlantic coast, and far inland from Boston, has a population of over 2.5 million. It is an industrial complex with large ethnic minorities. Even Cambridge, its academic suburb, is above all an industrial settlement whose slum population far outnumbers its academicians, and where votes are always to be won by berating the universities. In this complex environment, WGBH-TV began telecasting in 1955. For the first five years of its existence, it was almost purely a cultural station, broadcasting generally from 5:00 to 10:00 P.M. In 1960, however, it began school broadcasts in the mornings, and has become the originating station for such nationally circulated instructional programs as "Parlons Français." It broadcasts the Boston Symphony regularly, along with an impressive group of urbane and cultured programs, such as commentaries on the news by Louis Lyons, head of the Nieman Foundation at Harvard. WGBH operates with the advice and cooperation of the Lowell

Institute Co-operative Broadcasting Council, members of which include the Lowell Institute, Harvard, M.I.T., five other colleges and universities, the Boston Museum of Fine Arts, and the Boston Symphony Orchestra. Its financial support comes from the Lowell Institute, other foundations, and the community, and only in small part from the member educational institutions. It has attracted deep loyalties. When the studio building burned down in 1961, school children went from door to door soliciting money to rebuild, and newspapers, commercial television stations, and many individuals supported the campaign to get WGBH a new building. The station has a transmitter on high ground west of Boston, well-equipped studios, a mobile unit, and a network that connects it to all the New England ETV stations and to the new educational station in New York.

Pittsburgh sits in the rugged hills of western Pennsylvania, at the point where the Allegheny and Monongahela rivers form the Ohio River. Station WQED, like WGBH, is a community station. Pittsburgh is a prosperous industrial city, with nearly 2.5 million people living in more than 50 cities and towns within its metropolitan area. It is noted for its huge steel plants, for its ethnic groups, and for years for its smoky atmosphere. More recently, however, it has engaged in a remarkable program of urban renewal, eliminated much of the smoke that used to hang over it, and raised many handsome new buildings, notably in the once smudged and battered triangle where the Ohio River used to flood the city with monotonous regularity. The University of Pittsburgh and the Carnegie Institute, including the Carnegie Institute of Technology, are examples of the city's cultural strengths. Station WQED was the third educational station to go on the air, in 1954. It is owned by a community body called the Metropolitan Pittsburgh Educational Television Station. The studios are in an old mansion, remodeled with a special studio wing. The transmitter is on high ground elsewhere in the city. WQED occupies channel 13, and since 1959 has also operated a UHF station on channel 16 in order to meet the needs of the area for school broadcasts. These stations carry many hours for the schools, and also have been among the leading producers of programs for the educational network. WQED's financial support comes from gifts and grants, industry, schools, and so forth.

San Francisco. Station KQED went on the air about two months after WQED, in 1954. It broadcasts on channel 9, from a transmitter on top of a mountain at the edge of the city, and makes use of several translators to carry its programs over a wide area. It has also a microwave connection with the educational station in Sacramento, and anticipates a Pacific Coast network as soon as possible after Los Angeles gets its hoped-for ETV station. Like WGBH in Boston, KQED is fortunate to be in an area where the cultural roots are deep, and also where remarkable growth and immigration have taken place in the last ten years. The University of California, Stanford, and more than a dozen other universities and colleges are in the San Francisco Bay Area. San Francisco has a symphony and an opera, and well-known museums. The city itself is at the end of a peninsula, surrounded on three sides by the ocean and the bay. A string of suburbs has grown southeasterly down the peninsula and north across the Golden Gate. On the east side of San Francisco lie the city of Oakland and a number of smaller cities and suburbs. The total metropolitan population is about 2.8 million. Station KQED is one of the chief producers of programs for the educational network. Like WQED in Pittsburgh, it is well but not luxuriously equipped, and has more money to spend than most educational stations. Like WGBH in Boston and some other stations, it has attracted remarkable loyalties. It is the only ETV station that gets a substantial part of its budget from memberships.

Denver is in the heart of Colorado, ten miles east of the Rocky Mountains, at an altitude of exactly one mile above sea level. It was a cattle and mining town that became a state capital, and now is a prosperous and growing metropolis of half a million people. In its easy and relaxed manner, the city still shows its origin in the Old West. Station KRMA went on the air in 1956, with channel 6, and a transmitter on Lookout Mountain, west of Denver. Owned by the school district, with its studios in the adult school building, the station appeared at first to be chiefly a vehicle for school broadcasts and for extending the offerings of the adult school to the public at home. In the last few years, however, the community broadcasting of the station has been expanded and improved. Now, after devoting the daytime hours to serving classrooms, it goes back on the air with an evening program derived mostly from

NET and from its own excellent productions. Some of these latter—such as the lively "Ragtime Era," which was circulated nationwide by the educational network—are not precisely what one would expect from a school-board station, and that is all the more indication that the station has learned to serve the community as well as the schools. Some of its programing, though, is unmistakable in its origin. For example, the station frequently broadcasts repeats of classes heard in school during the day, and encourages parents to review these with their children! Except for program grants and similar resources, the station is financed entirely by the school system. The staff members are employed by the school system, and the director is an assistant superintendent.

Lincoln. Station KUON is licensed, operated, and supported by the University of Nebraska, in Lincoln. Lincoln is a city of about 125,000, on the rich, flat plains of Nebraska. The city is the capital of Nebraska, and the striking 400-foot tower of the Capitol can be seen from many miles away. Farmland comes up to the edge of the city, and the University feels a responsibility to serve the agricultural interests of the state. Unfortunately, the television station does not have power or antenna enough, or connecting translators, to serve more than the area immediately around Lincoln. However, the agricultural nature of the state, and its university sponsorship, are evident in the programs it broadcasts. Its most popular program is "Backyard Farmer." Faculty members are among its chief participants, and it broadcasts a number of courses. The studios are located in a university building, the antenna tower is on university land, and the staff members are university employees. KUON went on the air in 1954, and was the fourth university ETV station to begin broadcasting. It operates on channel 12.

Columbus. Like KUON, station WOSU is located in the state capital, and is operated by the state university. Columbus, Ohio, also has rich farmland around it, but is in a state where industry bulks larger, and Columbus itself is a larger city than Lincoln (nearly half a million people as compared with 125,000). As in Lincoln, the Columbus station has its studios in university buildings, trains students for broadcasting careers, and has a staff of university employees. Its director is influential in the university hierarchy. The chief difference between WOSU and the other stations we have talked about, however, is the channel it occupies. When WOSU prepared to go on the air in 1956, there was no VHF channel reserved for education in its area, and it was forced to make use of a UHF channel, number 34. This has been a cruel handicap for the station, because the commercial outlets were well established by 1956, and the community was saturated with VHF receiving sets. The only way people could hear the programs from Ohio State University was to buy an entirely new set that could pick up UHF signals or to buy a converter, which was not inexpensive and had the disadvantage of providing additional machinery to install and maintain. Only about 15 per cent of the people in WOSU's coverage area have so far equipped themselves to receive UHF. That station, however, maintains a long daily schedule, and now operates closed-circuit television carrying course broadcasts chiefly to university students. Financing, except for program grants and such things, comes from University funds.

Alabama. Nearly two-thirds of Alabama's population of 3.2 million are thought to be within the coverage area of the three stations that comprise the Alabama state educational television network. One of these stations is on Red Mountain, at Birmingham, in the north-central part of the state; a second is on the high ground in Mount Cheaha State Park, near Munford, in the east-central part of the state; and a third is near Dozier, in the southern part of the state. They operate, respectively, on channels 10, 7, and 2. The first two of these stations went on the air in 1955, the third a year later. A fourth one is now in use. The stations were established by an act of the State Legislature, which also established the Alabama Educational Television Commission to coordinate policy. The stations are connected by microwave. Network headquarters are in Birmingham, and the network is fed from three production centers—at the University of Alabama, Auburn University, and Birmingham (in connection with the school system). The financing comes from state funds.

To sum up, then, the stations we have studied include:

Three community stations operating on VHF: Boston, on the east coast; San Francisco, on the west coast; and Pittsburgh, on the slopes of the Appalachians;

Two university stations: Lincoln, in the heart of the Midwest, operating on VHF; and Columbus, near the eastern edge of the Midwestern plains, operating on UHF;

One school-board station operating on VHF, Denver, just at the eastern edge of the Rocky Mountains; and

Three VHF stations comprising the Alabama state network.[1]

The programs

We have tried to fill in some of the facts about these stations as they might look to a historian of ETV. One of the most important questions we have said very little about: How do they look on the air?

How many hours do they broadcast? The stations differ considerably from each other in program format. For one thing, the number of broadcast hours varies widely—from 70 hours per week to 24 hours per week—as will be seen in Figure 4.

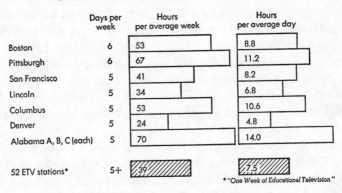

	Days per week	Hours per average week	Hours per average day
Boston	6	53	8.8
Pittsburgh	6	67	11.2
San Francisco	5	41	8.2
Lincoln	5	34	6.8
Columbus	5	53	10.6
Denver	5	24	4.8
Alabama A, B, C (each)	5	70	14.0
52 ETV stations*	5+	39	7.5

* "One Week of Educational Television"

Fig. 4.—Amount of broadcast time of selected ETV stations.

The educational stations are individualists. What Denver sees as its job is not what Pittsburgh sees. There is not much pattern in the figure here presented. The 14 hours a day that the Alabama state network broadcasts may be in part a reflection of the fact that there are three active production centers. On the other hand, San

[1] In addition to studies on these nine stations, there are recent studies of the ETV audience, one for Champaign-Urbana by Parker, and two of the Minneapolis-St. Paul audience by Carter and Troldahl. For other studies on the ETV audience, see Schramm, pp. 18–113.

Francisco has production facilities and staff comparable to Pittsburgh (and broadcasts fewer hours); and if a UHF channel is indeed a depressing factor, then it is a bit hard to explain why Columbus, which is on UHF, broadcasts so many more hours than Lincoln, which is also a university station but has a VHF channel. Financial support, concept of job, staff and facilities, all enter into determining how long the station is on the air, but our guess is that the job concept is most important.

The nine stations we have studied are on the air a total of 482 hours a week, which corresponds to a little over 25,000 hours a year. This is above the average of all stations, as can be seen from the comparative figure, taken from the Brandeis survey.

How do they divide up this time? There are considerable differences also in the proportion of time given over to school broadcasts, as is shown in Figure 5, although here the difference is of the order of 2 to 1, rather than 3 to 1.

Another way to look at this information is to ask how many hours on an average broadcast day an educational station devotes to in-school as compared with general broadcasts. See Figure 6.

On the average, then, we can count on an educational station to spend about three hours a day broadcasting to schools, and about five hours a day to its home audience. The San Francisco community station is almost exactly on that middle line. Keeping that in mind, we can see how the other stations deviate from the average. Pittsburgh has about twice as much school broadcast

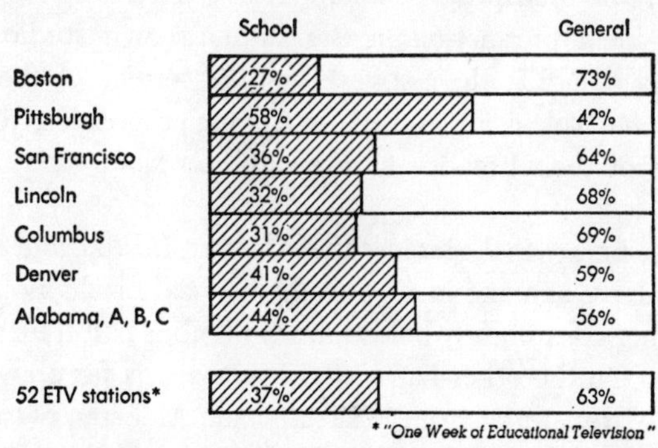

Fig. 5.—Proportion of time given to school and general broadcasts by ETV stations.

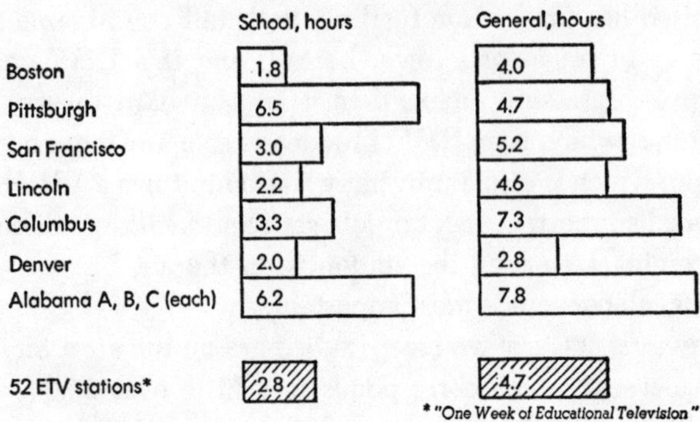

Fig. 6.—Amount of time given each day to school and general broadcasts by ETV stations.

time as the average, but no more general broadcasts than the average. Lincoln has about the usual number of general broadcasts but fewer school broadcasts. Columbus has about the usual number of school broadcasts, but more than the average number of general broadcasts. Denver, with its short schedule, has fewer of each. The Alabama network, with its long schedule, has more of each.

It will be interesting, when we come to audience measurements in the next chapter, to see whether size of home audience is related to amount of time spent on general broadcasts, and whether size of school audience is related to amount of time spent on school broadcasts.

Where do their programs come from? There are two principal sources—local production in the station's own studio, and the programs of NET, the network-by-mail service of the National Educational Television and Radio Center. Figure 7 gives the percentages of their broadcast time supplied from each of the two sources.

These figures make it clear that Denver, Boston, and Pittsburgh are far above average in percentage of local production, whereas San Francisco is slightly below and Columbus is still further below average. On the other hand, San Francisco is far above average in its use of material from NET, and the Alabama network is far below average. The reason for the low Alabama percentage may be that only one of its three production centers acts as the network's affiliate with NETRC, and only one production center has

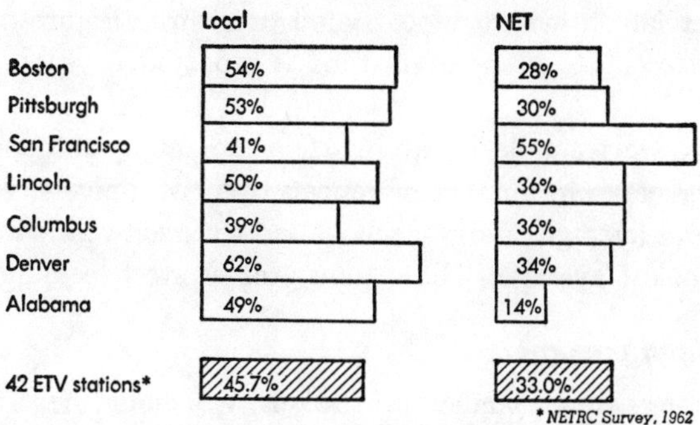

Fig. 7.—Proportion of time supplied from local and NET sources.

a videotape recorder for playing NET and other tapes. Let us postpone an attempt to explain the other deviations until we have more information before us.

The percentages for local production and network programs do not add to 100 per cent. Indeed, the average station gets only 88.7 per cent of its programs from those two sources. Where does the other 11.3 per cent come from? Most of these programs are from films or kinescopes. They are exchanged between stations, either by mail or by the microwave link that connects a number of pairs of educational stations. They may be rented from a film service, or furnished free by a corporation or educational institution. On the average, as we have seen, about one-eighth of all ETV time comes from sources like those.

How much do they repeat programs? This is one characteristic of educational broadcasting; it is easier for educational than for

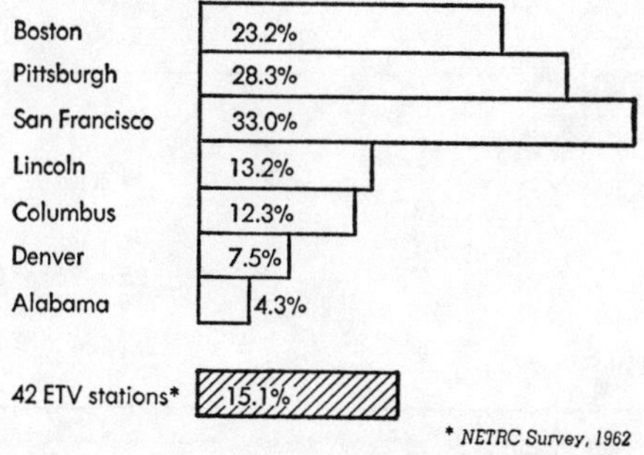

Fig. 8.—Proportion of time given to repeated programs by ETV stations.

commercial stations to repeat good programs. Figure 8 tells us what percentage of program time is repeated by each of these outlets.

Here we see a clear pattern: The community stations are far above average in number of repeats, the two university stations are about average, and the school and state network stations are much below average. The station profiles are becoming clearer.

Content of the programs

If these were commercial stations, we should describe their product in entertainment terms—Westerns, crime mysteries, domestic comedies, variety shows, and so forth. Inasmuch as they are educational stations, we find it easier to describe their program content in educational terms. Table 1 analyzes the *general* broadcasts—those directed to the general public rather than to the schools.

TABLE 1.—PROPORTION OF GENERAL BROADCAST TIME DEVOTED TO EDUCATIONAL CONTENT

Station	Science, Math., etc.	Social Science	Language	Literature	Children's
Boston	18%	19%	3%	2%	7%
Pittsburgh	10	13	0	2	15
San Francisco	13	10	3	2	17
Lincoln	28	12	0	2	0
Columbus	24	19	0	6	17
Denver	14	10	0	3	10
Alabama network	38	13	3	7	8
52 ETV stations*	18	20	3	5	12

Station	Arts	News	Public Affairs	How to Do It	Other
Boston	18%	15%	13%	0%	3%
Pittsburgh	28	3	18	3	8
San Francisco	33	3	7	0	12
Lincoln	32	1	25	0	0
Columbus	13	3	5	1	12
Denver	7	0	25	27	4
Alabama network	16	3	7	1	4
52 ETV stations*	18	3	11	2	8

* "One Week of Educational Television."

Now the differences are still clearer. Two of the community stations are strong on arts and children's programs. The two university stations are strong on science and mathematics; one of them (Lincoln) is strong also in arts and public affairs, but has no children's programs; the other (Columbus) is strong in children's programs and social science. The school-board station (Denver) is very strong in "how to do it" programs—in fact, the only station that has any considerable number of such programs—and also in public affairs programs, but it is the weakest of all the stations in arts. The Alabama network carries a higher proportion of science than any other of these stations—more than twice the national average for science programs. But before we yield to the temptation to say that community stations are characterized by strong arts and children's programs, university stations by strong science, and so forth, let us notice that there are about as many differences *within* classes—that is, between the other two community stations and Boston, or between the two university stations—as *between* classes, meaning, for example, between a community station and a university station.

The last line of Table 1 furnishes a bird's-eye view of the national content of educational television as it comes to the home. About one-fifth of all ETV's general broadcast time is on science and another fifth on social science and history. About a quarter of all the general broadcast time is on language, literature, and the arts. News and public affairs take up a little over one-eighth of the time, and children's programs take just under an eighth. The remaining tenth or so of the time is filled with a miscellany of program types. Perhaps the most noteworthy thing about it is the small amount of time (2 per cent) devoted to "how to" programs.

The general programs we have been talking about occupy, you will remember, nearly two-thirds of an average station's broadcast time. Now let us see, in Table 2, what content is being handled in the remaining third of the time—that is, in the programs that go into the classrooms.

Pittsburgh is the highest of these stations in literature, Boston in the arts. San Francisco and Denver concentrate on teaching foreign language; in fact they are almost three times the national average in that category. Lincoln concentrates on social science, with

TABLE 2.—PROPORTION OF SCHOOL BROADCAST TIME DEVOTED TO EDUCATIONAL CONTENT

Station	Science, Math., etc.	Social Science	Lan-guage	Litera-ture	Arts	Other
Boston	25%	17%	25%	8%	25%	0%
Pittsburgh	36	13	7	14	18	12
San Francisco	31	0	49	0	4	20
Lincoln	24	47	29	0	0	0
Columbus	66	3	29	0	2	0
Denver	26	7	46	5	6	10
Alabama network	57	11	14	0	11	7
52 ETV stations*	38	18	17	7	10	10

* "One Week of Educational Television."

a strong second in language; Columbus concentrates on science and mathematics (two-thirds of its school program time is in that field), and also has a strong second in language. The Alabama network concentrates on science.

How much of class broadcast time is directed to elementary school, how much to high school, how much to college?

These stations broadcast most of their classes for elementary school, regardless of whether the stations themselves are owned

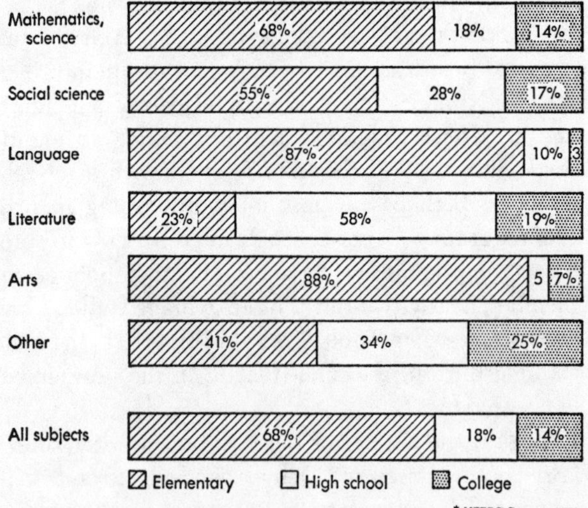

Fig. 9.—Proportion of school broadcasts at different school levels, 42 educational stations.

by school systems, universities, communities, or states. Only Columbus and Alabama broadcast any significant proportion of their classes to college students. San Francisco broadcasts all its classes to elementary schools, except for three in-service workshops for teachers. Denver broadcasts nearly 90 per cent of its classes to elementary schools; the rest to high schools. Pittsburgh broadcasts about 65 per cent to elementary schools, the remainder to high schools. Boston, Columbus, Lincoln, and Alabama divide their classes among the three levels, but in each case more than half the classes are for elementary schools. Over-all, these nine stations broadcast 65 per cent of the classes to elementary schools, 20 per cent to high schools, 8 per cent to colleges, and 7 per cent to in-service workshops for teachers. This is almost exactly the national average, as Figure 9 shows.

Summing up

Now, we are in a position to summarize some of the differences in the programing of these stations. See Table 3.

As we have noted before, the stations project different personalities. The Boston, Pittsburgh, and San Francisco stations, in large cities, blessed with VHF channels and loyal audiences, project a community image rather than an educational institution image. They catch up the tone and personality and stand for the best in the intellectual and cultural life of the cities. Their strategies for appealing to audiences are somewhat different from those of other stations, and even to some extent from each other. One thing in which they agree, however, is in programing a large number of repeats, so that viewers will have maximum opportunities to see the station's best programs. They are the only stations in the eight to make an extensive use of repeats. They agree also in fairly sophisticated programing and high production quality, and in being "arts" rather than science stations. Pittsburgh, however, creates an image of public service, with a long program day, a high proportion of school broadcasts, and an emphasis on public affairs programs. San Francisco, on the other hand, has only an average day and an average proportion of school broadcasts, but is distinguished by the large number of NET programs it airs, often with several repeats, and by its great attention to children's

TABLE 3.—PROGRAM DIFFERENCES, ALL STATIONS

Station	Broadcast Time	Proportion of School Broadcasts	Proportion of NET Programs	Proportion of Repeats	General Broadcasts High in	General Broadcasts Low in	School Broadcasts High in
Boston (VHF, community)	Average	Low	Average	High	News, social science, public affairs	Children, "how to"	Arts
Pittsburgh (VHF, community)	Long	High	Average	High	Arts, public affairs	Science, social science	Lit., arts
San Francisco (VHF, community)	Average	Average	High	High	Arts, children	Science, social science	Language
Lincoln (VHF, university)	Average	Average	Average	Average	Science, arts, public affairs	Social science, children	Social science, language
Columbus (UHF, university)	Long	Average	Average	Average	Science, children	Arts, public affairs	Science, language
Denver (VHF, school board)	Short	High	Average	Low	"How to," public affairs	Social science, arts	Language
Alabama A, B, C (VHF, state network)	Long	High	Low	Low	Science	Social science, public affairs	Science

programs. Boston, too, has only an average broadcast day and a lower-than-average proportion of school broadcasts, but stands out for its strong coverage of news, public affairs, and social science.

Compare with these the personalities of the two university stations. Columbus, you will remember, is a UHF station, and therefore greatly restricted in audience. Nevertheless it has a long broadcast day, and, like Lincoln, is a strong "science" station. Both these stations are about average in number of school broadcasts, use of NET programs, and repeats. Both of them teach a lot of language classes. Both make considerable use of their faculty resources. Both project a university image, and over-all the tone of their broadcasts tends to be a bit more "teachy" than the tone of Pittsburgh, Boston, and San Francisco.

The Denver station has still a different personality. Responsible to a school board rather than a community group, its first interest is in serving the schools of the city (which it does with a high proportion of schoolcasts). When it broadcasts to a nonschool audience, its first interest is in making available "how to do it" programs which relate to the adult school. Its general broadcast schedule is somewhat shorter than that of the other stations, which is doubtless also a reflection of its chief responsibility being to the schools. But the interesting thing about its concept of role is that it takes quite seriously the responsibility of offering some good nonschool programs to the general public. It produces one of the most entertaining of the programs circulated on NET ("Ragtime Era"), and it offers a high proportion of public affairs programs.

Finally, the Alabama network, supported by state financing and three production centers, projects a state service personality. It broadcasts long hours, has a high proportion of school programs, and airs many science programs (these doubtless reflecting the two university production centers). It makes little use of NET programs, seldom repeats, and provides a varied collection of classes for its schools and of adult education to fit all kinds of viewers.

These are the different personalities. We shall now see how the viewers respond to them.

4

How Big Is the Audience?

What size audience do we expect noncommercial educational television to attract? What would we consider a "good" audience?

Almost every operative receiving set is tuned sometime during the week to commercial television. Depending on how many stations there are available, each set may or or may not be tuned to each station every week. Where there are only two channels, both may very well be used. In New York, where there are seven channels in use, a viewer may go weeks without tuning in one or more of the seven stations. But if he is an average viewer, his set will be turned on, for one or more members of the family, five to six hours daily.

We have no reason to expect any such amount of viewing of educational television. ETV is a second service, added after television viewing habits and expectations were already established. It flies in the face of a well-established precedent that television should furnish entertainment and relaxation. One man told us, "When I want to lounge around in the evening, with my slippers on and my pipe lighted, this crazy station asks me to *come to school!* It wants to give me a lecture on something, or to start me worrying about problems!" This is exactly what educational television does. It offers work and challenge with the same picture tube from which people have learned to expect relaxation and escape. And there is little doubt that a great many more people, at the end of a hard day, prefer to relax than to go back to work.

Therefore, educational television asks for rather uncommon behavior. It asks for behavior one might expect of persons who, after a day's work, hurry off to a lecture or a symphony concert, or go to the library for a book on the history of Africa, or study mathematics because they feel they ought to know about modern notions like set theory. People who do those things are small minorities of their communities. Lectures are not notably well attended. Symphonies are forever ending the year with deficits because of an inadequate base of support. Only about 25 per cent of Americans read books regularly, and fewer use libraries. And if all the adults per hundred thousand who study set theory at home for fun were to be brought together, they would probably make no more than a comfortable dinner party. In other words, this is minority behavior. We are not arguing that educational television need restrict itself to these minorities; in fact, we shall argue just the opposite. But the fact remains that at present its underfinanced programing, its shortage of glamor and stars, the memories of school that its name calls up—all these make for restricted, rather than large, audiences and for specialized, rather than heterogeneous, audiences. Therefore, we have no reason to expect that ETV will be attracting more than a minority audience. What we want to know is, how big a minority? and what kind of a minority?

How many viewers?

Actually, ETV seems to be doing surprisingly well with its minority audiences. You will recall that we define a "regular" viewer as one who can give some proof he views the station at least once a week. We call "occasional" viewers people who say they view the station less often than once a week, or who say they view every week or oftener but cannot give information to prove it. All others are "nonviewers," although each of these has probably at least "tried out" the educational station at some time, if his set is able to receive it.

The figures on regular viewers, occasional viewers, and nonviewers that we obtained from the telephone interviews are presented in Figure 10.[1]

[1] In Boston the definition of viewing was having watched within the past four weeks; in the other studies it was the respondent's own estimate that he watches, on the average, at least once a week.

One-fourth of the Boston regular viewers had not watched within the last

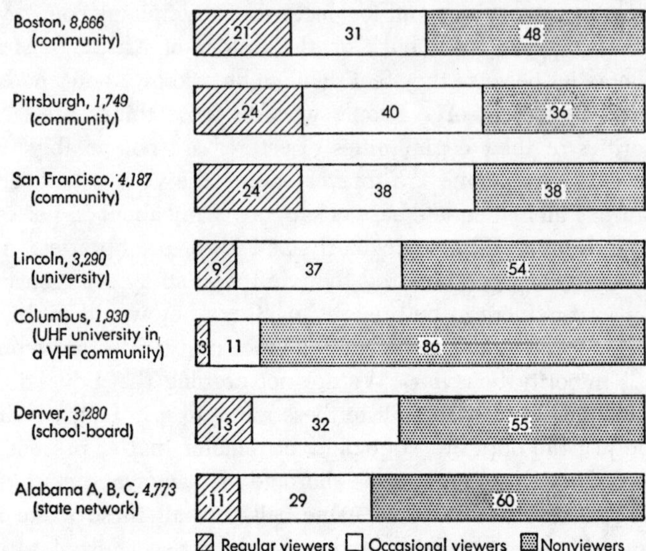

Fig. 10.—Percentage of regular viewers, occasional viewers, and nonviewers of ETV among set-owning adults. The figures in italic represent the number of telephone interviews on which the percentages in the chart are based.

As expected, the audiences vary greatly in size with the type and personality of the station. The community stations, old, well-established, projecting a community rather than an institutional personality, are able to attract close to one out of four adults at least once a week, and to get at least occasional use from up to two-thirds of all the adults in their communities. The school-

---

week. Thus the Boston one-week figure might be taken as 15 per cent, compared with San Francisco's 24 per cent and Denver's 13 per cent.

However, that would be misleading, for the Boston question was not a self-estimate of how often people watch ETV. It was a report on the most recent program viewed. And that deflates the respondent's tendency to overstate. Just one-third of all Boston respondents generalized that they see an ETV program at least once a week, but only two-thirds of those maintained that claim when asked about the latest week. In the other communities the bluffing test that required the respondent to show that he knew what the ETV program was, was applied to anyone who generalized that he watched once a week; in Boston only to those who dated the last program seen that recently. That suggests that Boston regular viewers, if the usual criterion had been used, would have been found to run somewhat over 20 per cent—or, in other words, thanks to compensating differences, about the same as the Pittsburgh and San Francisco figures.

board station, the state network, and the VHF university station all cluster between the 9 and 13 per cent figure; that is, they attract one out of eight to one out of eleven adults regularly, and almost half the community occasionally or oftener. In some respects, these are rather remarkable figures. A school-board station would seem to start life with a handicap, if one of its goals is to attract large audiences. A state network like Alabama must serve large rural and small town areas, rather than the centers of culture and education which surround Pittsburgh, San Francisco, and Boston. A university station like Lincoln likewise must suffer some handicap from its institutional personality in a not-very-large city surrounded by rural culture. And Columbus has to seek its audience entirely within the 15 per cent of TV homes that can receive UHF.[2] Furthermore, a number of the UHF sets and converters in that community had been purchased when Columbus was able to put university athletics on the air. It is seldom possible any more to broadcast important athletic events, because broadcasts are restricted by agreement of the National Collegiate Athletic Association, and therefore some owners of UHF sets are disgruntled because they are unable to get the kind of program that induced them to buy the set. Even so, Columbus attracts, as regular viewers, 20 per cent of the adults able to receive UHF. But the situation of Columbus points to the severe problem that all the educational stations on UHF face in trying to reach an audience in communities that have otherwise only VHF stations.

Are these figures representative of their station types? We have two other studies, made at about the same time and with much the same methods. One of these was a study made of the Minneapolis ETV audience.[3] The Minneapolis station is community-owned, but has studios on the University of Minnesota campus. It is apparently believed by a number of people in the Twin Cities to be a university station. Furthermore, it is a relatively new station. Its audience, therefore, might be expected to

[2] Only about 15 per cent of the homes in the area were equipped to receive UHF. Therefore, the figure of 86 per cent includes 85 who could not have received the UHF educational station even if they had wanted to.

[3] Carter, "Summary of Educational Television Inquiry in Minneapolis–St. Paul."

be more like that of Lincoln than like those of Pittsburgh or San Francisco. The study did indeed find that the regular viewers of that station were about 10 per cent of the adults in the community.

A study of a university station, WILL-TV, was made about the same time in Champaign-Urbana.[4] Unfortunately, the sample for this study included only the two cities, where university faculty members form a large part of the population. The figure for regular viewers was about 15 per cent. If extended into the farm regions around the two university cities, it would doubtless have come to a level comparable with that of Lincoln.

Previous studies of audiences of VHF educational stations, although made with somewhat different methods and designs and with different definitions of "viewer," have usually come out with figures between the low and the high percentages in this study.[5] Figures for the Michigan State University audience, when that University broadcast on UHF, were comparable with the Columbus figures. Measurements of the audience of the UHF outlet of the University of Wisconsin appear to give somewhat higher percentages than for Columbus, although it is very hard to compare the studies.

The advantage of the present studies is that they have all been done by virtually the same method, at the same time, with adequate samples. On the basis of what we have found, we can say with some confidence that a VHF educational station now typically attracts 10 to 25 per cent of the adults in its coverage area as regular viewers at least once a week and a somewhat larger group less often than once a week; that the older and well-established community stations are likely to be near the upper limit of the 10 to 25 per cent spread and the newer and the institutionally supported stations nearer the lower limit.

We see no necessary reason why community-owned stations should attract larger audiences than university or school or state

[4] Parker, "The Audience for Educational Television in Champaign-Urbana."

[5] These studies are reviewed in Schramm, pp. 20ff. The Michigan State study was I. R. Merrill, "Benchmark Television-Radio Study," 1956 (1,901 television homes in Lansing, Michigan). The Wisconsin study was B. H. Westley, "Attitudes toward Educational Television," 1957 (799 interviews in Madison, Wisconsin).

stations, except possibly that the community stations, by virtue of their sponsorship, *try* to attract larger audiences, whereas the institutional stations, by virtue of *their* sponsorship, are more content to deal with selected audiences. An additional reason for the difference between audiences in our data may be that the community stations we studied are in cities where cultural activities are well developed and where, particularly in the suburbs, there is a large percentage of highly educated persons; whereas the other stations are in smaller cities, and some of them cover large rural areas.

How long do they view?

We need also to know how much time the viewers spend on ETV. Are the "regular" viewers, for example, typically one-program-a-week viewers, or do they view a number of programs?

We tried to answer this by getting an estimate of the time viewers say they spend watching the educational station, and also by analyzing the viewing records obtained from home interviews. As might be expected, there is a wide variation. Some of the regular viewers do indeed watch little more than one program a week; others watch 15 or 20 programs. The average claimed by regular viewers is three to four programs a week (see Table 4). To be more specific:

1. Average time claimed to be spent per week by "regular" viewers varies from one hour and seven minutes, spent by men who are in the audience of the Alabama network, to three hours and fifteen minutes, spent by the women who regularly watch the

TABLE 4.—AVERAGE TIME "REGULAR" VIEWERS SAID THEY SPENT PER WEEK WATCHING ETV*

Area	Men	Women
Pittsburgh	1 hr. 13 min.	1 hr. 59 min.
San Francisco	1 hr. 49 min.	2 hr. 13 min.
Lincoln	1 hr. 39 min.	1 hr. 39 min.
Columbus	2 hr. 59 min.	3 hr. 15 min.
Alabama	1 hr. 07 min.	1 hr. 20 min.

* The time figures for Denver (Table 5) are of the same order, but cannot be readily compared with the others because they were obtained in a somewhat different way.

Columbus station.[6] The median is about one hour and 45 minutes.

2. Women who are regular viewers say they watch, on the average, about 20 minutes more per week than do men.

3. "Occasional" viewers, if we can trust their own estimates, average about 30 minutes per week watching the educational station, even though they do not watch it every week.

These figures are doubtless somewhat inflated. There is good reason to think that when people estimate the time they spend on ETV, they overestimate. We have some evidence on this from previous studies.[7] We also have some evidence from the present studies which would allow us to judge how much the estimates are probably exaggerated.

Table 5.—Average Time Spent per Week Watching ETV, in Denver; Comparison of Self-Estimates with Actual Records

During Week Watched KRMA	Men: Own Estimate	Men: Viewing Record	Women: Own Estimate	Women: Viewing Record
At least 1 hr.	100.0%	75.9%	94.0%	66.6%
At least 2 hr.	59.4	53.7	53.6	42.4
At least 3 hr.	38.8	25.9	32.2	17.8
At least 4 hr.	24.0	11.1	19.1	6.0
At least 5 hr.	12.9	5.6	15.5	1.2
Not at all	—	16.7	—	28.6
No check sheet	—	3.7	—	3.6

In the Denver study (Table 5), we compared self-estimates with actual records of viewing obtained from a detailed and checked schedule.

If the viewing record is, indeed, more reliable than the self-estimate, then we should conclude that the median viewing times are probably exaggerated between a quarter and a third.

In Boston the question was asked not in terms of hours, but in terms of numbers of programs. Taking the average program to be half an hour, the average time per week that regular viewers say they spent watching ETV was 73 minutes, or about one and a quarter hours.

[6] The Columbus viewers may average more time because the difficulty and cost of equipping one's set to view the UHF station selects out the most interested viewers.

[7] See Schramm, Lyle, and Parker, pp. 213–18.

Viewers also were asked about the one most recent ETV program they had seen. At the time of the interview, the median time that had passed since that broadcast was five days. Assuming the accuracy of that report and assuming a half-hour per program, that would lead to an estimate of 42 minutes per week per regular viewer instead of 73 minutes.

We have one estimate that is strictly objective. Since we conducted our 9,000 telephone interviews all in WGBH home broadcasting hours, we caught a certain number of people while they were actually watching a broadcast. This technique of coincidental interviews to establish ratings does not work well for ETV because the ratings are so low. Only about 50 respondents were watching WGBH when we called, giving a rating of 0.6 per cent. These were 2.3 per cent of the regular ETV viewers. Outside of school hours, at the date of our interviews, WGBH broadcast 64 half-hours per week. This suggests that the average viewer sees 1.5 programs per week ($.023 \times 64 = 1.47$). That we estimate to be 45 minutes of broadcast time.

The coincidental interviews thus confirm very closely people's estimates given on the basis of the last program they saw. They suggest that, in Boston at least, self-estimates of how many hours a week they generally watch ETV should be deflated by as much as 40 per cent.

If we conclude, then, that self-estimates may be inflated from 20 to 40 per cent, we should expect that the true figure for the eight-station sample would be not one hour and 43 minutes but somewhere between one hour and one hour and 20 minutes per week.

Talking about average viewing time may be misleading, however. The average ETV viewer is a composite of some avid fans and some very selective viewers. How much of the viewing is done by a small part of the audience? There are, of course, avid fans, but they are not many. In Boston 13 per cent of the regular viewers claim to watch six or more programs a week, and 18 per cent had actually watched in the past 24 hours.[8] The Boston audi-

[8] If it was a purely random process as to which regular viewers watched each day, then with 18 per cent viewing daily, only 17 per cent would not have seen ETV after nine days. Actually, 26 per cent had not watched ETV by

ence does not break sharply into avid fans and occasional viewers. Overwhelmingly it consists of mild devotees who give only a small part of their total viewing time to ETV.[9] The pattern demonstrable in Boston seems to hold for the other eight stations too.

Let us now translate the patterns we have observed into total hours. Suppose that a station like San Francisco has one million television-owning adults in its coverage area. We may suppose, then, that about 240,000 (24 per cent) of these will be regular viewers of the station, and will give about 360,000 hours per week to educational television (inasmuch as the San Francisco average for men and women is about two hours, which we shall reduce by 25 per cent to allow for overestimation). If we can suppose that, in addition to these, another 400,000 (40 per cent) are occasional viewers, and may average 15 minutes a week (reduced 50 per cent from their self-estimate), then these occasional viewers are giving another 100,000 viewing hours per week. Adding these two figures together, we can estimate that San Francisco is furnishing about 460,000 man-hours of educational television per week to the adults of its viewing area.

We are making the best estimates we can, based on the data so far available. But suppose that for some reason the figures were still exaggerated, and should be reduced by 25 per cent more. Even so, San Francisco would be supplying something like 300,000 hours of adult education a week to its area. To realize how enormous this figure is, add up the lectures, the concerts, the discussion groups, the adult evening classes, and other adult education events held in the area during a typical week, and multiply each of them by the time it lasts and by the number in the audience. You will find that educational television contributes far more adult education to its community than all these other sources combined.

---

then, showing the effect of the differences in habits, but this is an extraordinarily small difference. If 14 instead of 18 per cent had viewed daily, then the weekly accumulation would have been accounted for by random processes. Thus only 4 percentage points of the 18, or two-ninths of WGBH's audience, was accounted for by the avidity of its fans. Without any fans, but only average regular viewers, it would still have had seven-ninths of its audience.

[9] For more detail on this matter see Pool and Adler, pp. 50–61.

How big is the school audience?

So far we have been talking wholly about the adult audience. However, these stations spend the daytime hours broadcasting programs for the schools. How big are their school audiences?

Some of the figures on school coverages are actual figures, and others are rough estimates. In the case of San Francisco, we have actual figures. Schools in the coverage that make use of classes from the station are expected to pay a small fee per pupil in the classes taught by television. This fee has been paid for 151,000 students. It is probable that the service is being used by other pupils in other schools without paying the fee. But in any case, we can be quite sure that at least 151,000 children in the San Francisco area are getting some of their teaching by television.

If they get an average of one hour of television teaching per week, that is another 151,000 hours which San Francisco is contributing to community education each week.

Here are the best estimates on school audience that the directors of our nine stations were able to make. Some of these estimates (as in the case of Lincoln and Denver) are quite sound; others (as in the Alabama network, where no fee is collected and schools do not have to report their use of the service) are educated guesses only.

	Number		Number
Boston	300,000	Columbus	100,500
Pittsburgh	291,450	Denver	26,000
San Francisco	151,000	Alabama network	200,000
Lincoln	29,132	Total	1,098,082

Thus, these nine stations are helping to teach perhaps 1,100,000 students. The overwhelming majority of the students are in the elementary schools. College and university students in this audience apparently number between 5,000 and 7,500. The number of secondary students is probably around 20,000. This means that only about 2½ per cent of all this television teaching goes to high school students, less than 1 per cent to college students.

How big is the national audience?

There is no way, at this moment, to estimate the national ETV audience in such a way as to give much confidence in the result.

It is possible to make a rough estimate, however, by projecting the available figures to the other stations.

We now have studies made about the same time and in about the same way on 11 ETV stations—the nine here reported on, and Minneapolis–St. Paul (by Carter) and Champaign-Urbana (by Parker). By using the best current figure on television homes and adult population in each of these areas, and the percentages obtained in the television surveys, it is easily possible to obtain an estimate of regular and occasional adult viewers. By adding the school-broadcast figures to these adult figures (which, of course, takes no account of children who view the station but do not get part of their teaching by television), or by adding an arbitrary figure based on other audience measurement (such as, for example, one child for every three adults), we can arrive at an estimate for the total number of individual viewers.

Suppose, now, that one projects the 1961 figures from those 11 stations to 52 more in this way:

1. Divide the stations by type: community-owned VHF, university VHF, school-board and state-owned VHF, and UHF stations regardless of ownership.

2. For each of these types, take a high and a low estimate based on the highest and lowest figures available from the 11 stations recently studied:

a) Community VHF stations: *high,* 24 per cent regular and 40 per cent occasional (Pittsburgh); *low,* 10 per cent regular, 11 per cent "proved" occasional viewers (Minneapolis–St. Paul).

b) University VHF stations: *high,* 14 per cent regular (Champaign-Urbana) and 32 per cent occasional (Lincoln); *low,* 9 per cent regular (Lincoln) and 23 per cent occasional (Champaign-Urbana).

c) School- and state-owned stations: *high,* 13 per cent regular, 32 per cent occasional (Denver); *low,* 11 per cent regular, 29 per cent occasional (Alabama network).

d) UHF stations, all types: *high,* 3 per cent regular, 11 per cent occasional (Columbus); *low,* those same figures multiplied by 0.8 (inasmuch as only one estimate of UHF coverage was available).

3. Obtain the best estimates possible of adult population in

coverage area of each of the remaining stations, corrected for incidence of television homes. Multiply these population estimates by the viewer estimates for the appropriate type of station.

4. Add one child for every three adult viewers.

We present the results of this process, not as a definitive set of figures,[10] but merely as the best conservative estimate it was possible to make in 1962, when 63 educational stations were on the air. It will suggest the order of magnitude of the audience, but should be considered only as a rough estimate pending a more complete set of measurements. Our estimate is: In the spring of 1962, ETV could reach about 14 million television homes.[11] In those homes, it is attracting somewhere between 4.5 and 7 million regular viewers (depending on whether the high or the low estimate is more nearly right) and between 8 and 13 million occasional viewers (again depending on whether the high or low estimate is more nearly true).

This is a conservative projection, but is still presented most tentatively. In considering these figures, it should be remembered that 17 of the 63 stations are on UHF channels and consequently are doomed for the time being to small audiences. It should also be remembered that the two largest communities in the country—New York and Los Angeles—had no ETV station at the time of this estimate; the New York ETV station went on the air in the fall of 1962, and, although no target date has been set, a Los Angeles citizens' committee has announced its intention of purchasing and programing a station. These two stations alone might double the ETV audience. If other large communities, like Philadelphia, could obtain a VHF channel for their educational station, that too would make a great difference in the size of the audience. And it is to be expected that the new program of federal aid to ETV construction, and the requirement that new receiving sets be equipped to receive UHF, will in the course of a few years make a considerable difference in the potential audiences for ETV.

[10] The danger in this method of projection, of course, is that it may compound errors by multiplying incorrect figures together.

[11] It must be remembered that many of the stations are on UHF, and the number of UHF homes, where the commercial stations are on VHF, is only a small fraction of total TV homes.

But even at the moment, it appears that ETV is being used in homes *at least occasionally* by 12.5 million viewers (if we take the most conservative estimate) and *regularly* by at least 4.5 million viewers. It is helping to teach between 2 and 3 million children in school.[12] It is apparently furnishing, at the lowest estimate, about 10 million man-hours of educational and informative material per week to Americans.[13]

[12] This is the present estimate by the U.S. Office of Education.

[13] This supposes that 5 million regular viewers view one hour each per week, that 8 million occasional viewers average 20 minutes each, and that 2.5 million students get one hour each of TV teaching.

5

Who Is in the Audience?

We have described the audience of noncommercial educational television as a minority audience. *What kind* of minority is it?

It is not a minority in the sense that a small religious or racial group can be called a minority, that is, a group in which every member possesses some characteristic that every nonmember does not possess. Quite the contrary. The feature of the ETV audience that first comes to one's attention is that there are all kinds of people in the audience. There are young people and old ones, well-educated people and little-educated ones, parents and childless couples, nuclear physicists and manual laborers. There are eggheads and businessmen. It is a minority of choice rather than a minority by determination. The only common trait that seems even to promise to distinguish all regular viewers of educational television from all others is that the viewers enjoy watching ETV. And even this is not a clear test, because some people like ETV but cannot get it; and even among viewers there are differences of opinion about how enjoyable it is.

What we are talking about is minority behavior, rather than minority characteristics. And yet in the ETV audience there are a series of characteristics that occur as trends rather than as absolutes. That is, a viewer of educational television is *more likely than* a nonviewer to have certain characteristics. These characteristics occur in different combinations, and viewers who seem to deviate from one part of the pattern usually are in accord with another part of it. When this minority behavior is viewed against a group of trends or traits occurring in different combinations, then it is seen that the traits have a great deal of power to predict from a large number of individuals who *will* and who *will not*, given an equal opportunity, become a viewer of ETV.

Among these traits we do not find some that, at one time or another, have been advanced as probable characteristics of an educational audience. There is no difference pattern in age that consistently distinguishes viewers from nonviewers. There is some slight indication that the age group 30–39 produces a larger proportion of ETV viewers than do other age groups, but the trend is slight, and even if it were larger we should discount it on the grounds that people of that age have a lot of energy and tend to be generally more culturally active than older or younger people. It is also clear that parenthood does not make people any more likely to be viewers of educational television. *Number* of children makes some difference, but not the mere fact of having children. And there is no evidence that either the nonviewers or the viewers think of the ETV audience as "egghead" or "snobbish." The semantic differentials show only an insignificant difference between viewers and nonviewers on that point, as we shall have occasion to illustrate later.

The traits that have proved to be the best predictors are these:

The viewers of ETV are more likely than nonviewers to be well educated and of high socioeconomic status

The people who watch WGBH, for example, have a median income about $1,000 higher than nonviewers, are three times as likely to have gone to college (40 per cent for viewers compared with 14 per cent for nonviewers), and are more likely to live in the suburbs (65 per cent of viewers are suburban, against 57 per cent of nonviewers).

The specialty of the viewers becomes more dramatically highlighted if we look at the figures the other way around. What are the chances that persons of different sorts will become WGBH viewers? We can see in Table 6 that the odds are one in three that a member of a professional family will be a viewer; for an unemployed person or his family, the odds are one in 17. With nothing but time on his hands, the unemployed person still does not watch. It is socioeconomic status, and the personality that goes with it,

Except as noted, the numbers of cases in the charts and tables on audience characteristics which appear in this and following chapters are the same as those in the Interview Samples, Appendix B. These N's will not be repeated, in order to simplify the presentations.

that most clearly separates the public of ETV from its neighbors.

Indeed, a person with a postgraduate education and a family income of $7,000–$10,000 a year is more likely to be a viewer than not. A person with only a grade-school education and less than $5,000 in income has only one in 11 chances of being a viewer. But people of this type are four times as numerous as the first type, so these poor and uneducated ones add 2 per cent of WGBH's total audience, while the well-off, highly educated add only 2½ per cent—not a great difference for the broadcaster who must recognize that both kinds of people are watching.

A station manager may be interested in thinking about the percentages not as they are presented in Table 6, but with the total audience as the base. He wants to know the composition of his clientele, and in Boston, while 42 per cent are from professional and managerial families, it is still true that nearly one-fifth (19 per

TABLE 6.—THE VIEWERS OF WGBH, BOSTON
(*Per cent of possible viewers who are actual viewers*)

Category	Per Cent	Category	Per Cent
		Occupation of head of household:	
Education:		Professional	32
Grade school	10*	Managerial	26
High school	15	Retired	22
Vocational school	24	Sales	21
College	32	Student	18
Postgraduate	37	Clerical	18
Family income:		Farm	17
Under $5,000	16	Craftsman	17
$5,000–$7,000	21	Housewife	15
$7,000–$10,000	30	Service worker	13
Over $10,000	34	Operative	12
Urbanization:		Laborer	9
Highly urbanized	17	Unemployed	6
Suburban	22		

* This table should be read: "10 per cent of grade school graduates in the WGBH area are actual viewers; 15 per cent of high school graduates are viewers"; etc.

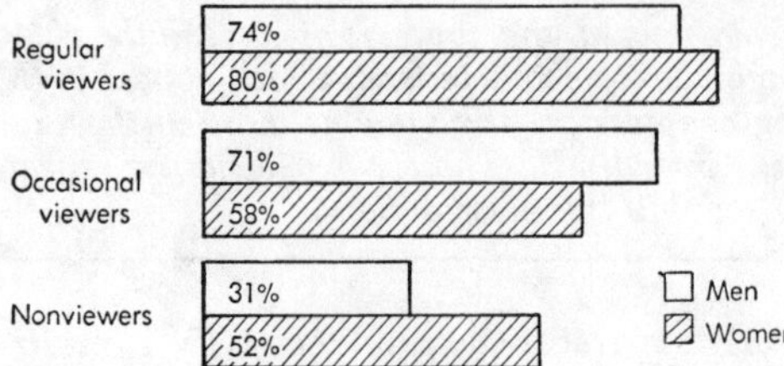

Fig. 11.—Proportion of regular viewers, occasional viewers, and nonviewers of ETV who come from white-collar group in San Francisco.

cent) are blue-collar people. But what Table 6 tells us is that these few blue-collar people are recruited from a large base, only a few of whom choose ETV, while the professional families, who form but 16 per cent of the population, provide one-fourth of the WGBH audience.

Is this picture generally representative of ETV? So far as we can tell from our other eight stations, it is. Figure 11, for example, shows the patterns of viewing by occupation in San Francisco. We can let San Francisco represent the other stations. By white-collar occupations we mean professional, managerial, sales, clerical, and supervisory personnel. By blue-collar occupations we mean production, service, laborers, and farm workers. It is obviously much more likely that a resident of the San Francisco Bay Area will tune in KQED if he comes from the white-collar group than if he comes from the blue-collar group. This trend is consistent over all our stations except with the Pittsburgh and Columbus men. In other words, 16 out of 18 comparisons support it.

Figure 12 is a chart of the regular viewers, occasional viewers, and nonviewers of each station who (*a*) have some college education, and (*b*) have less than a high school diploma.

With one exception, these trends are strong and consistent: the more education a group has, the more likely a member of this group is to be a viewer of educational television. The one exception is the sample of men from Pittsburgh. The Pittsburgh women fit the pattern perfectly, but the men do not. Since the Pittsburgh men also represent blue-collar workers in much higher proportion than the other eight stations, we must conclude either (*a*) that men of lower socioeconomic status in Pittsburgh are somehow dif-

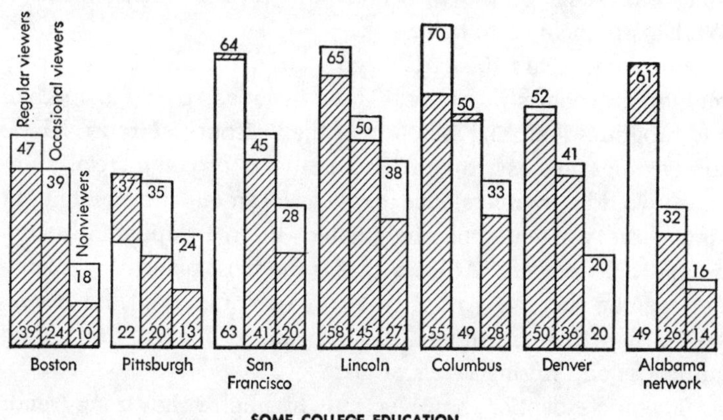

SOME COLLEGE EDUCATION

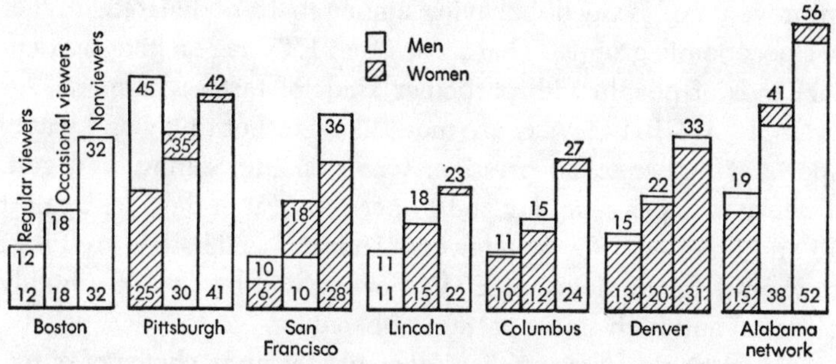

LESS THAN HIGH SCHOOL DIPLOMA

Fig. 12.–Comparison, in per cent, of regular viewers, occasional viewers, and nonviewers of ETV according to education. The figures, starting at the top left, are to be read thus: In Boston, 47 per cent of the men and 39 per cent of the women who were regular viewers had some college education, etc.

ferent from their opposite numbers in eight other cities or (*b*) that something about the programing of WQED in Pittsburgh is especially attractive to this particular group of men.

We can find nothing in our data to indicate a basic difference between the Pittsburgh men and the other men. Is there, then, anything essentially different in WQED's programs that would account for the number of low-education, blue-collar men in the audience? Here we have a hypothesis. It is impossible to prove it without duplicating the conditions, but it at least sounds believable, and some of the personnel and former management of WQED are inclined to believe it.

For some years the Pittsburgh station broadcast some very high-quality sports programs. These included some Pitt football and programs featuring members of the Pittsburgh Pirates. These sports programs, as we know from studies of commercial audiences, would attract less-educated viewers among the men but not among the women. Once habituated, the men apparently continued to be viewers. At least, that is the most plausible explanation we can suggest. And if true it is very important, for it suggests a way that educational stations can be effective in building audiences and raising levels of taste.

The one exception, however, only highlights the strong trend: Watching ETV is much more common, and apparently much more approved and valued behavior among better-educated, higher socioeconomic groups. That means that ETV is reaching particular kinds of people with particular kinds of tastes. In sports, for example, WGBH viewers are more likely to both play and watch sports of higher social prestige: tennis, skiing, sailing, and golf. Twenty-four per cent play and 17 per cent watch these, as against 15 and 8 per cent for nonviewers. Unless special steps are taken to change the audience of ETV, viewing will be part of a highly cultured and high-status pattern of behavior.

Education, income, and social status act upon choice of entertainment not only directly but also through the social milieu. People associate with others of their kind and adopt their habits. A person who moves in educated, prosperous groups finds himself in a milieu that supports ETV viewing; a person outside those groups does not. To see how this works, consider the talk about television that goes on in these different groups.

People do talk a lot about TV. Twenty-five per cent of WGBH viewers and nonviewers alike reported that within the preceding 24 hours they had talked to someone outside their own household about something they had seen on TV. And 80 per cent (for viewers and nonviewers alike) of conversations about TV were described as conversations about a show both parties had seen. This seems an extraordinary proportion; let us discount it a bit for possible response bias; but no matter how much we discount it, a pattern seems clear. People do talk about TV and they talk about shared TV experiences. If initially one friend in a pair "discovers" a show, before long both share the habit or both drop it. And when the habit is shared, talking about TV is then usually not a matter of imparting fresh information. It is a way of sharing and confirming one's own experiences. It is analogous to the pattern observed in various studies that people who have seen a sporting event are the ones most likely to read newspaper accounts of it, and that people who have just bought a product are the ones most likely to read the ads for it.

So the man who is the one out of 11 in his milieu to watch WGBH is doing a harder thing than the man half of whose friends do the same. The density of viewers in a population stratum is a critical fact in assessing the prospects for audience growth within it. It is harder to stimulate additional watching where word-of-mouth support does not exist than in those circles where a good ETV show will be discussed among friends.

The viewers of ETV are more likely than nonviewers to be "achievers"

In recent years a number of studies have shown that communication behavior in general, and television viewing in particular, have a normative quality; that is, they are considered good or bad things to do, depending on the norms of the social groups to which one belongs. The norm that seems most important in separating commercial and educational television watching is a set of related beliefs or values that have been variously called "deferred gratification norms," "delayed reward values," work orientation, future orientation, need achievement, and aspiration levels.[1] The people who hold these beliefs value work and self-improvement very highly, as contrasted with pleasure and relaxation. They tend to be ambitious and upwardly mobile. They value learning (it leads to self-improvement). They work hard in the present to reach future goals. In other words, they are the "achievers."

[1] See Schneider and Lysgaard, pp. 142–49, for a review of these theories up to ten years ago. The chief book on achievement motivation is McClelland, *The Achievement Motive.*

Achievers are more numerous in the middle class than in the lower class. They are more numerous in some cultures than in others and in some religious denominations than in others. They correspond closely in our society with the people who read books and other serious print. They are scarce among the people who have a high intake of entertainment television or film. And they apparently include a very large proportion of the viewers of ETV.

High TV Low print	High TV High print	Low TV Low print	Low TV High print
16%	26%	18%	40%

Fig. 13.—Television and print use by regular viewers of ETV.

Geiger and Sokol documented the normative quality of ETV viewing. Later studies, including the volume by Schramm, Lyle, and Parker, were able to sketch in the full pattern of what some called the "ETV syndrome"—high use of print, low use of entertainment television and film, high likelihood of being a viewer of ETV—and all this connected to a strong achievement norm.[2] It was found that even children 12 years old in many cases had already absorbed this achievement norm and already showed the high-print, low-TV pattern and were more likely to view ETV.

In this study we have found the same pattern. Although the viewers of ETV are on the average low viewers of commercial television, they are extremely heavy readers of books, and fairly heavy readers of magazines. By dividing our samples into above- and below-average users of television, and of books and magazines, and then combining the resulting groups, we separated out four groups to study, with the results that are seen in Figure 13. In other words, it is quite clear that the viewing of ETV seems to ally itself more closely with high use of print than with high use of commercial television. It tends to be an approved activity of the upper socioeconomic levels, the more highly educated people who, as the recent CBS study and other recent works show, are still critical and suspicious of entertainment television.[3] There is every

[2] Geiger and Sokol, pp. 174–81; and Schramm, Lyle, and Parker, *passim.*

[3] The study by Steiner repeatedly demonstrates that more outspoken and more severe criticism of television comes from the better-educated part of the

reason to believe that these better educated and higher-status groups think of educational television as being quite different from commercial television, more akin to serious reading, and something that can be sanctioned by their norms much more easily than commercial television. And whenever we have been able to measure the norms and values, we find that this print-ETV behavior tends to be accompanied by a strong achievement norm.

In our data almost any measure of aspiration level, work orientation, or social striving separates ETV users from nonusers. WGBH viewers, for example, belong to more organizations,[4] but they particularly exceed in attending meetings of professional, civic, political, and PTA organizations. Thirty per cent of viewers list membership in such purposeful groups, as against only 11 per cent of nonviewers.

Finally, although the difference in social striving between ETV viewers and nonviewers has been often noted in earlier studies, there are related social differences between them that have usually been missed. Most notable among them is religion.

Boston is a predominantly Catholic city. Fifty-seven per cent of our cross-section sample were Catholics. Boston also has a substantial Jewish population—about 10 per cent. These two groups provide the extreme patterns of ETV use or nonuse. The Catholic population is so large in Boston that two-fifths (39 per cent) of the ETV viewers are Catholic even though only one Catholic in seven watches. The small Jewish population watches so heavily that it provides another one-fifth of the WGBH audience. See Figure 14.

The results match many other findings on religion and education. Catholics are few among scientists or doctoral candidates.[5] Jews are typically high. And among Protestants certain denominations, represented in our coding by Episcopalians, Universalists,

---

populace. See also W. Schramm's analysis of the Milwaukee Journal Consumer Survey questions on parents' opinions of television. This shows that better-educated parents are much more likely to be able to name some undesirable thing they feel their child has learned from television. Eleanor Maccoby has also documented the different feeling toward television in low and high socioeconomic groups. See Maccoby, pp. 239–44.

[4] Sixteen per cent attend meetings of three or more associations, as against 4 per cent for nonviewers; 36 per cent attend none, as against 49 per cent for nonviewers.

[5] O'Dea, *American Catholic Dilemma.*

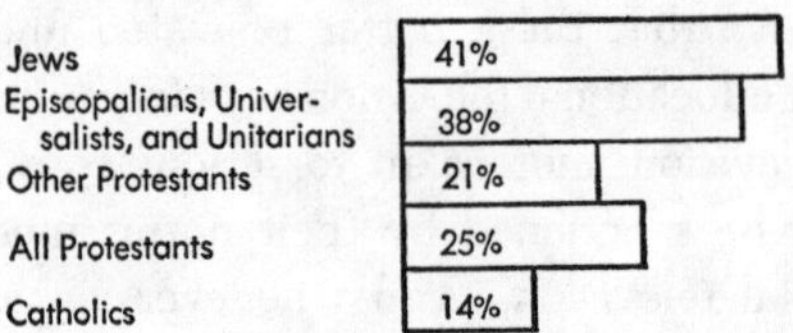

Fig. 14.–Proportion among different denominations who are WGBH viewers.

and Unitarians, provide larger proportions of professional and intellectual leadership.

The pattern of religious differences, which we note for use of ETV, is one that social scientists since Max Weber and R. H. Tawney have recognized as reflecting an ethic of achievement. David McClelland has documented by careful tests and measurements such differences in need to achieve among these religious groups. The response to ETV, or the lack of it, in some denominations is but one manifestation of a response that is much more general. It is aspiration, need for achievement, desire to learn, and gratification in work that ETV satisfies for many people.

The viewers of ETV are more likely than nonviewers to be fans of high culture

Of all the differences between ETV viewers and nonviewers, none stand out more prominently than interest in culture and interest in information.

Whatever the criterion, ETV viewers are more cultured people, as is shown in Table 7.

Most dramatic is the difference in reading. The median ETV viewer in Boston claims to have read four books in the past year, admittedly not an enormous number (30 per cent of the ETV viewers claim to have read 11 or more books). Among the nonviewers the median reader has read just over zero books; 47 per cent concede that they have read no book at all.

This characteristic of ETV viewers is not peculiar to Boston. We have ample confirmation of it from all our other studies. Figure 15, for example, is a chart of reading behavior from the Alabama samples.

With the exception of the Pittsburgh men, all our samples show

TABLE 7.—PROPORTION OF BOSTON VIEWERS AND NONVIEWERS OF ETV WHO ENGAGE IN VARIOUS CULTURAL ACTIVITIES

Activities	Viewers	Nonviewers
Play musical instruments	27%	15%
Play classical and semiclassical music	19	7
Collect classical records	34	17
Have FM radio sets	37	21
Listen to the more cultural stations on the radio	46	24
Like to play chess or do crossword puzzles	11	6
Read more cultural magazines	14	4
Have been reading a book in the past month	55	28
Are reading a difficult book (classical fiction or such nonfiction as philosophy, international affairs, and poetry)	14	7
Read about hobbies as well as practicing them	55	35
Have taken adult education courses	66	44
Have taken adult education courses in academic subjects	29	8
Have participated in a discussion group with some intellectual content	24	12

more ETV viewers than nonviewers going to concerts, hearing lectures, taking adult education courses, and otherwise demonstrating a deep interest in cultural activities.

The results become even more striking when we put a number of these cultural behaviors together in an index. Any one taste, say reading books or liking classical music, might be shared by a non-ETV viewer. But the person who participates in several of them and is still a nonviewer is rare.

On a seven-point scale of cultural interests covering music, TV, radio, books, and discussions, 61 per cent of the nonviewers scored 0 or 1, meaning that they had a substantial interest in no one of

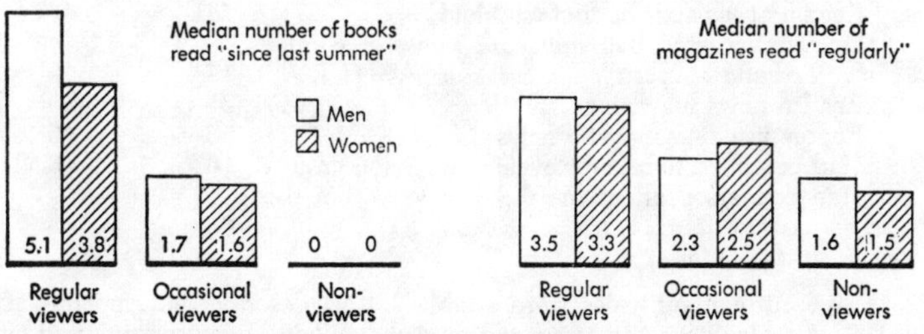

Fig. 15.—Reading behavior of regular viewers, occasional viewers, and nonviewers of ETV, Alabama network sample.

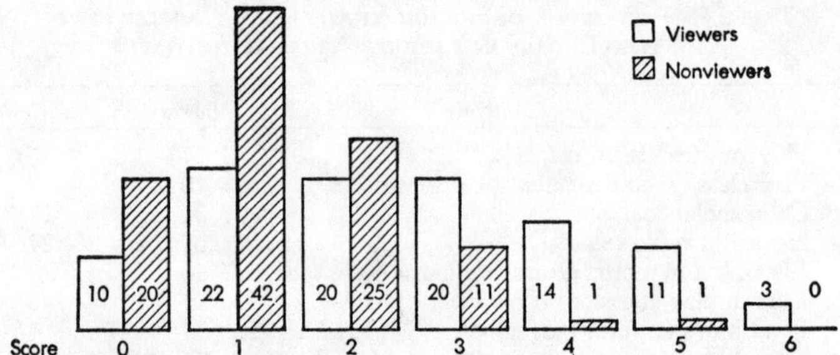

Fig. 16.—Distribution of viewers and nonviewers along a seven-point scale of cultural interests. Per cent at each level, from the low end of the scale (0) to the high (6).

these areas of culture or in one only. Among viewers, on the other hand, about two-thirds (68 per cent) showed a substantial cultural interest in two or more of the topics explored, and about half (48 per cent) in three or more of the topics.[6] ETV viewers have a taste for culture which the nonviewers seldom share. See Figure 16.

The viewers of ETV are more likely than nonviewers to be seekers of information

Only slightly less dramatic than the difference between viewers and nonviewers in their eagerness for culture is the difference in their interest in news. The day's news is part of the life of most people, whether viewers or nonviewers. But the viewers go after more informative sources, such as the better newspapers. To a substantial degree they talk and think about the news more, as is shown by some figures from the Boston study:

	Viewers	Nonviewers
Read a newspaper but not a tabloid	78%	48%
On Sunday, read the *New York Times* or *Herald Tribune*	14	2
Read a news magazine	31	19
Report listening to radio news	53	46
Had belonged to current events discussion groups	10	6
Had conversed about the day's news within the past 24 hours	66	48

[6] Six Guttman subscales were established, as described in Appendix D, p. 199. A scale of scales was created by dichotomizing between high and low scorers on each subscale. This also turned out to be a Guttman scale with a coefficient of reproducibility of .87.

There is an interesting difference between viewers and nonviewers in their use of print versus gossip for getting the news. The difference is partly blurred, because for all types of respondents the newspaper is the most important news source and TV the next most important. Asked about their main source of information about politics other than newspapers, word of mouth is clearly next to TV for nonviewers, but ETV viewers also use magazines and books:

	Viewers	Nonviewers
Cite magazines and books	23%	10%
Cite word of mouth	23	29

Reviewing the last two tabulations we find that although they use news media less, our nonviewers are more nearly, though not quite, on a par with ETV viewers in all ways of getting the news that do not require reading: radio, TV, and word of mouth. The ETV viewers gain their edge in news consumption via the printed word.

These data come from Boston, but the other studies are in full agreement, although they took up this question in less detail.

The WGBH audience follows the news, and so it is no surprise to learn that, when asked, they expressed more interest in acquiring information. We gave our respondents a closed-choice question on what they "like about the newspapers." Two of the choices on the card were "I like the human interest. I like to read about people"; "I learn about things in the world and about important news."

It was the latter choice, learning, that was overwhelmingly chosen, but by ETV viewers even more than by nonviewers, as a reason for liking newspapers:

	Viewers	Nonviewers
Human interest	17%	31%
Important news	73	58

We asked the same sort of question on what they "like most about the meetings" they attended. Once again the desire to learn came through strongly, but for ETV viewers more than for nonviewers. Among the alternatives on the card were: "I learn things from speeches and discussions I hear"; "It gives me a change from everyday activities"; "I see people I know."

Learning was the chosen motive of most ETV viewers, social contact was the motive of nonviewers, as a reason for liking club meetings:

	Viewers	Nonviewers
Learning	40%	29%
Change	23	30
People	28	41

The eagerness to learn shown by the WGBH viewers had one odd and interesting result. Although they were supporters of a noncommercial station that carries no ads, they had no more antipathy to ads than did the nonviewers. If they had any bias against commercialism, it was fully offset by their responsiveness to information in whatever form it might come, even in ads. Note that there were no real differences between viewers and nonviewers in their replies to three different questions about ads:

	Viewers	Nonviewers
Did *not* choose "too many commercials" from a list of terms which they could use to characterize various CTV channels	55%	53%
Said they watched the commercials and evinced no dislike	53	56
Said they learned something from newspaper ads	65	59

WGBH was not chosen by its audience as an escape from commercialism, but for what it added to their culture and knowledge.

And add to their knowledge it certainly did. We have only sparse and relatively inconsequential information on what particular items of knowledge particular viewers acquired from WGBH. It is often hard for a person to know where he learned a particular fact, and with the small audiences WGBH has for any given show, one has to hunt far before spotting in our data two individuals who had first acquired the same fact from WGBH. We forgo the detective job of tracking such clues and simply note that our viewers do report learning things.

Being eager learners, they were also learning from reading and from other media, which, as we have seen, they used a great deal. We gave our respondents a ten-item information quiz. Each respondent was asked to identify the following:

Fidel Castro
Jim Arness
Nigeria
Tony Curtis
J. Robert Oppenheimer
Brigitte Bardot
Robert Frost
Ralph Bunche
Betty Furness
Mao Tse-tung

Arness, Curtis, Bardot, and Furness were thrown in partly to sustain the morale of respondents who might on the public affairs items find themselves failing every time. But they were also thrown in for a much more serious reason. We did not wish to label those persons who were ignorant of the things we knew as ignorant men. They might know something else instead. An objective study of knowledge cannot start with the assumption that someone who knows of Robert Frost but not Tony Curtis is *per se* more informed than someone who knows of Tony Curtis but not Robert Frost. There was at least the possibility that, rather than dealing with informed and uninformed people, we were dealing with two cultures the members of which were each informed in their own sphere and not in the other.

Is that the case? Here are the figures for the four popular-culture characters on our quiz.

	Per Cent Replying Correctly	
	Viewers	Nonviewers
Jim Arness	56%	56%
Tony Curtis	57	58
Brigitte Bardot	80	77
Betty Furness	74	56

The nonviewers were not better informed about these people. For three of the four entertainers the results were virtually identical for ETV viewers and nonviewers. The WGBH viewers do not look down their noses at comedy or the comics, baseball or the twist, Hollywood or slick magazines. They are not aesthetes in a world of their own. They are simply people much like their neighbors in broad interests, who have enough wit to enjoy stretching their minds occasionally, and enough taste to get annoyed and bored by arid stretches of pure banalities. We are not dealing with two cultures. The WGBH viewers are, for much of their lives, part of exactly the same culture as the nonviewers. They share to exactly the same degree as the rest of the population the popular circuses of our society.

A note about Betty Furness. She had been selling Westinghouse appliances on the political convention telecast half a year before. The political conventions attracted many of our news-hungry ETV viewers. Her polished but trivial performances punctuating the cosmic hamming of the politicians made her a culture heroine of sorts for the more politically interested sectors of the American public. It is ambiguous whether she belongs in the list of popular-culture figures or of public-affairs figures.

So we find that our viewers and nonviewers were at one in sharing a popular culture. What of their knowledge of public affairs? Here the picture is very different. The ETV viewers took off from the shared base and also knew about a lot of other things little known to the nonviewers. In the public-affairs field the ETV viewers were much better informed.

	Per Cent Replying Correctly	
	Viewers	Nonviewers
Fidel Castro	92%	84%
Mao Tse-tung	56	23
Robert Frost	51	18
Nigeria	43	18
Ralph Bunche	48	16
J. Robert Oppenheimer	36	10

Treating these six items as a test, the average score obtained by viewers was 55 per cent (one-fifth of them scored 100). The average score of nonviewers was 30 per cent (less than 4 per cent of them scored 100). The average nonviewer could identify Fidel Castro and one of the other five items.

It is easy to deplore human ignorance. It is easy to be shocked that two-thirds of our WGBH viewers had forgotten who Robert Oppenheimer was, if they ever knew, and that more than half were stumped by Nigeria and Ralph Bunche. But they were alert compared to the nonviewers, who must have found this test incredibly hard. Except on Fidel Castro, not even one-fourth of our nonviewers gave a right answer on any one item.

The results on Castro are useful in discouraging overquick generalization. Except for him, no political item on the list is known to more than one-fourth of the nonviewers, and even among the viewers the best-known other item is known to no more people than the least-known popular-culture figure. One would be tempted to generalize that public affairs information gets far less widely known than the acts of entertainers do. But then we note Fidel Castro, who substantially outpoints everyone else on the list including Brigitte Bardot. The valid conclusion would seem to be that for the nonviewers the range of attention for public affairs is an extraordinarily narrow one. The scope of their knowledge of public affairs reflects accurately the coverage in the news sources they use. The tabloid, the five-minute radio news bulletin, and word-of-mouth conversation are not devoid of political and world news. But it is the one or two top stories of the day that are given space in their small news hole. Berlin, Cuba, a spaceman in orbit, outbreak of a local war may capture the banner headlines or may be talked about by friends over coffee. What gets lost in this kind of limited news coverage is the wealth of subordinate stories found in a great newspaper or in a rounded broadcast schedule of documentaries, panels, and commentaries. Years may go by without Robert Frost, Nigeria, or Ralph Bunche rating the banner head in the daily papers. Recurrently important, still they are always important at the second level. And it is the second-level stories that get filtered out of the inferior media. The WGBH viewers, like the news sources they use, throw a wider net. For them in public affairs, as for everybody in popular culture, the world of interest is a large and complex place with many interests to choose from. The average ETV viewer is not an expert or professionally committed to following the news, so he will miss half of the easy items on our quiz. But the things he does know range over a wide scope of possible foci of interest, corresponding to the numerous departments and story categories of a large metropolitan daily paper or news magazine.

The viewers of ETV are more likely than nonviewers to be very active people

The results already obtained foreshadow our next point: ETV audiences are energetic, active people—doers. We have already noted that they participate more in high culture (music, books, etc.) and in public affairs information. Now we are about to present evidence that they also participate more than nonviewers in an additional series of activities, and in particular that they are more active in the cultural and civic affairs of their communities.

The astonishing thing is that they seem to achieve this greater participation without any less participation in anything else we have measured so far except total television time (which, for ETV viewers, was a few minutes less per day than for nonviewers of ETV).

This can only go so far. The day is 24 hours long for everybody and time must be found somewhere. But to some degree people of greater energy, drive, and capacity will pack more into the same hours. Our research question is how far this is the case. What are the things ETV viewers do more of, and what are the things that get displaced to make room for their special tastes?

The general conclusion is that very little gets displaced. The special interests of ETV viewers get packed in on top of a base of interests and activities shared by the whole society. The tastes of the viewers are catholic and their energy is such that they can consume what their less motivated neighbors consume and something else besides. This has its implications for ETV programing. It means that the viewers of ETV for the most part are not rebels against the enjoyments of the masses, but rather they are people who share those enjoyments but want something else too.

The picture of intense activity is seen in every one of our nine-station audiences. In Figure 17 the Columbus comparisons stand for the rest of the eight studies outside Boston. Table 8 gives more detailed figures from the Boston study.

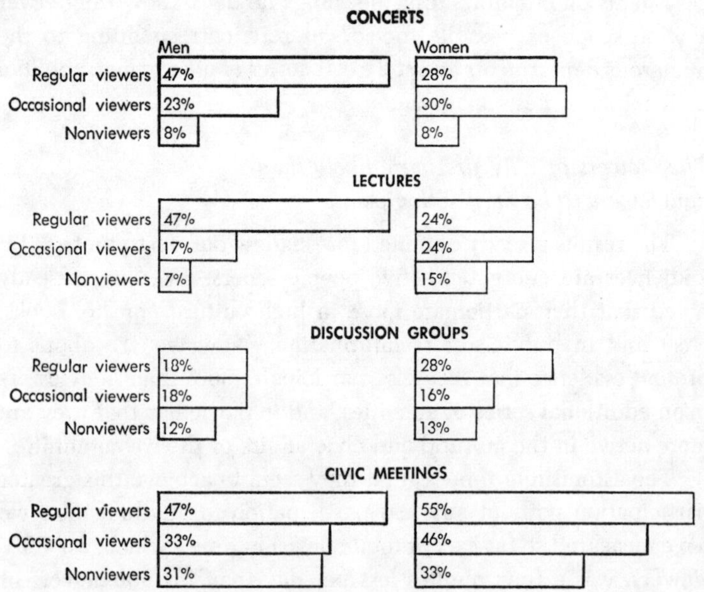

Fig. 17.—Per cent of viewers, occasional viewers, and nonviewers participating in various activities in a winter season in Columbus.

TABLE 8.—ACTIVITIES OF BOSTON VIEWERS AND NONVIEWERS OF ETV

Activities	Viewers	Nonviewers
Go to lectures	33%	13%
Have gone in past week	7	3
Go to the legitimate theater	42	24
Have gone in past week	4	1
Take evening courses*	17	8
Have attended in past week	8	4
Occasionally take part in discussion groups*	18	10
Have taken part in past week	6	3
Attend club or organization meetings	64	51
Attend meeting of three or more groups	16	4
Have ever been active in politics	23	14
Are active now	4	2

* Adult education courses and discussion groups were asked about in slightly different ways in the 9,140 telephone interviews and in the 511 personal interviews. However, the picture is consistent. The figures from the telephone interviews were as shown above, and the personal interviews were as follows: have ever taken adult education course, viewers 66 per cent, nonviewers 44 per cent; are doing so currently, viewers 11 per cent, nonviewers 7 per cent; have ever belonged to discussion group, viewers 32 per cent, nonviewers 16 per cent; are in one currently, viewers 10 per cent, nonviewers 4 per cent.

TABLE 9.—OTHER ACTIVITIES OF BOSTON VIEWERS AND NONVIEWERS OF ETV

Activities	Viewers	Nonviewers
Go to the movies	54%	48%
Have gone in past week	10	9
Have a hobby	75	64
Have two or more hobbies	42	29
Attend sporting events	43	35
Have attended in the past week	12	10
Like to watch sports	88	83
Have played at a sport in the past year	53	55

Those were activities in which one might expect to find more participation by educated and alert men and women. But there are other activities about which our stereotype of the educated man does not tell us what to expect. And in these, too, WGBH viewers participate as much as or more than nonviewers. They have more hobbies, go to the movies as much, and follow athletics as much as the nonviewers. See Table 9.

We have yet to find any significant area of life from which the ETV viewers slice the time to do all the extra things they do.[7]

[7] One suspicion might be that while ETV viewers do more different things, they spend less time on any one of them. That is not the case for most activities. WGBH viewers spent as much of the last week at sports events and movies as did nonviewers.

In player sports WGBH viewers pick up a little time. Virtually as many of

The data contain one other item of great importance concerning the activities and energies of the ETV audience. The relation between viewing ETV and cultural, informational, and civic activity holds, not only for the upper socioeconomic group, but also for that *blue-collar group* who are viewers. We shall discuss those deviants on p. 84. Their participation serves to reinforce our conclusion that activity of these kinds is one of the truly distinguishing characteristics of the ETV viewer.

If there is one viewer of educational television in a family, there are likely to be other viewers in the family also

Viewing of ETV goes by families. In the large study of children and television mentioned earlier,[8] it was found that television viewing is most often a family affair. In particular, parental viewing is a great predictor of, and apparently a strong influence on, children's viewing. These studies of the educational television audience show that the viewing of ETV follows this same pattern. In each of the nine communities, if one member of a family is an ETV viewer, the odds are quite good that other members of the family are also viewers. Conversely, if a person is not a viewer, the chances are strong that no one else in the family is a viewer. The following figures are from the Alabama network interviews:

If Person Interviewed Is	Proportion of Cases in Which Someone Else in Family Views ETV
Regular viewer	85%
Occasional viewer	61
Nonviewer	14

It is interesting to note that the wife seems more often to be the focus of "ETV contagion" in a family than does the husband. For example, when we ask a husband who is a regular viewer whether anyone else in the family watches educational television, the chances are a little better than even that his wife will also be a viewer of ETV; but if we are talking to the wife, then the chances

---

them play some sport, but there are fewer real enthusiasts who play weekly or daily among the viewers. Those who estimate that they had played 41 or more times in the past year were 16 per cent, against 26 per cent of the nonviewers.

[8] Schramm, Lyle, and Parker, pp. 47–48.

are only about four in ten that the husband will be a viewer. For example, figures from Denver show:

When husband is regular viewer	Wife is viewer in 51% of cases
When wife is regular viewer	Husband is viewer in 40% of cases

And if the mother alone is a viewer, it is a bit more likely that the children will be viewers than if the father alone is a viewer.

This "social contagion" seems to spread not only through the family but among the family's friends also. Over half the viewers said they knew that some of their friends watched educational television. By contrast, only a small minority of the nonviewers could say they knew that some of their friends viewed ETV. This is not surprising, because people tend to make friends in their own social and cultural groups. If one person has the education, the tastes, the interests, the norms that lead him to watch ETV, his friends are likely to have those characteristics also.

Educational television viewers are more likely than nonviewers to go purposefully to the receiving set for a single program which they know will be on at a certain time

We observed this in interviewing people to find out the programs they watched during the previous week. There were very few ETV viewers who reported that they simply turned on the educational station and "let it play" for the evening. Most viewers seemed to know when a particular program was coming, and went purposefully to the set at that time. They tended to be "one program" viewers. They would watch the desired program, then turn the set off or tune to another station. This is not to say that all ETV viewers behaved this way, and it is also worth noting that sometimes the program to which they went so purposefully was one like "Open End," which lasted two to three hours. But they typically went for single programs.

To supplement this evidence we asked the respondents in five studies to reflect back on their use of educational television and to answer the question: "When you view educational television, do you usually tune in the station to see what is on, or tune in to hear a specific program that you know is on?" The results are shown in Table 10.

The question is whether this television behavior is characteristic

TABLE 10.—METHOD OF SELECTING ETV PROGRAMS

Station	Tune to See What Is On	Tune for Specific Program	No Answer
Boston*	18%	74%	8%
Pittsburgh	14	74	12
San Francisco	17	74	9
Lincoln	25	73	2
Columbus	10	80	10
Alabama network	27	65	8

* The Boston question concerned the mode of choice of the most recent ETV program seen, rather than asking for the respondent's usual behavior. In this instance the question form made no difference.

of the kind of people who view ETV, or whether it is an effect of the kind of programs that are to be found on ETV. Our conclusion, after talking to a number of viewers in an attempt to answer this question, is that it is probably a function of both. Viewers with more education are more likely to exhibit this purposeful selection of programs, whether with educational or entertainment television. On the other hand, it seems that viewers, regardless of education, are likely to be more purposeful and selective with ETV than with CTV.

If viewers tend to go to educational television for specifically preselected programs, then it becomes important to know how they inform themselves of the programs. About two out of three who sought information said they relied on the newspaper. About one in five said he depended on the station's program guide.

Detailed information on this topic was secured in the Boston study. Like other ETV users, WGBH viewers usually turn to the station to pick up a preselected program. Most often, 40 per cent of the time, they had picked the last program they had seen from a newspaper listing, and if one adds *TV Guide* (7 per cent) and WGBH's own guide (only 1 per cent), then almost half of the viewers claimed to have picked it from a printed listing. Word-of-mouth recommendations added another 9 per cent. The two remaining modes of choosing a program, dial flipping and habit, were used in 18 and 17 per cent of the cases, respectively. Twenty-three per cent claimed to watch some program regularly, while 64 per cent said they picked programs one at a time.

There is one other way in which people get to see programs.

Someone else in the household may pick them. The average size viewing group of a WGBH program, as found in our telephone coincidental interviews, was 1.8 persons. Any 100 average groups would have, besides 100 respondents, 27 other adult females,[9] 20 other adult males, 10 children over 14, and 25 children under 14. Under these circumstances the respondent might often watch ETV programs he did not choose to watch as well as sometimes fail to watch programs he would like to see. But in practice our WGBH viewers were not particularly conscious of such compulsion. Family tastes are reported to be reasonably homogeneous. They may not have started out that way. Some one member may initially have set the family's viewing habits. But by the time of the interview people felt that they were seeing the programs they wished to see. Only 17 per cent of viewers reported that they saw WGBH programs bcause they were picked by someone else. Sixty-eight per cent said the choice was their own.

Thus the viewing pattern is predominantly one of conscious selection of individual programs. Such a pattern would never lead to very large amounts of viewing or, more important, would not allow for audience growth if it were the only pattern of viewing. For the audience to grow, people somehow have to experience programs that they have not seen before. Fortunately, preselection from published lists is not the only mode of choosing. About one-tenth of choices are, it will be recalled, recommended by someone else; one-sixth are explicitly chosen by another member of the household, and another sixth are chosen by dial flipping. These mechanisms provide enough fresh exposure to programs other than established favorites to allow effective audience building.

Other differences between viewers and nonviewers

The main factors that distinguish ETV viewers from nonviewers we have found to be higher social status, higher aspiration level, higher cultural level, higher interest in public affairs, and

[9] While females were in the majority, as they are in the population, men were actually better represented in the WGBH audience than in the CTV audience. Nineteen per cent of women with TV sets and 23 per cent of men with TV sets were ETV viewers.

higher energy. We have also noted that viewing ETV goes by families, and that ETV viewers tend to be purposeful rather than "let's see what's on" users of television. In the course of our studies we also noted a few other differences which might be briefly noted.

In a majority of the studies, families with adult ETV viewers tend to have more children than non-ETV families. However, the difference was slight, and it did not hold in Boston, probably because of the large number of Catholics in the city. Catholics, who often have large families, are less likely than Protestants to be ETV viewers.

ETV viewers are slightly more likely to engage in activities along with their families. They are also slightly more likely to engage in them all alone, leaving nonviewers slightly more likely to "go out with the boys" or otherwise play with friends.

ETV viewers like foreign movies. Fifty-one per cent go to them in contrast to only 19 per cent of nonviewers.

ETV viewers, at least in Boston, are politically slightly more liberal than nonviewers. See Table 11. But the differences are not great. Ideology is not one of the things that sharply differentiate viewers from nonviewers.

One further difference should be mentioned. In all the nine communities, we find that ETV viewers spend a little less time on TV of all sorts than do nonviewers, but very little less. In Boston, the telephone interview was used to estimate (by asking whether the set was on when the interviewer called) the proportion of the evening hours that sets were on. In the homes of ETV viewers, sets were on about two hours and 28 minutes an evening (only a small part of that on WGBH). In homes of nonviewers of ETV,

TABLE 11.—BOSTON VIEWERS AND NONVIEWERS OF ETV AND THEIR POLITICAL VIEWS

Political View	Viewers	Nonviewers
Choose the label liberal for themselves	53%	47%
If in charge of radio station, would let someone continue a speech attacking America, rather than cut him off the air	64	50
Rate personal contact between people of different countries as important in solving world problems	39	30
Fail to select military might as important in solving world problems	71	63

sets were on about 18 minutes longer. In San Francisco, nonviewers of ETV claimed to spend about 15 minutes a day more on television than did ETV viewers. In Lincoln the difference was slightly larger. On a week night in Lincoln the estimated time spent on all TV by regular viewers and nonviewers of ETV was as follows:

Men, regular viewers	1 hour 33 minutes
Men, nonviewers	1 hour 59 minutes
Women, regular viewers	1 hour 49 minutes
Women, nonviewers	2 hours 14 minutes

This was the general order and direction of difference.

The fact has some significance because TV viewing is the first field we have found in which ETV viewers are actually less active. That may be an indication of the extent to which TV watching is sometimes not an activity at all but a passivity. Television watching may be just a way of filling time, not a conscious seeking of something. If it is that, it may expand to whatever amount of time is available, which for busy ETV types is less. So the slightly lower TV-watching figure for ETV viewers is interesting. But even more interesting is the fact that it differs so little from that of nonviewers.

Previous studies of audience characteristics

These findings about the nature of educational television agree with the great majority of previous studies of individual station audiences, so far as these studies go into the variables that we have discussed. Thirteen of these studies are reviewed in *The Impact of Educational Television.*[10] The results of these earlier studies can be summarized this way:

Ten out of the 13 studies concluded that ETV viewers are better educated, on the average, than nonviewers.

Ten of the 13 studies concluded that ETV viewers are more likely than nonviewers to come from the white-collar, middle- and upper-class part of society.

All the nine studies that went into this matter concluded that viewers are more likely than nonviewers to participate in community cultural and civic events.

All the nine studies that went into it concluded that viewers of

[10] Schramm, p. 30 and *passim.*

ETV are also more likely to indulge in serious reading and other "highbrow" communication.

This is an encouraging amount of agreement, but it is not unanimous in all respects. In particular, the three studies that do not follow the general trend seem to demand some explaining. One of these studies is of station WQED in Pittsburgh. Another is of the Houston university station, and a third is of ETV viewing in a small southern town. These studies lined up as follows:

Study	Education	Social Status	Cultural, Civic Participation	Serious Mass Media
University	No relation	No relation	Related	Related
Small town	No relation	No relation	Related	Related
Pittsburgh	No relation	No relation	Did not consider	Did not consider

It has been somewhat puzzling that these three studies do not agree with the great majority of the others in the conclusion that more education and higher social status are more likely to go with the viewing of educational television. We are in a position to reconsider why these studies might have come out as they did, in terms of the much greater amount of data we now have available, and especially in view of our ability, with these data, to study the viewers who seem to be deviants from the general pattern.

What about the deviants?

There are many people in the educational television audience who would seem, on the basis of the characteristics we have so far identified, not to belong there. These people do not have many years of education. Or they are of blue-collar, rather than white-collar, status. Or they are not active in cultural or civic affairs. Or they are not readers of books or other serious prose. And still they are viewers of ETV. We call these people deviants, because they seem to deviate from the pattern.

The most interesting of these deviant groups is made up of the people who are in blue-collar jobs and who, for the most part, have less than college education. As we have already pointed out, there is good reason for thinking that norms regarding television differ as between these lower-status people and the higher-status people, who, mostly, hold white-collar jobs and have college education.[11] The difference seems to run like this:

[11] For this evidence, see Schneider and Lysgaard; see also Schramm, especially the article by K. Geiger and R. Sokol.

Higher status	Values work and self-improvement—"delayed gratification"	Therefore is suspicious of entertainment television	But approves educational television and serious reading
Lower status	Values enjoyment and relaxation—"immediate gratification"	Therefore is suspicious of mass media that demand work and study	But is grateful for and approves of entertainment television

To the extent that this is true, blue-collar workers are going against their class norms when they view ETV. And yet there are a number of such persons who are regular viewers of ETV. How can we explain this?

It is interesting to find evidence that a number of the blue-collar viewers of educational television are upwardly mobile—that is, persons trying to raise their position in the community, and to that extent, at least, rejecting their own group. Here, for example, are the answers to a question asked of a number of such deviants. These were people who held (or whose husbands held) a blue-collar job, and who had less than college education, but who nevertheless were regular viewers of ETV. They were asked whether they would rate themselves as belonging to the upper class, middle class, or working class. The answers are shown in Figure 18.

Clearly a much larger proportion of viewers than of non-viewers, in the blue-collar group, rate themselves higher than the

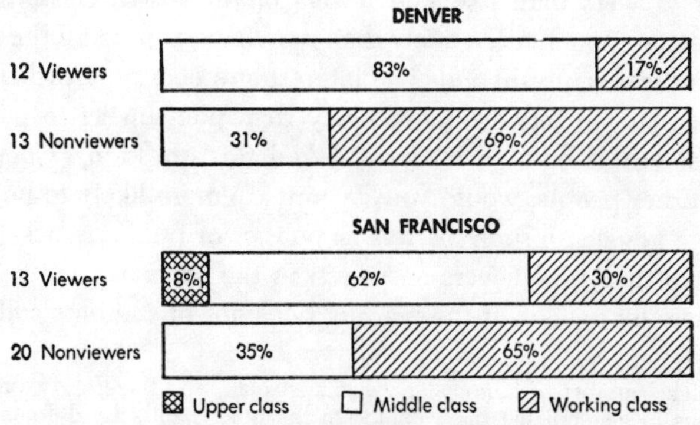

Fig. 18.—Blue-collar viewers and nonviewers of ETV rating themselves by class.

social status to which they objectively seem to belong. There is no such difference in the white-collar group; they distribute themselves among classes in about the same proportion, whether they are viewers or not. Therefore, a perfectly good hypothesis to explain some of the deviance is that a certain number of these blue-collar ETV viewers are yearning upward in the social structure and are therefore really operating under the norms of the higher-status class.[12]

Now let us look at Table 12 for some of the evidence on cultural, civic, and political activity on the part of these blue-collar viewers of ETV.

TABLE 12.—CULTURAL AND CIVIC ACTIVITY BY BLUE-COLLAR VIEWERS AND NONVIEWERS OF ETV

	Attended Concerts		Attended Lectures		Attended Discussion Groups		Attended Civic Meetings	
Area	V	NV	V	NV	V	NV	V	NV
Pittsburgh	16%	2%	8%	1%	20%	6%	41%	19%
San Francisco	19	4	18	10	22	4	30	17
Denver	22	7	17	4	18	6	17	7
Alabama network	11	7	20	5	20	5	42	28
Lincoln	9	1	9	5	18	3	25	19

Note: These percentages are based on the following sample sizes of viewers and nonviewers, respectively: Pittsburgh, 49 and 248; San Francisco, 83 and 150; Denver, 167 and 258; Alabama network, 179 and 504; Lincoln, 56 and 150.

These are impressive trends. They indicate that blue-collar viewers of ETV tend in this respect at least to be more like white-collar viewers than like nonviewers of their own class; that is, viewers are much more likely than nonviewers to do all the things that indicate cultural and civic interest and energy. Furthermore, blue-collar viewers are more likely than nonviewers to perceive themselves as opinion leaders. Asked this question, "Compared with other people, would you say you are more likely to be asked to give advice on such matters as politics or public issues?" more viewers than nonviewers answered in the affirmative.

Now let us look at the reading behavior of the blue-collar de-

[12] The number of blue-collar viewers is small, and therefore we must be cautious in generalizing these data. On the other hand, the differences are very large, which should give us some confidence.

TABLE 13.—READING BEHAVIOR OF BLUE-COLLAR GROUPS

Area	Median Number of Books Read in Last Six Months		Median Number of Magazines Read Regularly	
	Viewers	Nonviewers	Viewers	Nonviewers
Pittsburgh	—	—	2	1
San Francisco	5	—	3	—
Denver	4	—	2	1

viants, in Table 13. Here, once again, we find the blue-collar viewers behaving in the white-collar pattern. This is shown in yet another way by Figure 19, which divides the blue-collar sample on the basis of television and print use. These are striking differences. Within the blue-collar group, nonviewers conform to the expected pattern: the majority of them fall into the high TV—low print category. But the percentage of blue-collar *viewers* is little more than one-fourth as large as that of nonviewers. The blue-collar *viewers,* just like the white-collar viewers, tend to be high users of print.

So what do we find? The blue-collar deviants are deviants by classification, rather than by behavior. By occupation and education they are classified with a social group that does not especially value educational television. But they yearn, many of them, to be upwardly mobile in society. They not only reject their class; they also reject many of its norms and customs. They not only go against its norm with regard to television; they also behave unlike most blue-collar people in their use of print, and in their cultural and civic activity. In other words, these deviants are classified as blue-collar workers, but they behave in all these other respects like white-collar people.

If a person has a college education and a white-collar job, the odds are good that he may also read books, be active in cultural and civic life, and view educational television, if it is available to

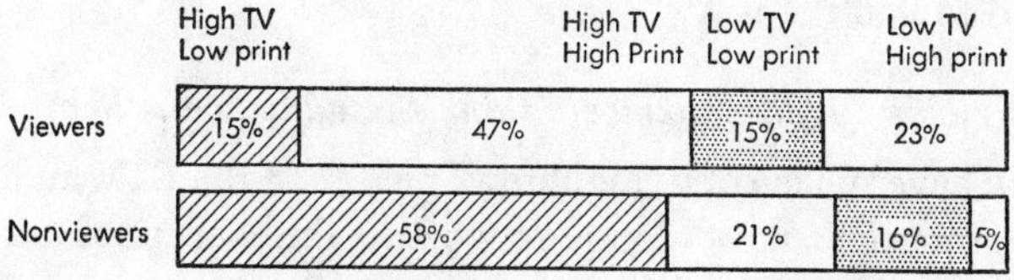

Fig. 19.—Television and print use by viewers and nonviewers of ETV in blue-collar group.

him. If he has less than college education, and if he has a blue-collar occupation, then the odds are good that he may not view ETV *unless* he engages in the rest of the behavior we have now come to associate with ETV viewing—cultural and civic activity and serious reading. If he does demonstrate this part of the "ETV syndrome," then, regardless of his education or his occupation, we have good reason to suspect that he is rejecting the norms we might expect him to follow, and will very likely be a viewer of ETV, if it is available to him, and if he tries it.

We have at least an idea, then, as to how blue-collar people fit into what might be a predominantly white-collar, high-education audience. But how was it possible that three stations would attract such people in large enough numbers to skew their educational and occupational distribution? We suspect that such people often tend not to "find" ETV, or not to give it a serious trial. But for the Pittsburgh station we have the hypothesis previously stated: that blue-collar men were attracted by the station's athletic programs, and a number of them liked what they saw and stayed in the audience. We know that the Houston station also programed athletics and exciting civic events which could have helped attract viewers. For the third station we have no programing information. But this, at least, seems to stand out in our brief look at the deviants: there are doubtless many more potential viewers of educational television than we should expect to find, on the basis of our rather highbrow picture of the audience—high education, high occupation, high cultural behavior, high civic activity, highly serious use of the mass media, and so forth. We must remember that not every viewer has all those characteristics, or even most of them. People who *do* have all or most of those characteristics will probably find their way to educational television unassisted. Those who do not have all or most of these characteristics must often be helped to find the way.

What viewers and nonviewers think the audience is like

We have spoken of a "highbrow" picture of the ETV audience. It is appropriate, now, to inquire whether the concept of the ETV audience as "highbrow" is a common one.

In the Stanford studies, we asked respondents in the home

interviews to fill out a series of descriptive statements of the semantic differential type.

They were given 13 adjectives taken from previous unstructured comments concerning educational television:

ambitious	intellectual
interesting	public-spirited
youthful	insecure
snobbish	successful
"egghead"	dull
comfortable	"going places"
highly educated	

For each of these they were asked to say whether "people who watch educational television" are *not at all, somewhat, quite,* or *very* (ambitious, interesting, and so forth). Then they made corresponding judgments on "people who watch regular commercial television but do not watch educational television."

The most interesting point, of course, is how the viewers and nonviewers, respectively, of ETV saw the ETV audience. Neither viewers nor nonviewers saw the audience as "egghead" or snobbish or dull, epithets that have plagued many cultural endeavors. To each of these adjectives the most common response, from viewers and nonviewers, was "not at all." This despite the fact that both groups see ETV viewers as "quite intellectual" and "highly educated." It may have been, of course, that the respondents were averse to speaking unpleasantly of anyone in the presence of the interviewer. On the other hand, the respondent *himself* filled out these answers, and handed them to the interviewer folded.

In general the two pictures are surprisingly alike. Both viewers and nonviewers tend to see the viewers of ETV as

quite interesting	somewhat youthful
quite intellectual	
quite public-spirited	not at all snobbish
quite ambitious	not at all "egghead"
quite successful	not at all insecure
quite comfortable	not at all dull
quite highly educated	
quite likely to be "going places"	

How do they compare the viewer with the nonviewer? They agree that the nonviewer of ETV (the viewer of commercial television) is a little less highly educated, a little less intellectual, a little less ambitious,[13] a little less likely to be "going places," and a (very) little less public-spirited. In regard to all these, the modal response applied to ETV viewers was "quite"; to the non-ETV viewer (but commercial viewer) it was "somewhat." They did not entirely agree as to how interesting, successful, and youthful the non-ETV viewer is. The nonviewers of ETV described a non-viewer as quite interesting, successful, and youthful; the viewers of ETV described the nonviewer as "somewhat" interesting, successful, and youthful. It is interesting that all the standard traits of white-collar norms are attributed unanimously to the viewers of ETV, but not so unanimously to the nonviewers.

A remarkable audience

This is a remarkable audience, strongly representing the best educated people in the community, the people with the professional and managerial jobs, the people who are most active in civic and cultural affairs, the people who are the serious and purposeful users of the mass media. It is an audience that any television broadcaster should be happy to have, and that any community organization, educational institution, or state commission should be proud to serve. Yet we must note what this audience is *not.* For one thing, it is not large, by commercial standards; it is a selective rather than a mass audience. Second, it does not represent equally all levels of society. From time to time there has been talk about educational television coming to be the device by which the less educated members of society can make up for missed opportunities. This it has not so far proved to be. It is serving chiefly the better educated members of society, the members who are already more socially and culturally active and who have learned already to use the mass media as a source of high culture and serious and thoughtful information.

13 This is interesting in view of what we have said about upward mobility and about the self-betterment norm.

6

What Programs Do They View?

If the stations we have studied are representative ones, then the educational television broadcaster can expect that his big program of the week in any given week will attract 30 per cent or more of his regular viewers. He can expect two or three of his programs to attract 20 per cent or more of those regular viewers, and perhaps 12 programs to attract more than 10 per cent.

Translating these figures into percentages of *total* audience, we see that a program like "Open End," which attracts about 40 per cent of the regular viewers of the San Francisco station, would therefore be attracting about 9 or 10 per cent of the total adult audience in San Francisco. We have supporting evidence for this, because "Open End" has been frequently given a program rating of 5 to 10 in San Francisco by the commercial rating agencies.[1] On the other hand, a program like the Civil War series, which attracts about 16 per cent of the regular viewers of the Alabama network, would have a little less than 2 per cent of the total adult audience in the coverage area of the three Alabama stations. A program like "Ragtime Era," which attracts about 30 per cent of the regular viewers of the Denver station, would have about 4 per cent of the total Denver adult audience.

This is the order of magnitude of program audiences on educational television. A community program rating of 10 is rela-

[1] In Boston, "Open End," though it attracted very unevenly from week to week, likewise has had ratings like 5. What this means is that 75,000 to 80,000 people are viewing it, in contrast to the well-under-10,000 for an average WGBH program.

tively enormous for an ETV program. A rating of 4 is extraordinarily good. Most ETV programs have an over-all sets-in-use rating in the neighborhood of 1—meaning that about 1 per cent of sets are tuned to them. The average coincidental rating in Boston for WGBH programs was 0.6. The programs that educational television puts in its prime time are competitive in program rating with *daytime* commercial television (ratings of 2 to 10). There is nothing on ETV that attracts the large audience that commercial television gets with its favorite Westerns, crime mysteries, and adventure and popular music programs.

These figures should be kept in mind throughout this chapter when we talk about the audiences for educational programs, because we shall be talking in terms of percentages of an ETV station's *regular viewers*—these being the percentages we have, and any projection from them to over-all program ratings being necessarily less reliable than the basic figures themselves.

In pointing out that ETV program audiences are smaller than the audiences of many commercial programs, we are not implying that things should be otherwise. As we said early in this report, television is both a great entertainment medium and a great educational medium. Educational television does a large part of its educational job in the daytime hours broadcasting to school classes, multiplying the effect of expert teaching and outstanding teaching demonstrations. In this service, as in all school teaching, it has a captive audience. When it extends its educational service into the late afternoon and evening hours, when it no longer serves a captive audience, when it competes in the hours of relaxation with entertainment television, then it cannot realistically be expected to attract large numbers of the general public away from less demanding alternatives. Yet we are concerned with ascertaining what ETV programs are most competitive in the entertainment hours, because the goal of ETV is still to furnish an educational and informative service to the largest number of people who can profit by it.

At the time we made these studies, "Open End," David Susskind's weekly discussion program, was apparently the leader among ETV programs. It was offered in four of the areas we studied. In San Francisco it was the most popular ETV program, attracting 40 per cent of the station's regular viewers. It was also the most popular ETV program in Boston and in Pittsburgh, where it gained 24 per cent of the regular viewers. In Denver, with 29 per cent of the regular viewers, it was a close second to another ETV program.

Table 14 shows some of the other most popular programs, as follows:

Public affairs programs—such as "Profile Bay Area," a program discussing currently hot public issues, which drew 30 per cent of regular viewers in San Francisco.

Practical programs—"Backyard Farmer," which drew 40 per cent of regular viewers in the Lincoln audience; "House and Home," which drew 23 per cent of regular viewers in the same audience; "Legally Speaking," which drew 18 per cent in Pittsburgh.

Musical programs—"Casals Master Class," which, with two repeats,[2] in one week drew 27 per cent of the San Francisco regular audience; "Capstone Concert," which drew 21 per cent of regulars in the territory of the Alabama network; "Ragtime Era," a program of popular music of 40 years ago, which drew 30 per cent of regular viewers in the city of the program's origin, Denver.

Dramatic programs—"Robert Herridge Theater," which drew 23 per cent in San Francisco.[3]

Popularized science programs—"Animals of the Seashore" and "Moon, Planets, Stars," which drew 19 per cent each in Lincoln and San Francisco, respectively.

Popularized history—"Civil War" and "Redman's America," which drew 16 per cent each in the Alabama network and Denver areas, respectively.

General cultural program—"Heritage," a series of visits with great Americans, which drew 18 per cent of Lincoln regular viewers.

Among others, only slightly less popular than the ones we have

[2] The extraordinary audience this program was able to draw during the week seems to justify the San Francisco policy of repeating an outstanding program several times.

[3] It was unfortunate that "The Age of Kings" was not yet on the air during the period of our study. This outstanding dramatic series (distributed by NET) apparently attracted large and enthusiastic audiences.

Table 14.—Most Popular Programs of Five ETV Audiences

Per Cent of Regular Viewers	Pittsburgh	Alabama Network	Lincoln	Denver	San Francisco
40 or more	—	—	Backyard Farmer	—	Open End
30–39	—	—	—	Ragtime Era	Profile Bay Area
20–29	Open End	Capstone Concert	House and Home Great Plains Trilogy	Open End	Casals Master Class Robert Herridge Theater
10–19	Legally Speaking Farm Facts The Greeks Had a Word for It Children's Corner Allegheny Roundtable Face the People	Civil War Stones and Bones Living Arts and Crafts Music Box Let's Learn More Time to Grow Family Challenge	Evening Prelude Animals of the Seashore Casals Your Unicameral Religions of Man Heritage Shakespeare Layman's Guide to Modern Art Band Concert Conference on World Tensions University News Elementary Science	Redman's America Spanish Decision Income Tax Guide Invitation to Art	Concert Hall Moon, Planets, Stars World Press Review Kaleidoscope Scotch Gardener Science Reporter This Week in Science Portrait in Music Heritage UN Review Inquiring Mind

named, are a review of the world press, a program on the religions of man, a program on archaeology, and a series of miscellaneous interviews.

Altogether, it must seem to be a most extraordinarily diverse list of programs. This, however, is a characteristic of television. Everyone who studies program audiences is amazed at the diversity of individual choice. Thus Dr. Himmelweit, studying several thousand English children of nearly the same age, reported that she could not find 10 per cent who agreed on a favorite program.[4] We ourselves have been examining lists of "five favorite television programs" selected by a large sample of residents of Milwaukee, Wisconsin. There is so little agreement in the lists that it is hard to find enough correlation for the factor analysis we had hoped to make in order to cluster the choices.[5] It is a fact of life that television program tastes are diverse.

Therefore, the fact that 30 or 40 per cent of the viewers of an educational station can agree on watching a particular program is really remarkable. Such a program must have characteristics that appeal to the central tendency we have noted in educational television viewers, and if it is desired to enlarge program audiences for ETV these characteristics might well be studied in detail.

Favorite programs and programs viewed

In the Boston study, an effort was made to see whether the programs that people called their favorites were also the programs that they actually watched, or whether watching and verbal endorsement were different. Each respondent who watched WGBH was asked whether he and each person in his family had a favorite program broadcast on it. He was also asked whether he had personally seen each of a dozen programs that were then of leading interest to the station. The results are shown in Table 15.[6]

There are various reasons why some programs are seen but not chosen as favorites. First—a trivial matter—some were specials that were on just once or only during a brief period. People may

[4] See Himmelweit, Oppenheim, and Vince.

[5] This is from data gathered in connection with the Milwaukee Journal Consumer Analysis, and made available by the Milwaukee Journal Company.

[6] Thirty-nine per cent of viewers and 83 per cent of marginal cases had no favorite program.

TABLE 15.—PROGRAMS WATCHED BY BOSTON ETV AUDIENCES

Program	Viewers		Marginal Cases	
	Had Ever Seen	A Favorite	Had Ever Seen	A Favorite
Boston Symphony	58%	10%	33%	6%
Open End	52	16	25	8
Louis Lyons News	49	10	22	0
President's Press Conference	44	0	27	1
Science Reporter	40	1	19	1
Eliot Norton Reviews	34	2	17	0
Ask the Candidate	28	0	14	0
Grass Roots Voters 1960	21	0	7	0
Gardener's Almanac	19	1	11	0
Performance	14	0	11	0
Julius Caesar	10	0	6	0
Make Believe Clubhouse	8	0	6	0

enjoy these, but do not name them as favorites. These included "Julius Caesar" and the two special 1960 election items, "Grass Roots Voters" and "Ask the Candidate." Perhaps "President's Press Conference" belongs in the same category of programs people think of as an occasional special rather than as a recurrent program. Or perhaps, in addition, people watched it out of respect and awareness of its importance without enjoying it very much. Eisenhower conferences were hardly dramatic.

"Make Believe Clubhouse" is a children's program, presumably seen by adults in the household while the children watched, but hardly the adults' favorite.

Thus we are left, among those programs not spontaneously picked as favorites, with two programs that nonetheless get a wide audience, "Science Reporter" and "Eliot Norton Reviews," and two that do not, "Gardener's Almanac" and "Performance."

These results are odd but instructive. They demonstrate once more how very different the audiences for different programs may be.

"Science Reporter" and "Eliot Norton Reviews," the programs that cast a wide net, both share the "Open End" formula of an MC and interesting guests.[7] "Science Reporter" is an M.I.T. pro-

[7] It is worth noting that about one-third of our WGBH viewer respondents named some program that uses this format as among their favorites, whether on ETV or CTV. "Open End," the most often mentioned, was closely followed by "Jack Paar."

gram in which scientists are interviewed about and demonstrate current research. Eliot Norton, who followed Louis Lyons on Tuesdays, reviews a theater opening, bringing into the studio with him an actor, author, or other guest connected with the show. These two programs are both at a considerably more technical and specialized level than "Open End" and do not feature personality appeal as much. But to some degree, at least, they share its character and broad appeal.

In contrast, "Gardener's Almanac" is straight information, undoubtedly of interest to a portion of the audience, but to a very special portion. To the management of WGBH its small audience is a surprise, for no program produces more letters. As many as 1,000 letters have been received in a single week, requesting from the station the Department of Agriculture pamphlets it offers. By our figures, these correspondents in a single week amount to about 2 per cent of the regular viewers who remember ever having seen the program. Its small audience is deeply responsive. It seems possible that most of its regular viewers have at some point or other written to the station. So the small audience of "Gardener's Almanac" may well be worth the station's time. The same kind of specialized audience probably follows the live chamber music broadcast on "Performance" on those weeks when "Boston Symphony" is off the air.

It is, however, the three runaway successes, "Boston Symphony," "Open End," and "Louis Lyons News," that are most instructive to us. They drew not only the station's regular viewers, but even a substantial number of those marginal cases that we here use as a comparison group for the viewers, since nonviewers are irrelevant. These programs have the ingredients to make ETV audiences grow. Unfortunately, it would not be easy to produce, two or three times over, material of the quality of these three programs. The talents are rare that are represented in each of them. It is hard to come by the combination of warm human being, personality, showman, professional expertise, wide knowledge, and sophisticated interpretation represented, for example, in a newscast by Louis Lyons, the curator of the Nieman Fellowships at Harvard. Yet it is equally clear that if programing of that level could be doubled or tripled, there would be a real demand for it.

The bulk of that one-fifth of the public that is the WGBH audience is looking for entertainment and information, not in a program formula very different from that on commercial TV, but at a much higher level of quality. Favorite programs and the programs people watch the most are precisely those that could equally well appear on commercial TV, and indeed sometimes do. They are programs distinguished only by excellence, not by belonging to a special educational category. A station that could, and would, provide that sort of programing most of the time would absorb more of their time and become their favorite.

Program preferences—entertainment versus educational

In the Boston study, both viewers and nonviewers were given an opportunity to name favorite programs across the board, regardless of whether on WGBH or on commercial outlets. The favorite programs of viewers and nonviewers did differ, but, unfortunately, not because WGBH viewers found most of their favorites on the educational station.

The favorites for WGBH viewers were mostly found among standard commercial offerings. Forty-five per cent of WGBH viewers listed either a variety or MC personality show among their favorites. Second in order, 31 per cent mentioned a mystery. And third, 22 per cent mentioned a Western.

But while this is sobering and makes us realize that ETV viewers share with nonviewers that standard set of American or human passions that Hollywood and Madison Avenue cater to, we should not conclude that the tastes of viewers and nonviewers are alike. There are some program types that show no differences. Variety shows and sporting events are equally popular with both. Mysteries, quiz shows, and situation comedies get on the order of 50 per cent more elections as favorites from nonviewers than from viewers. On the other hand, educational programs (including ones not on WGBH) are noted as favorites by 11 per cent of viewers, 1 per cent of nonviewers. Art and music, panel discussions, news reports, and news specials are in general named about twice as often by WGBH viewers as by nonviewers. The most frequently noted category among those, panel discussions, contains a favorite program of 20 per cent of WGBH viewers. Most people named two or three favorite programs, though a few named four or five. Suppose that we score a person one point for naming a panel program, a news program, an art or good music program, or an educational program as a favorite. WGBH viewers scored on the average 0.7 such choices apiece, while nonviewers averaged 0.3 such choices apiece—a difference, if not an enormous one. The average viewer made his 0.7 high-level choices while also choosing 1.7 lower-level favorite programs. The average nonviewer made his 0.3 high-level choices while also choosing 2.2 lower-level favorite programs. The lower-level material is preferred by both viewers and nonviewers, but it is significantly leavened in the favorite diet of the viewers, not in that of the nonviewers.

The viewers' comments about their favorite programs are confirmed by data on what they actually did. We asked each respondent in the personal interview in Boston to list all programs seen in the preceding 24 hours. In the particular weeks during which we interviewed, Louis Lyons came out on top in frequency of mention of WGBH programs, but no WGBH program compared in frequency of mention with the leading commercial ones. In the first place, 48 per cent of WGBH viewers had seen nothing but commercial entertainment and/or news reports in the past 24 hours. To these must be added 20 per cent who had not turned their sets on, leaving 32 per cent who had watched an educational or informational type of program in the past day. And of these, the great bulk of programs named were interview or discussion programs on commercial TV. Dave Garroway's "Today" show got almost as many mentions as all of WGBH's programs combined.

Significantly different as the tastes of typical ETV viewers may be from those of the general public, they are clearly not as different as the programs on ETV are from those on CTV. While the ETV viewers complain about CTV more than do their less urbane fellow citizens, nonetheless it is among the vast panoply of programs offered by CTV that they find their favorites. And it is on CTV that they spend the bulk of their viewing time. Our estimate for Boston is that all but three-quarters of an hour out of 15 to 20 hours of viewing time per week by ETV viewers went to CTV. What the largest number of them seem to want most is something not so different in concept from CTV, but just done more intelligently and better.

ETV stations differ in the degree to which they meet this prescription. These are the predominantly cultural stations, often community-owned, whose aspirations, at least, are along such lines, though even these present but little pure—while intelligent—entertainment. There are also stations whose emphasis is more largely instructional. How much difference does it make in the response of their audience—or more accurately of their *audiences*?

Different kinds of audiences

Different educational stations, because they are the kinds of stations they are and serve the kind of cultural area they serve, doubtless attract different audiences. Different kinds of programs also attract different audiences, regardless of where they are presented. An interesting question is whether the chief audience differences are between stations or between programs. We are not prepared to say which makes the greater difference, but we can say that both factors are operative. Station audiences are different, and program audiences are different.

Let us first analyze some of the differences between station audiences. Suppose we take the four general categories of educational programs on each of which considerable segments of the educational audience reported that they spent some time during the previous week. These figures are comparable for four of the studies—Alabama, Lincoln, Denver, and San Francisco. For each category of programs we shall record what percentage of the viewers in each area spent no time on those programs, and what percentage spent half or more of their ETV time on it.

Figure 20 strongly supports the argument that there are audience differences between stations. It is apparent that the Alabama network audience is more interested than the others in television adult courses. The Lincoln audience is more interested in practical aid programs (as their heavy viewing of "Backyard Farmer" and "House and Home" suggests). Lincoln and San Francisco seem more interested in cultural programs (art, music, and drama), whereas Denver and San Francisco seem more interested in information and public affairs programs. (See also Appendix C,

FORMAL EDUCATION (COURSES)

	Spent no time watching	Spent 50% or more of ETV-viewing time watching
Alabama	27%	44%
Denver	67%	14%
San Francisco	64%	6%

PRACTICAL AID PROGRAMS

	Spent no time watching	Spent 50% or more of ETV-viewing time watching
Alabama	59%	8%
Lincoln	44%	25%
Denver	77%	14%
San Francisco	64%	2%

CULTURAL PROGRAMS (ART, MUSIC, DRAMA)

	Spent no time watching	Spent 50% or more of ETV-viewing time watching
Alabama	55%	14%
Lincoln	30%	35%
Denver	66%	7%
San Francisco	36%	19%

INFORMATION AND PUBLIC AFFAIRS

	Spent no time watching	Spent 50% or more of ETV-viewing time watching
Alabama	71%	5%
Lincoln	35%	21%
Denver	48%	41%
San Francisco	34%	43%

Fig. 20.—Choice of program categories by audiences of different stations.

Table A3.) In order of interest, the four station audiences could be ranked as follows:

	Alabama	Lincoln	Denver	San Francisco
1.	Courses	Cultural	Information	Information
2.	Cultural	Information	Courses	Cultural
3.	Practical	Practical	Practical	Courses
4.	Information		Cultural	Practical

Thus the Alabama audience seems to be an education-seeking one, expressing no very great interest in any of the other types. The Lincoln audience is considerably interested in cultural, informational, and practical programs; its interests are wider and more even than the other audiences. Denver is interested in informational programs, with the other types far behind. And the San Francisco audience seems to be what we have called a "culture audience," deeply interested in public affairs and the arts, caring little about practical help programs and courses.

There are interesting differences between stations in the proportion of viewers the same program is able to attract. "Open End" gets 43 per cent in San Francisco, 29 in Denver, 24 in Pittsburgh. "Heritage" gets 18 per cent in Lincoln, 13 in San Francisco, 8 in Pittsburgh, 4 in Alabama. "Casals Master Class" draws 27 per cent in San Francisco, 15 in Lincoln, 4 in Alabama. "Origami," a program on Japanese paper-cutting, gets 9 per cent in San Francisco, 7 in Lincoln, 1 in Alabama. "Great Problems of Conscience" draws 8 per cent in San Francisco, 2 in Pittsburgh.

In three station areas—San Francisco, Pittsburgh, and Denver—we have enough viewers of "Open End" to compare the station audiences for the program. The only fair way to do this, of course, is to compare the viewers in each city who watched the program with the viewers in the same city who did not, inasmuch as the three station audiences contain different proportions of college graduates, heavy readers, and the other classifications on which we want to make comparisons. When we do that, we find a considerable amount of similarity in the audiences. For one thing, they all contain more men than women. They all contain book-reading people. The age medians are not far different. But look carefully at the comparisons of people within the separate station audiences who do and do not view the program, and you will find evidence that "Open End" seems not to mean quite the same thing to San Francisco as it does to the other two cities. In Pittsburgh and Denver, "Open End" selects out of the regular viewers the more highly educated, the people who are more likely to attend lectures, the people who say their purpose in watching television is to "keep better informed," and the high-print users. In San Francisco it does no such thing. Figure 21, for example, shows the print-television indexes for San Francisco and Denver. It is obvious that there is very little difference between the viewers and nonviewers of the program in San Francisco, whereas there are considerable differences in Denver. Either the San Francisco audience is more homogeneous than Denver's, or else the program has a somewhat different meaning and attraction to the two audiences.

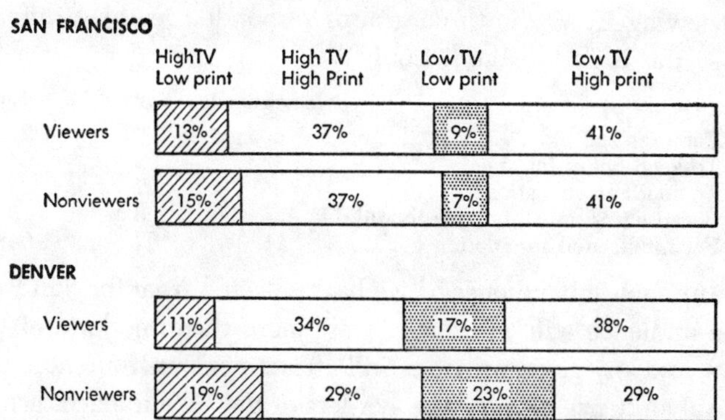

Fig. 21.—Television and print use by viewers and nonviewers of "Open End" in San Francisco and Denver.

Now let us look at some of the audiences that different programs attract on the same station.

In San Francisco there appear to be three distinct audiences, the cultural, the informational, and the instructional (see Appendix C, Table A4). They are interestingly different. The cultural audience is youngest, the instructional oldest. The instructional group is more likely than the others to have no children at home. The instructional audience is more active than the others in attending concerts, plays, lectures, and discussion groups, although the cultural audience is more likely to go to civic meetings. Both the instructional and cultural groups watch more ETV than the informational audience. The answers to what specially interests them on educational television can be tabulated as follows:

	Audiences		
	Instructional ($N = 19$)	Cultural ($N = 37$)	Informational ($N = 85$)
Practical information	65%	32%	44%
The arts	55	67	51
Public issues	75	76	88
Serious music	60	65	59
General knowledge	80	67	66

As we might expect, the instructional audience is interested more than the others in practical information and general knowledge, the cultural audience in the arts and serious music, and the informational audience in public issues. Given a list and asked to check on it the statements that came closest to describing their reasons for viewing ETV, the three groups responded in these different ways (this is part of the list only):

	Instructional	Cultural	Informational
For practical aid	40%	0%	21%
To keep better informed	45	62	64
To continue education	45	27	28
Because it is something one should do	15	8	8
For intellectual stimulation	75	67	64

Any such subaudience as we have selected from the San Francisco audience will, of course, view more than one kind of program, and any given program will attract persons from more than one subaudience group. The borders of the subaudiences are not so clear that members do not cross them. Although programs may attract different types of audience, still there will be some overlaps between audiences. How much overlap is there? Table 16 shows what percentage of the audience for a given one of five favorite programs on the Pittsburgh station also views another given program of the five, and what percentage of the audience of each program does not view *any* of the others. It is apparent that there is a great deal more overlap between some programs than others. But perhaps the most interesting column in the table is the one to the far right, which shows that nearly one-third of the persons who viewed "Open End" and "Famous Features" did not view *any* of these other four programs.

We can tell something about the difference in audiences for these programs by noting what proportion of male and female viewers they attract. This is shown in Figure 22. Furthermore,

TABLE 16.—PER CENT OF AUDIENCE SHARED BY FIVE TOP PROGRAMS ON PITTSBURGH STATION

Of the total who watch	The Per Cent Below Also Watch					
	Famous Features	Legally Speaking	Face the People	Open End	The Greeks Had a Word for It	None of the Other Four
Famous Features (N=26) ..	100%	11%	10%	30%	28%	31%
Legally Speaking (N=35) ..	15	100	65	35	44	23
Face the People (N=20) ...	8	37	100	17	24	15
Open End (N=46)........	54	46	40	100	52	30
The Greeks Had a Word for It (N=25).....	27	31	30	28	100	20

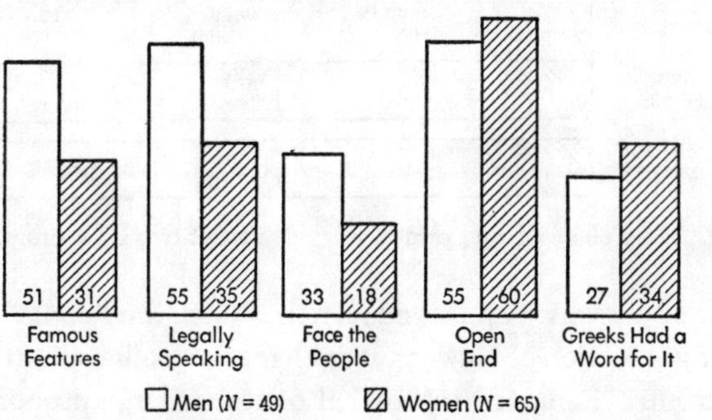

Fig. 22.—Sex composition, in per cent, of audience of five top programs on the Pittsburgh station.

there are interesting differences in educational level, as Figure 23 shows. The fact that these educational distributions are so strikingly different suggests the possibility of deliberately programing so as to broaden the ETV audience beyond the high educational, culturally active group who are its chief components. As is seen in Figure 23, "Open End," although nearly half its audience in Pittsburgh are college-educated, still attracts a large

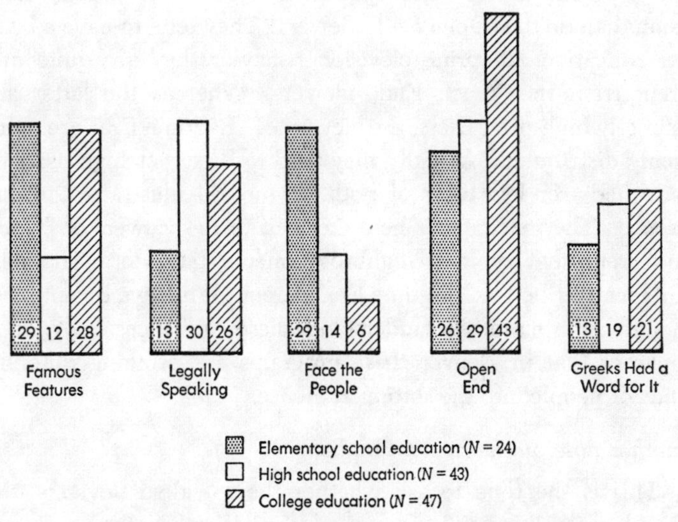

Fig. 23.—Audience, in per cent, by educational level of five top programs on the Pittsburgh station.

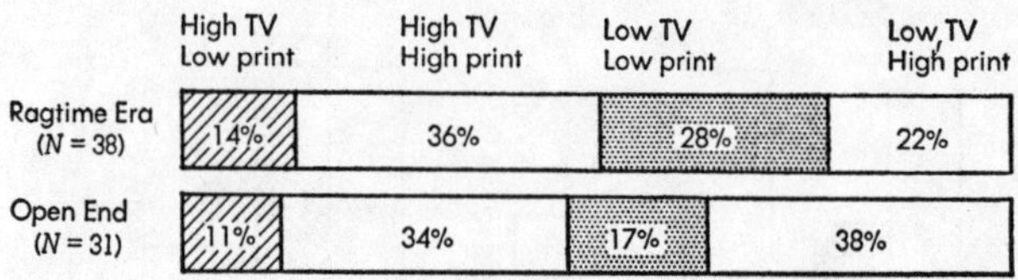

Fig. 24.—Television and print use by viewers of two ETV programs.

number of persons with less education. "Face the People" attracts a larger proportion of viewers with elementary education than any other group. "Famous Features" also attracts large proportions of the less-educated viewers, and "Legally Speaking" is popular with the group with high school education. If programs like these can be judicially mixed with the others, and suitably promoted, it should be quite possible to broaden the audience.

This is apparently what the Denver station does by presenting both "Open End" and "Ragtime Era," and may help to explain why Denver, for a school-board station, has such a comparatively large audience.

These two are Denver's top programs. Each attracts nearly one-third of the viewers, but by no means all the same viewers. The "Ragtime Era" viewers spend less time on educational television than do the "Open End" viewers. They tend to have a little less education. In print-television behavior they are quite different from the "Open End" viewers. Whereas the latter are definitely high-print users, the viewers of "Ragtime Era" are more evenly distributed. Actually they tend to be either high users of both media or low users of both. Figure 24 illustrates the difference. The percentages here credited to the viewers of "Open End" represent typical "highbrow" media behavior. The percentages ascribed to "Ragtime Era" do not. While we do not have enough information to understand these audiences fully, it is apparent that in Denver these programs are bringing different kinds of people into the station audience.

Another note on the deviant audience

This is the time to ask whether the so-called deviants—the less-educated, blue-collar group of viewers—when they are once attracted to the station by programs such as sports, remain in the audience to view more intellectual programs. Among our audiences, the one that is heaviest in this deviant group is Pittsburgh. And here the best evidence we can assemble indicates that such viewers apparently are found in substantial proportions in the audiences of serious intellectual programs.

Let us focus, for the moment, on the group of Pittsburgh viewers who have had only elementary schooling. From Figure 23 it is evident that the elementary school viewers (though smaller in absolute numbers) are very well represented in those audiences. In two audiences, "Face the People" and "Famous Features," the percentage of this group is actually higher than the percentage of either of the other groups. In the case of "The Greeks Had a Word for It," the percentage of elementary school viewers is close to that of high school viewers and college-educated viewers. In the case of "Open End," the percentages follow the expected pattern—rising with education—but the difference between the elementary school and high school groups is quite small.

Until we have evidence to the contrary, therefore, we are prepared to assume that if an educational station can attract a "deviant" audience of this kind, there is a very good chance that a considerable portion of this audience will come to like the serious intellectual programs of the station. It goes without saying that this is a very important hypothesis for ETV program directors who are seeking to broaden their audiences.

The audience for adult courses

Most of the adults watching educational television are not seeking formal courses. They want programs that, if they have to be called "educational," are only informally educational. They mean programs that offer wide swatches of information and ideas, that fill in the background of events, that present art and culture in such a way as to make them understandable and exciting. These are the programs that get most of the ETV audience. The audiences for formal courses are always small. Even in Chicago, where an entire junior college curriculum is on the air, the audience at any given time can still be counted in thousands; and the Laubach literacy course in Memphis draws audiences that are smaller yet. The people who take these courses are usually highly motivated, and very few things the station does will probably have more impact. But it will be impact on a limited audience. Therefore it is interesting to have 9 per cent of the Alabama network viewers,[8] 22 per cent of Denver viewers, 17 per cent of San Francisco viewers, 18 per cent of Columbus viewers, and 16 per cent of Lincoln viewers report that they had watched all or some of an adult course. (The question was not asked in Pittsburgh.) Throughout the five stations, about half the viewers, on the average, said they had watched at least one program of a formal adult course. Some of these percentages represent numbers of considerable size. For example, they would mean that in the San Francisco area perhaps 40,000 persons had watched all or most of an adult course on television.

However, let us say frankly that we think these numbers do not refer only to persons who have taken formal televised courses. There seems little doubt that respondents took a very liberal view of "formal courses" when they answered this question. We asked them, in some cases, to tell us what courses they had followed on television. They would often name such program series as "Japanese Brush Painting," which is not a formal course at all, and is not given for credit. Therefore, we believe that these "course viewers" include large numbers of persons who have followed systematic presentations of a topic—not formal courses as such.

Who are these viewers of courses? If we can generalize from the San Francisco audience, they are likely to be persons who have had some college but have not received a degree; to judge from the Alabama network audience, they are more likely to be persons who have not finished high school. Many of them are people who say that the chance to continue their education is their reason for viewing ETV. More women than men are course viewers. They tend to be less interested than the average ETV viewers in public issues, but more interested in acquiring general knowledge and practical information. As might be expected, they are a bit more likely than other viewers to attend evening classes. And they spend more time than does the average viewer on ETV.

[8] We are rather puzzled that this figure should be so low for the Alabama audience, inasmuch as the Alabama network carries more course work than any others of our stations; and the Alabama audience reported spending considerable time on adult courses.

Some implications

For the station manager, program director, or supporter of educational television, three of the findings in this chapter are of great importance. One is that "wide-band" programs, like "Open End," are available and have proved their ability to attract sizable audiences to educational television from different levels of society. A second is that different educational television programs attract different kinds of audiences, so that, within limits, a manager can choose the kind of audience he wants to reach by choosing the kind of programs he broadcasts. A third is that less educated groups can apparently be brought into the audiences of serious high-level programs if they can be attracted to the station by programs they like.

The strategy for educational television, if it wants to build its audiences, should probably include both of these approaches. There should be an attempt to develop widely popular and still educational programs like "Open End." There should be a judicious balancing of programs to serve different segments of the audience. Admitted that we don't know all we need to know about the kinds of audience different programs attract; still we have a good start toward that knowledge, and we do know that the educational audience is a varied thing, composed of groups who are seeking different things and have different education, abilities, and standards. The combining of programs to reach them and satisfy them is a test of the highest skill of the programer.

7

Why Do They View?

Human beings are typically not very articulate in explaining why they do anything—except that they "like it" or think they "ought to" or "want to." It is not easy, either for the layman or for the scholar, to understand and explain the reasons for such complex behavior as deciding to view educational television rather than watching entertainment television or selecting any of the other behaviors possible at the moment. Nevertheless it would greatly help us to understand what ETV means in the lives of people, and how it might be made more useful to them, if we could only understand more clearly *why* they choose to view it.

As a matter of fact, throughout the previous chapters we have been making assumptions about motivations for viewing. For example, we have talked about the middle-class norm which values self-improvement through work, and therefore tends to cast suspicion on entertainment television and approval on educational television. We have implied that some people may be in the educational television audience because they have accepted the norm and therefore regard ETV as a "good thing"—as something "one ought to do." But one of the advantages of studying human beings, as contrasted to studying animals or things, is that they can answer questions. There are certain great *dis*advantages about studying human beings rather than these other subjects, but at least one can ask them to consider and explain. And this is what we have tried to do with reference to the question of why they view educational television.

What we want to know, of course, is what (if anything) they are seeking when they turn their dials to the educational channel, and what rewards or benefits (if any) they feel they receive from viewing educational programs. We should like to know whether these motivations and rewards are different for different segments of the total audience, and for different kinds and patterns of ETV.

It might only seem necessary to ask the viewers directly why they view ETV. We did this, but were not satisfied to stop there. The motivation for viewing is probably a complex matter, and one that has not been consciously weighed by most viewers. Therefore, a direct answer of this kind would almost certainly be incomplete, and might be misleading. For this reason we tried to approach the problem from several directions. We inserted a number of questions, some structured, some unstructured, dealing with rewards and motivations, at various points in the interview and in different contexts. Then we studied the answers, one against the other, and analyzed them with such statistical tools as seemed justified. The results of this analysis are what we are going to report in this chapter.

The direct question

In four cities of the eight-city study we asked the viewers, in the course of their home interviews, the straightforward question "What would you say are the main reasons why you watch station YYYY when you do so?" ("YYYY," of course, was replaced by the call letters of the particular educational station in that community.) Our interviewers then took down, as nearly verbatim as possible, the respondents' answers.

These respondents were quite varied, and the distribution of answers was somewhat different in different cities, but well over 90 per cent of all the answers could be fitted into eight categories, as shown in Table 17.

While the large vote for the educational quality of ETV is impressive, still we must use caution in interpreting it. People may have had quite varied things in mind when they made such statements as "because it's educational." In Chapter 5 we saw that only a minority actually followed formal courses on ETV; therefore it seems unlikely that these persons are referring to the *formal* educational function of ETV. Viewed informally, "education" or "adult education" means different things to different persons. To some people in our sample, it may simply have meant

TABLE 17.—MAIN REASONS GIVEN BY RESPONDENTS IN FOUR CITIES FOR WATCHING THE ETV STATION

Reason	Per Cent of Respondents*
Because of its educational value (I can learn something from it—it's educational—it has something to teach anybody—the kind of programs you can learn from—it stretches your mind—and similar responses)	33%
Because I like specific programs on the station	20
Because it provides something not available on commercial television (it is more satisfying than the other television—it gives me things I can't get on commercial—it gives me programs I don't get enough of on the other stations—and so forth)	16
Because it suits my personal interest (I'm specially interested in ———, and the ETV station is good at that—it's the only place I can get a good program about my hobby—I can find more programs on it that really interest *me*—and so forth)	15
Because it entertains me: I enjoy it	13
Because it keeps me better informed	8
Because it's good for the children	6
Because it's intellectually stimulating	4

* Some respondents answered in more than one category.

"informative"; to others it may have called up the image of popularized science; to others it may have meant discussion groups or panels on public issues; and to still others it may have meant exactly what some respondents called "intellectual stimulation." Beyond that, we cannot help expecting that when a person is asked a question about something called *educational* television, the logical, appropriate, and easiest response may be to say that he views it for its "educational" value. Therefore, it is important to try to see what ideas and wishes lie behind that response.

We have some interesting information along this line from the Boston study. For this study, a question was borrowed from the study of commercial TV viewing being done by Gary Steiner.[1] This was a schedule of reasons for watching TV.

[1] For this question, the M.I.T. study thanks the Columbia University Bureau of Applied Social Research. Bernard Berelson, its director, was starting a study of CTV viewing at the time that Pool was starting the Boston study, and Berelson asked Pool to conduct some interviews for him in Boston. Pool did this, and also incorporated in the M.I.T. study a few questions from the Steiner study. The initial intent was a technical one—to provide an estimate of the extent to which possible differences in conclusions of the two studies were due to the fact that Pool was working only in Boston, whereas the Columbia study was a national one.

Each respondent was handed a form and told: "Now let's talk for a moment about *reasons* for watching television. Here is a list of possible reasons. When you watch TV, how often does each of these reasons apply to you?"

Some 15 reasons were listed. Among them a few might be taken as use of TV for social purposes. Fewer ETV viewers admitted they used TV in that way either "usually" or "occasionally."

	Viewers	Nonviewers
I turn the set on just to keep me company when I am alone	32%	42%
I watch because everyone I know is watching and I want to be able to talk about it afterwards	22	26
I watch mainly to be sociable when others are watching	46	58

A couple of other reasons might be taken as use of TV as an escape, that is, something to relax into when tedium, anxiety, or insomnia attack. TV was used for this purpose substantially as much by ETV viewers as by nonviewers:

	Viewers	Nonviewers
I watch because there is nothing else to do at the time	35%	38%
I watch to get away from the ordinary cares and problems of the day	37	37

Giving a number of other reasons might be taken as an indicator of television addiction. Such replies are given less often by ETV viewers.

	Viewers	Nonviewers
I watch because I'm afraid I might be missing something good	22%	29%
I keep watching to put off doing something else I should do	14	19
I start on one show and then get stuck for the rest of the evening	30	40

A closely related set of replies, which are also more common among nonviewers of ETV, assert a liking for television as such, though we should perhaps avoid the word "addiction" because no psychological compulsion is suggested by the wording of these reasons:

	Viewers	Nonviewers
I watch just for background while I am doing something else	22%	34%
I watch just because I feel like watching television	59	77
I watch just because it is a pleasant way to spend an evening	66	83

Only one reason draws a positive reply, especially from WGBH viewers: *"I watch because I think I can learn something."* That is asserted to be usually or occasionally true by 85 per cent of the viewers and also by 73 per cent of the nonviewers. For both viewers and nonviewers alike, this is a very substantial magnitude of reply, which we are willing to discount somewhat for a halo effect, since everyone knows that learning is a good thing. But it cannot be discounted completely. The desire to learn is a strong motive for watching TV, particularly strong among the ETV viewers but present among the nonviewers too.

We have some further evidence that this is the case. It will be recalled that we asked each respondent to tell us about the most recent conversation outside his household which he had had about a TV program. Three-quarters of the respondents could recall such. Many of the programs they discussed were informational programs. Among ETV viewers informational programs actually outpointed entertainment programs 39 per cent to 34 per cent in the conversations. Among non-ETV viewers, discussion of entertainment programs predominated, but not overwhelmingly. Informational programs were the subject of 26 per cent of the conversations, entertainment programs the subject of 44 per cent. This is presumably a smaller difference than in the average ratings of the two sets of programs, a result suggesting that people may think and talk more about the relatively few serious programs they see than about the entertainment that fills their evenings.

Let us add still more evidence that for ETV viewers and nonviewers both, but to different degrees, TV is a substantial information source. We asked each respondent to name something he had learned from TV apart from the news, and then we also asked each to generalize: "Do you feel you learn things from watching TV?" By either test most people were apparently learning. Two-thirds (68 per cent of viewers and 66 per cent of nonviewers) affirmed, in reply to the general question, that they were learning, and they generally could prove it by citing something.

In such citations of specific learning experiences the ETV viewers do differ from the nonviewers. Though both equally claimed that they were learning, the ETV viewers were better able to cite examples, a difference that may be attributable to nothing more than IQ. Although only 34 per cent of nonviewers had said they did not learn from TV, a few more, 40 per cent, could not give any examples. Among the viewers, on the other hand, while 32 per cent said they learned nothing from TV, all but 26 per cent could cite examples of things they had learned even with the news excluded. At least 6 per cent disproved their own critical generalization!

The viewers and nonviewers learned from different programs. (Note that these are answers covering all of TV, not just ETV.) In more than half of the instances where a nonviewer indicated the specific program from which he had learned, it was either live coverage or a drama (and about equally for those two). In more than half the instances in which a WGBH viewer indicated the specific program from which he had learned, it was either an instructional program or a documentary.

The kinds of things they claimed to learn differed between the viewers and the nonviewers. Political information (by 21 per cent of viewers and 19 per cent of nonviewers) and fashions and fads (by 10 per cent of each) were the things both cited. But viewers also cited facts about art, literature, and music (15 per cent), science (15 per cent), and foreign countries (9 per cent). Nonviewers less often cited these.[2] The emphasis among the nonviewers was on information and technique, politics, fashions, and science. The attention of the viewers encompassed these items too, but also culture and the arts.

How they feel the station helps them

Attempting to dig a little deeper into these motivations for viewing, respondents in the eight-station study were asked to say in what ways, if any, they felt their local ETV station helped them. An overwhelming proportion of their responses fell into four categories, which are rather similar to the categories used in previous questionnaires. Table 18 presents these results, showing some interesting differences between stations and within station audiences.

There were also a few other types of answers—among them,

[2] Art, literature, music, 1 per cent; science, 9 per cent; and foreign countries, 4 per cent.

TABLE 18.—IN WHAT WAY OR WAYS, IF ANY, DOES STATION YYYY HELP YOU?

Area	Adds to My Education	Intellectual Stimulation	Keeps Me Informed	Entertainment, Enjoyment	General Positive	General Negative
San Francisco						
Men	21%	19%	30%	10%	9%	6%
Women	20	21	33	16	9	9
Lincoln						
Men & women	37	6	27	11	8	4
Denver						
Men	32	20	32	20	20	0
Women	38	19	23	0	27	0
Alabama network						
Men	41	8	18	1	10	13
Women	47	5	18	6	10	10

"gives me relief from commercial television," "furnishes cultural programs," "provides helpful [how-to-do-it] programs," and so forth—but these were in every case less than 5 per cent of the total answers, and have been omitted from the table. The "general positive" remarks were statements like "oh, it's a good station." The "general negative" remarks were like "it *doesn't* help me."

The most interesting feature of this table is the extent to which the answers cluster around other things than the station's educational function, narrowly conceived. The answer "keeps me informed" is given by almost as many people as give the more generalized response about education. In San Francisco, particularly, this is the case; "keeps me informed" is mentioned by half again as many persons as mention "education," and "intellectual stimulation" is mentioned by practically the same number as mention "education." It is interesting, though, to notice that the Alabama stations, which carry the largest proportion of courses, also draw the largest "education" response. And there are some differences between men and women—for example, the fact that 20 per cent of Denver men say that ETV provides enjoyment and entertainment, whereas *none* of the Denver women give this answer—that are fascinating though puzzling.

These answers, of course, are "open-end." The respondent is asked the question, and his answer is recorded in whatever form he gave it. Later on we shall report what happened when we gave respondents a choice between answers already prepared for them. But the significance of the answers we have just given is to re-emphasize that there are dimensions of "education" beyond formal education in the minds of ETV viewers when they speak of the station's educational value to them.

What they would miss most about the station

Viewers were asked also what they would miss most about the station if they had to do without it. The responses to this question still further subdivided the broad category of "education," as Table 19 shows.

TABLE 19.—WHAT WOULD YOU MISS MOST IF YOU HAD TO DO WITHOUT STATION YYYY?

Area	Educational Aspects	Specific Programs	Intellectual Stimulation	Cultural Programs	General Quality	Nothing
San Francisco						
Men	17%	19%	19%	23%	23%	5%
Women	11	26	13	17	21	4
Lincoln						
Men & women	21	25	11	15	15	8
Denver						
Men	12	26	24	8	24	8
Women	27	15	8	8	19	0
Alabama network						
Men	28	4	11	11	13	4
Women	33	12	9	10	11	4

Only in the Alabama network audience and among the women of Denver is the educational category now the dominant one. The men in Denver are more likely to say they would miss specific programs—principally "Ragtime Era" and "Open End." They are also much more likely to mention intellectual stimulation and the station's general quality than to talk about its educational value. In San Francisco specific programs ("Open End," in particular), intellectual stimulation, cultural programs, and the general quality of the station, all draw more frequent mention than the educational aspects of the station. In Lincoln specific programs are likewise more likely to be missed than the educational contribution of the station.

What happens to the "keeps me informed" and "entertainment,

enjoyment" categories in the responses to this question? It seems likely that this question elicits viewers' ideas of the *unique* contribution of ETV. The programs on educational television, the qualities of intellectual and cultural stimulation on educational television, are more nearly unique to it. The qualities of informing and entertaining people are shared to a much greater degree with commercial television; and entertainment obviously is much more central in commercial television than in educational.

Answers to this question, however, are significant to persons who work in educational television and to other persons who want to understand it, quite apart from any comparison with other answers. These answers say that the viewers of educational television would miss ETV for specific programs, for the educational element it adds to television, for the intellectual stimulation and cultural experiences it offers, and because of its general high quality as television.

How would they recommend the station?

This question also was asked: "If you were going to make the strongest argument to get friends and other people to watch Channel YYYY [the educational station], what would you say?"

This question proved to be one that elicited generalized rather than specific arguments. Educational aspects were more often mentioned, although "to be informed" was a close second. "Because it is more worth while than commercial television" was also very frequently mentioned, as were specific programs. A small but significant number said they would argue that ETV is good for children. The differences between the station audiences stood out in this instance as in the others: the Alabama network people were the most likely to talk about educational values, and the San Francisco audience was least likely to talk about education, most likely to mention information and culture.

Their rationales for viewing

On the basis of information like this, and considering some of the chief categories of educational programing, a structured question was then devised that read like this:

"Here is a list of statements different people have made when asked why they watch educational TV stations like Channel YYYY.

Would you look through them and give me the number of those statements that come closest to your reason or reasons for watching Channel YYYY?"

The respondent was handed a card on which appeared the following statements:

(1) It is of practical aid in teaching things I want to do.
(2) It helps to keep me better informed.
(3) It helps me to continue my education.
(4) It is more satisfying than commercial TV.
(5) It offers good cultural programs not often available on commercial TV.
(6) It is something people like me should do.
(7) It sets a good example for my children.
(8) It is intellectually stimulating.
(9) It fills a void in the cultural life of the community.

You will see that these were written so as to separate the *formal* education on ETV from the practical aid, on the one hand, and the general informational and cultural advantages, on the other. They also were intended to sharpen the comparison with commercial television and to give people a chance to express any general feeling that they "ought" to be viewing ETV.

Because these answers are rather significant, we are going to reprint the entire table and also the orders of frequency in which the various responses were given by the different audiences (Tables 20–21).

A little study of these tables will show that the responses clearly divide into four groups. The most frequent responses were the same in every city, with the exception of one category in one city. We shall therefore call these

Group One

(5) It offers good cultural programs not often available on commercial TV.
(2) It helps to keep me better informed.
(8) It is intellectually stimulating.

There is a second-order group of responses almost as clearly set off as the first one:

Group Two

(3) It helps me to continue my education.
(4) It is more satisfying than commercial TV.

Next in order of preference is

Group Three

(9) It fills a void in the cultural life of the community.
(1) It is of practical aid in teaching things I want to do.
(7) It sets a good example for my children.

TABLE 20.—RATIONALES FOR VIEWING EDUCATIONAL TELEVISION

Area	(1) Practical Aid	(2) Better Informed	(3) Continue Education	(4) More Satisfying	(5) Cultural Programs	(6) Something One Should Do	(7) Example for Children	(8) Intellectual-Stimulation	(9) Fills Cultural Void
Pittsburgh									
Men	25%	62%	28%	32%	62%	15%	32%	52%	35%
Women	19	47	22	45	57	13	24	43	24
San Francisco									
Men	21	51	23	37	60	6	13	51	22
Women	24	63	28	40	62	13	16	60	23
Lincoln									
Men and women	21	56	35	30	62	15	20	46	25
Columbus									
Men and women	18	58	42	25	72	8	10	58	12
Denver									
Men	30	56	24	32	65	24	26	65	30
Women	44	45	31	34	56	27	37	65	30
Alabama network									
Men	30	71	40	23	47	12	24	32	13
Women	32	63	37	21	54	22	31	45	18

TABLE 21.—RANK ORDER OF FREQUENCY OF THE NINE RESPONSES

Response	Pittsburgh		San Francisco		Lincoln	Columbus	Denver		Alabama Network	
	Men	Women	Men	Women	Men and Women	Men and Women	Men	Women	Men	Women
(1) Practical aid	8	8	7	6	7	6	5	4	5	5
(2) Better informed	2	2	2	1	2	2	3	3	1	1
(3) Continue education	7	7	5	5	4	4	8	7	3	4
(4) More satisfying	5	3	4	4	5	5	4	6	7	8
(5) Cultural programs	1	1	1	2	1	1	2	2	2	2
(6) Something one should do	9	9	9	9	9	9	9	9	9	7
(7) Example for children	6	6	8	8	8	8	7	5	6	6
(8) Intellectual stimulation	3	4	3	3	3	3	1	1	4	3
(9) Fills cultural void	4	5	6	7	6	7	6	8	8	9

And, finally, at the bottom of every list except one:

Group Four

(6) It is something people like me should do.

This is an interesting grouping. Group One, everybody's first choice, seems to indicate that the basic rationale for viewing ETV every place is an intellectual-cultural one: for cultural programs not readily available elsewhere, for intellectual stimulation, and to be kept well informed. Group Two, however, is a mixed group, and it is not surprising to find that the station audiences are divided on it—San Francisco and Pittsburgh giving higher place to the fact that ETV is more satisfying than commercial TV, the two university audiences and the Alabama network stressing that it helps to continue education. Group Three is also a mixture of practical and cultural purposes. Practical aid by ETV is emphasized by two audiences considerably more than the others. These are in Denver and Alabama. And Group Four is interesting, too. The very great degree of agreement in putting the "something we should do" rationale at the very bottom indicates that if the social norm of educational television being a "good thing to do" is indeed active, it isn't being talked about.

The individual station audiences are set apart really by how they stand on three items: number 3 (continuing one's education), number 4 (more satisfying than commercial TV), and number 1 (practical aid). Alabama, Columbus, and Lincoln are high on the continuing educational value (3). Pittsburgh and San Francisco are high on the satisfying quality of ETV in comparison with CTV (4). Denver and Alabama are high on the practical aid they get from ETV. Thus we seem to have four different kinds of audience, if these responses on rationale are to be taken seriously. Every audience bases its viewing on a desire for the cultural and intellectual programing of educational stations. But in addition to that, we have what we might call a *noncommercial audience* (Pittsburgh and San Francisco), a *continuing education audience* (Columbus and Lincoln), a *practical aid audience* (Denver), and an audience that combines interest in *continuing education and practical aid* (Alabama network). See Figure 25.

This inevitably reminds us of what we found out about how

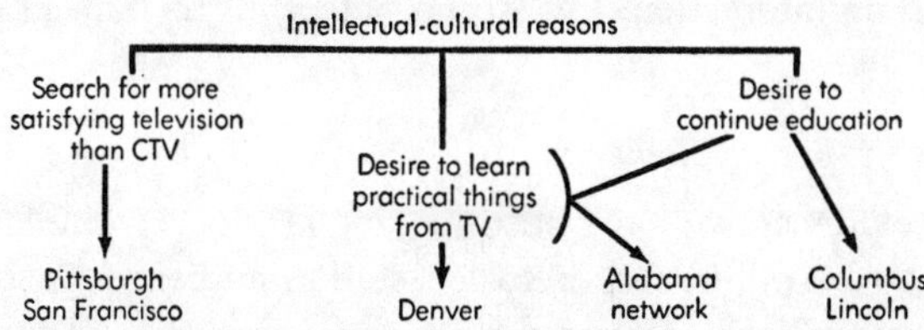

Fig. 25.—Rationales of audiences for viewing ETV.

the stations program (Chapter 3). The two stations whose audiences seem to find them outstandingly "more satisfying" than commercial television are community stations, skillful in production, repeating many programs, and with large audiences. They are what we called "arts stations," because of the number of art and culture programs they carry. By contrast, we called Columbus, Lincoln, and the Alabama network "science" stations. These stations broadcast many courses and make frequent use of professors from the universities associated with them. It is not altogether surprising to find out that the audiences of these stations are the ones who see ETV as especially important in helping them continue their education. We recall that the Denver station specialized in a large number of "how to do it" programs, and are not surprised that the Denver audience should give a high rating to the "practical aid" available on educational television. And the Alabama network not only is strong in its continuing education programs, but also has an audience of which a sizable part claims to spend more than half its ETV time on practical programs. So if we then speak of Pittsburgh and San Francisco as an *intellectual-cultural* audience, of Columbus and Lincoln as an *intellectual-cultural-education* audience, of Denver as an *intellectual-cultural-practical* audience, and of the Alabama network as an *intellectual-cultural-education-practical* audience, we have some support both in the programing and in the audiences' expressed reason for viewing.[3]

It is an interesting question whether a station programs as it does because the people want what they want, or whether the people learn their tastes from what the station gives them. Prob-

[3] Let us not lose sight, in thus naming these groups of station audiences, that all the audiences are interested in all these kinds of programs, and all the stations offer the several kinds of programs. We are talking only of *emphasis*.

ably it is an interaction, but we do not have the data in hand to prove it.

Are there types of viewers?

The evidence we have been looking at seems to indicate that there may be differences between station audiences in terms of what they are seeking from the educational station. The obvious next question is whether there are types of viewers, so that Audience A would be different from Audience B because it contains more viewers of Type X, fewer of Type Y. There undoubtedly *are* types of viewers, but we have not known how clearly they are distinguished from one another, or what different kinds of patterns exist.

We tried to answer that question by analyzing the *patterns* of response to the question about rationales for viewing. Since respondents were instructed to list all the rationales that approximate their own reasons, it is possible to consider the omission of a rationale as a negative answer. Thus, the question becomes a kind of true-false test, wherein the respondent picks those statements he believes to be true, and the remainder are the ones he regards as false. This approach enabled us to construct a correlation matrix and analyze it so as to find whether the various rationales fit together into repeated clusters. This was done by calculating phi coefficients, and we shall not interrupt the report to give the raw data or details of the method here; the correlation matrix will be found in Appendix C, Table A10.

Suffice it to say that when we did find the intercorrelations of all the rationales, the first conclusion that came out of the analysis was that there are really no sharply divided clusters of persons by rationale. That is, there is not a large group of persons interested *only* in continuing their education and becoming better informed, or in practical aid and filling a cultural void, or any other sharply differentiated group of interests. One characteristic of ETV viewing seems to be that the reasons for viewing are usually multiple, and they are usually interrelated. In other words, we conclude that there are probably not a number of separate and distinct reasons for viewing ETV, but, rather, one group of related reasons, some of which are emphasized by some viewers, others by other viewers. The difference is one of emphasis rather than kind.

Nevertheless, there are some reasons more closely related, more central in the act of seeking ETV, than others. Let us take only the rationales that are correlated strongly—phi equals .30 or above. The strongest relationship of all is between the motivations to seek cultural programs and intellectual stimulation (rationales 5 and 8). Number 8 is also strongly correlated with the statement that ETV fills a void in the cultural life of the community (number 9) and that it is more satisfying than commercial television (4). In turn, the filling of the "cultural void" is closely related to the seeking of intellectual stimulation and cultural programs. Thus, as shown in Figure 26, we have a tight little cluster of reasons all interrelated at a level that is statistically highly significant. The seeking of cultural programs is also related to trying to fill the cultural void, as we should expect, but not quite at the level of a .30 correlation.

Now, suppose we include all correlations of .20 or above. All of these will be statistically significant at the .05 level or better, so we judge that these are not chance relationships. If we expand the model to include the relationships of .20 or above, we find the pattern shown in Figure 27. Now only "example for children" stands isolated from other rationales. A second-order cluster has appeared, composed of the first cluster plus "keep better informed," which is quite closely related to "cultural programs," and is in turn related closely to "continue education" (which is closely related to "fill cultural void" and less closely but significantly to "intellectual stimulation"). There is also a third-order linkage, a long arm of weak but significant relationships that connects "practical aid" to "continue education" and "something one should do" to "practical aid."

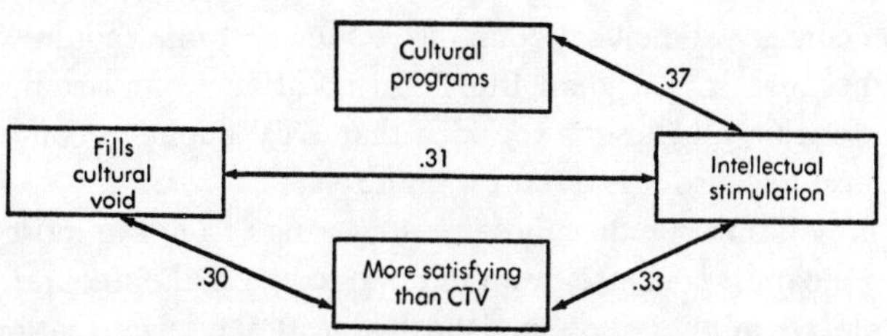

Fig. 26.—Reasons for viewing ETV. Correlations of .30 or above.

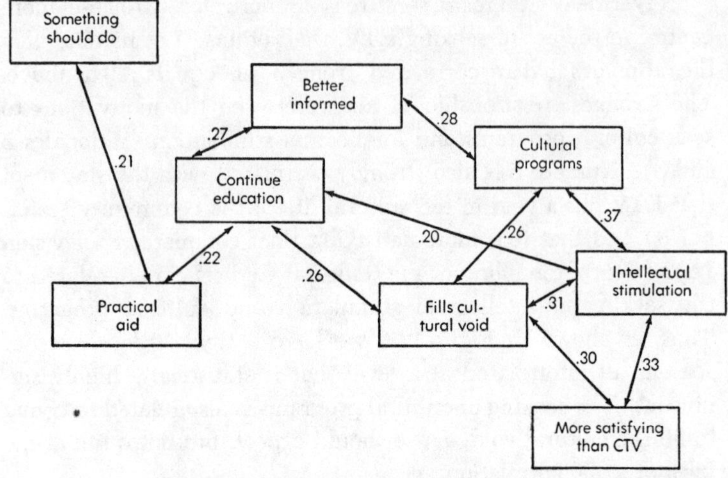

Fig. 27.—Reasons for viewing ETV. Correlations of .20 or above.

The most reasonable interpretation of these results is as follows: The most prevalent reason for watching ETV, so far as answers to this question reflect the reasons, is that ETV offers high-level programs which give the viewers intellectual stimulation, programs of a nature they do not find (or do not find as many as they would like) on commercial television. Closely related to this is the reason that ETV informs its viewers—adds to their knowledge and understanding of cultural, scientific, and public affairs matters.

Another reason for viewing that is closely related to the idea of being informed and being intellectually stimulated is the desire for substantive and usually formal education. Another reason, closely related to the desire for formal education, is the desire for "practical aid" on everyday problems. And along with this last reason comes a somewhat compulsive idea that one should watch ETV because it is a good thing. In addition to and somewhat separate from all these is the idea that ETV ought to come into the house because it is good for children.

You will observe that these reasons range from the most general to the most concrete, from internal to external outcomes. For example, we might impressionistically locate the several rationales on two axes, as in Figure 28.

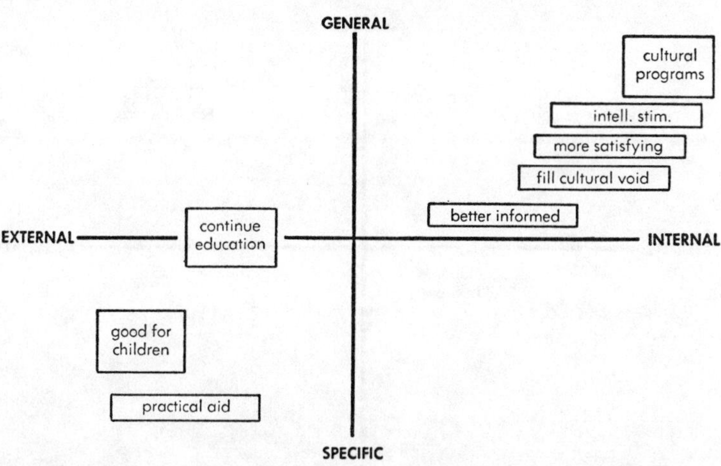

Fig. 28.—Reasons for viewing ETV: from general to specific, from internal to external satisfaction.

The answers in the upper right-hand corner of the figure are mostly in terms of satisfaction, enjoyment, and what ETV will do to one's intellectual and cultural understandings. The most specific and external of these is the idea of being "better informed," which conveys the implication that one can then do something about it—discuss, or vote, or read more wisely, or whatever. When one gets as far as "continue education," however, one is talking of a product directly usable. Education will help a person get another job, or a higher salary, or something tangible. And down in the left-hand corner of Figure 28 are two rationales which are clearly specific, external, and usable. "Practical aid" programs will help one re-cover the furniture, or make a better garden. Children's programs will help one bring up healthier and happier children.

It is doubtless true that educational stations program for all these interests, and educational audiences represent all these interests. The difference comes in emphasis. The large audiences of the community stations in Pittsburgh and San Francisco tend to put their emphasis (for adult education, not school broadcasts!) in the upper right-hand corner. The audiences for the two university stations emphasize that corner also, but in addition they emphasize an interest in continuing education, which is a more external and specific interest. The audiences for Denver and the

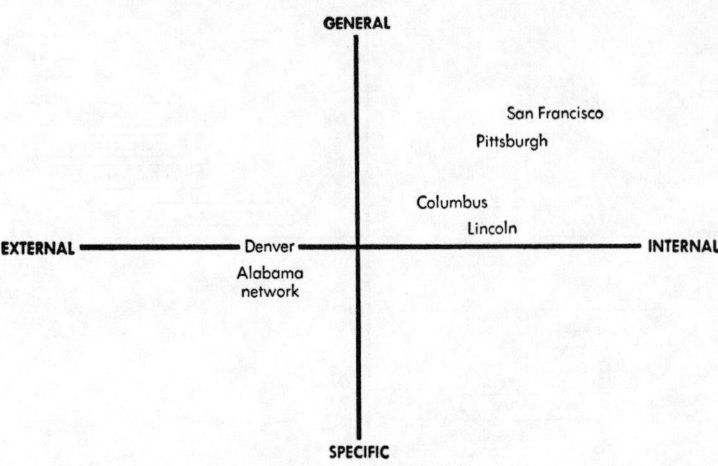

Fig. 29.—Emphases of ETV audiences.

Alabama network emphasize also the need of practical aid, and thus move farther toward the external and specific corner. Impressionistically again, we might locate the "center of gravity" of the various station audiences as in Figure 29. Another way to distinguish these audiences is by means of the correlation diagrams we looked at earlier, Figures 26 and 27. The different audience emphases might be drawn as shown in Figure 30. In other words, it seems to us that the San Francisco and Pittsburgh audiences are, more than the others, "culture audiences"; the Denver and

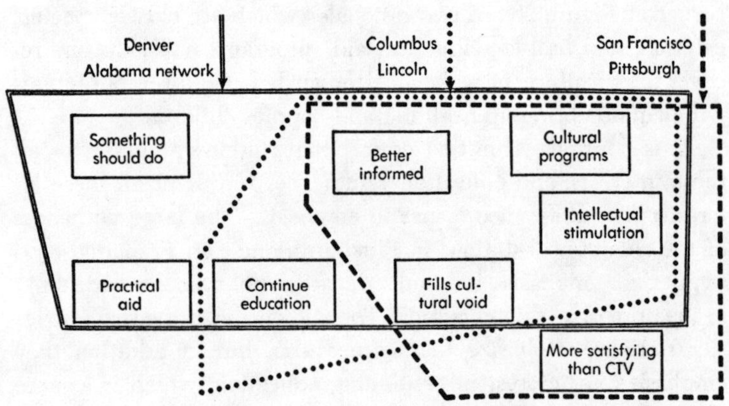

Fig. 30.—Correlations of emphases of ETV audiences.

Alabama network audiences, more than the others, are "practical audiences"; and the university station audiences are in between.

But let us emphasize again that the significant thing about ETV viewers is not how different the several audiences are, but rather how alike they are. There is a common core in all these ETV audiences which might be described as a seeking of high-level programs, programs that they feel have a value beyond entertainment, that offer artistic or intellectual excellence, that both inform and please, that stimulate and edify as well as entertain.

Defining "education"

We are now in a position to define "education" in "educational television" as it must look from the standpoint of the audience. Some viewers clearly are seeking formal instructional programs, but they are a minority. To most ETV viewers, "education" must mean the kind of material in the upper right-hand quarter of our fourfold chart (Figure 28), or the right-hand side of our correlation chart (Figure 27). Intellectual, artistic, significant, informative—these must be the kind of adjectives most viewers connect with the educational quality of the medium. Educational television is probably considered "educational" in the same sense that a trip to a museum, a lecture on modern science, a Greek drama, or a symphony orchestra concert would be considered educational. This is what must have been in the minds of most of the viewers whom we quoted earlier in this chapter as citing the "educational aspects" of ETV as the chief reason for watching it.

Does rationale predict behavior?

We should like to know, now, whether these expressed rationales are parallel to the actual television behavior of audiences. Do they view the kinds of programs they say they want?

It might seem easy to answer this question, but it is far from easy. For one thing, a regular viewer of ETV may see only three or four programs a week. We have only a week's viewing record, which provides hardly enough viewing to test whether a person really lives up to all the rationales he expressed. Furthermore, his choice of programs will depend not only on what he thinks he wants, but on what the station offers him. For example, he might choose a very excellent program in a category that is not his first choice, rather than a mediocre program of the type he is seeking. Therefore, we put together some items of evidence so as to find something about whether rationale for viewing predicts viewing.

We divided the viewers into heavy and light viewers of ETV. We found that, as a general thing, the heavier a person's viewing, the more rationales for viewing he was able to cite. This sounds reasonable. The more ways a person finds a medium satisfying or helpful, the more likely he is to increase his time with the medium. (Or, if one reverses the relationship, the more time one spends with a medium, the more he will tend to rationalize his behavior by seeing himself as benefiting in more ways from the time he spends.) We also found that three rationales for viewing were consistently cited more frequently by heavy than by light viewers. These were "for cultural programs not available on commercial television," "for intellectual stimulation," and "it fills a cultural void." As we have seen, these are three of the basic or core rationales, and we should expect them to go with heavier viewing.

Another way to test this relationship is to take the groups of viewers who said they spent 50 per cent or more of their ETV time on a given kind of programing, and find out what rationales they gave for viewing. We did this, and found a number of encouraging results. For example, of the people in San Francisco who said they spent the majority of their ETV time on cultural programs, only 13 per cent gave "practical aid" as one of their reasons for viewing; but on the other hand, 40 per cent of the viewers who said they spent the majority of their EVT time on instructional programs cited "practical aid" as a reason. We have seen that "continue education" and "practical aid" are related reasons. Similarly, "intellectual stimulation" was given as a reason by only 32 per cent of the practical aid audience in the Alabama network territory, whereas 52 per cent of the cultural program audience cited "intellectual stimulation." Fifty-three per cent of the Alabama instructional program audience gave "continue my education" as one of their chief reasons, compared with 40 per cent of the cultural program viewers. The relationships were by no means always clear, but there were enough patterns such as we have just

TABLE 22.—REASONS FOR WATCHING ETV GIVEN BY VIEWERS (V) OR NONVIEWERS (NV) OF THREE EDUCATIONAL PROGRAMS*

Rationale	The Greeks Had a Word for It ($N = 25$)	World of Music ($N = 22$)	Open End ($N = 43$)
Practical aid	NV	NV	NV
To be informed	V	NV	V
Continue education	NV	—	—
More satisfying	—	NV	V
Cultural programs	—	V	V
Something I should do	—	—	NV
Example for children	—	—	NV
Intellectual stimulation	V	NV	V
Fills cultural void	—	—	V

* The top left-hand cell is interpreted as follows: "Among the ETV audience a significantly higher percentage of nonviewers than viewers of 'The Greeks Had a Word for It' replied yes to the question 'Do you watch ETV for practical aid?' "

cited to encourage us to believe that these rationales do tend to be reflected in viewing choices.

Perhaps the most effective place to test the relationship is in the audiences for specific programs. In several of the studies we have large enough program audiences to be able to do this (see Table 22). We find that in Pittsburgh the audience for the program "The Greeks Had a Word for It," compared with its nonviewers, cited two rationales significantly more frequently. These were "to be better informed" and "it is intellectually stimulating." In the same city the audience of "World of Music" scored higher than this program's nonviewers on only one rationale: "it offers good cultural programs not available on commercial television." And the "World of Music" audience scored much lower than its nonviewers on "practical aid," "to be better informed," "more satisfying," and "for intellectual stimulation." Intuitively, these differences make very good sense.

"Open End" scored consistently higher, viewers over its nonviewers, on "more satisfying," "for cultural programs," "for intellectual stimulation," and "fills a cultural void." These were the same in all three cities where the program was being shown at the time of these studies. The consistency also encouraged us to believe that rationales may predict viewing. In *two* of the three cities the "Open End" viewers also scored higher on "to be better informed." In all the cities "Open End" viewers scored lower on "practical aid," "something I should do," and "example for my children." There was little difference between viewers and nonviewers of the program in any city on "continue my education."

When the viewer rationales for "Open End" are compared with those for "Ragtime Era" in the one city where both programs were currently being broadcast, the general profiles are about the same, but the "Open End" audience scored higher on "to be informed" and "intellectual stimulation." This, too, makes intuitive good sense when we compare a lively discussion program with a program of ragtime music.

Finally, we separated in two cities the viewers who said they had never followed a course, those who had watched a course "a few times," and those who had watched "all or most" of a course. We then analyzed their choice of rationales for viewing, and found this interesting pattern in the percentage of viewers who said that they watched ETV "to continue my education":

	Never Followed a Course	Watched a Few Times	Watched Most or All of a Course
San Francisco ($N = 159$)...	20%	31%	47%
Alabama network ($N = 328$)	36	46	57

We conclude that these rationales, though not perfect predictors, do relate very closely to viewing patterns, and are therefore more than polite and proper answers.[4]

It is worthy of note that broad cultural experiences, which

[4] We also ran these rationales against a measure of socioeconomic status—blue-collar vs. white-collar or a close equivalent. In Columbus and San Francisco there was very little difference between the rank order of rationales given by the two socioeconomic groups. In Pittsburgh and Denver, however, there were considerable differences. The high SES groups in both cities had the same top choices as the viewers in Columbus and San Francisco—"to be informed," "cultural programs," and "intellectual stimulation." But the low SES group in Pittsburgh cited "to be informed," "more satisfying," and "example for children" as their top three. The low SES group in Denver cited "something I should do," "example for children," and "intellectual stimulation." The high SES group invariably had a high score on "cultural programs." In general, our belief is that the more highly educated, higher socioeconomic viewers tend to cluster toward the "general, internal" end of the rationale scale, and the less educated ones probably tend to cluster toward the other end. (See Table A9, Appendix C.)

form the core of what ETV viewers call education, are provided most heavily by the educational stations that have built the largest audiences for themselves. This is hardly surprising, for people who most often gave cultural reasons for watching ETV were the most typical ETV viewers rather than the deviant cases; they were the heavy users of ETV rather than the light users; they were expressing in another form the capability of deferred rather than immediate gratification. They were the people who had a taste which CTV was not satisfying. Overt condemnation of CTV did not loom large in the replies we have quoted above. The ETV viewers themselves used CTV for escape. They also shared the interests of the nonviewers in current news and useful knowledge, some of which CTV supplied. But they had a further set of desires summarized in the notions of intellectual stimulation and good cultural programing which they could not satisfy elsewhere. That is what educational television meant to most viewers, while also meaning information, instruction, and practical advice.

8

What They Think of ETV

Merely being in the educational television audience is, of course, a favorable opinion ballot. Coming to ETV for "intellectual stimulation," for "cultural programs," to find something "more satisfying than commercial television"—coming to the audience seeking those rewards, and *remaining* in the audience—is at least an inferential kind of approval. Beside this inferential evidence we can now set some evidence of a more direct kind.

This chapter is concerned with what the viewers of ETV think of it, whether it is fulfilling the expectations with which they came to it, and how satisfied or dissatisfied they are.

What is ETV doing well?

When the Stanford study was trying to find out why people view educational television, interviewers asked respondents to indicate which of nine possible rationales reflected their own reasons for viewing. We report the results in Chapter 7. Reasons most frequently indicated in all the test cities were: (1) ETV keeps me well informed, (2) it offers good cultural programs not available on commercial television, (3) it is intellectually stimulating. Following at a little distance were: (4) it helps me to continue my education, and (5) it is more satisfying than commercial television.

The next question in the interview asked the respondent to name any of the nine rationales he believed his ETV station was fulfilling especially *well*. In each of the test cities, an average of about 15 per cent of the respondents either said they did not think the station was doing any of the things well or declined to answer the question—which may or may not be a negative answer. The other 85 or 90 per cent, however, were quite specific in their answers. They listed fewer of the nine rationales than they did when citing reasons for viewing, and appeared to have fairly clear ideas of where they felt the station was doing well and where not.

Although the percentages varied from city to city, the rank order of judgments was quite uniform. Table 23 shows the high items from each test area.

TABLE 23.—REASONS FOR VIEWING THAT ARE BEING SATISFIED ESPECIALLY WELL BY ETV

Area	As Named by 30% or More of Respondents	As Named by 20–29% of Respondents
Pittsburgh	Provide cultural programs	Be better informed; help continue education
San Francisco	Intellectual stimulation; provide cultural programs	Be better informed; help continue education
Lincoln	Provide cultural programs	Intellectual stimulation; help continue education
Columbus	Provide cultural programs; intellectual stimulation; help continue education	Be better informed
Denver	Practical aid	Intellectual stimulation; be better informed
Alabama network	Provide cultural programs; be better informed	Help continue education; practical aid

These responses are remarkably uniform. In five of the six areas, "provide cultural programs" is named by more than 30 per cent of the viewers, and it might well have been named in all six cities, except for the reason that it was not included in the list in Denver.[1] "Intellectual stimulation," "be better informed," and "help continue education" follow close behind. Thus the list of things the station is doing well matches quite closely the list of most common reasons for viewing ETV. It is interesting to notice that the only one of the favorite rationales that did not reappear on the "well done" list is "more satisfying than commercial television." A little later in this chapter we can see in more detail how the viewers compare ETV with CTV.

[1] The Denver study was made a little earlier than the others, as a large preliminary test.

It is interesting to notice that Denver gets a high audience endorsement for its series of practical aid programs, and that the Alabama network also draws praise for practical aid. These are the two audiences that listed "practical aid" highest in their inventory of reasons for viewing ETV.

It is hardly surprising, of course, that there should be this agreement between reasons for viewing and perceptions of a good job being done, but it is at least encouraging.

What is ETV not doing well?

Respondents were also asked to indicate any of the nine rationales that the station was not fulfilling as well as the respondent thought it should. In only two instances did more than 10 per cent of any sample mention a given area of dissatisfaction. Nineteen per cent of the men in the Alabama network audience and 15 per cent of the viewers in Columbus felt that their ETV stations were not doing enough to "fill the cultural void" in their communities. This may seem rather odd, inasmuch as both audiences praised the station for "providing cultural programs." Possibly this is merely a reflection of a very deep wish for cultural improvement: even though the station is doing well in this respect, there is still much to do. Or it may reflect a minority group opinion of some kind. In any case, the most important result of this question was an overwhelming vote of confidence in the station's performance. Figure 31 shows the percentages in each audience that said they knew of *no* area where the station was not doing as well as it should.

ETV compared with other media

Another question of considerable interest is how educational television fits with the other media into the use-patterns of a viewer. For information on this, both viewers and nonviewers of ETV in the eight-station sample were asked how interested they were in five kinds of service the media provide—practical information; art, literature, and poetry; public issues; serious music; and general knowledge. Then we asked each to tell us which of the mass media were of real help to him in each of these areas. We asked viewers of ETV to distinguish in their answers between commercial and educational television. Then we separated the

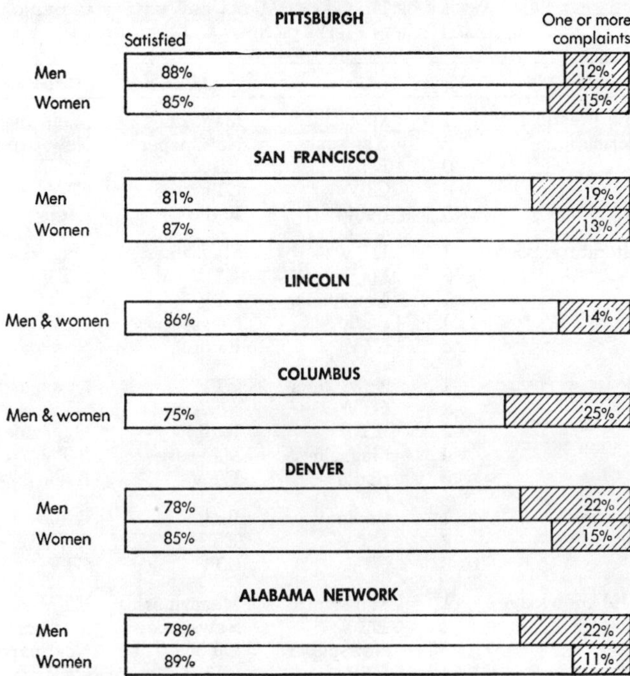

Fig. 31.—Proportion of audience satisfied with performance of station.

persons who said they were "very" or "intensely" interested in each area of content, and analyzed what they had said about the help they got from different media.

Detailed information is in Appendix C, Tables A5–7, but Table 24 shows what the answers were like. This table represents the answers of *ETV viewers* only.

One's first reaction upon looking at Table 24 concerns the highly specialized role into which radio has been forced by the coming of television. Before television, radio would certainly have rated very high in each of the five categories. Now it is first in bringing serious music to the audience, but rather uniformly last in all the others. Commercial television has taken over much of radio's responsibility for bringing public issues to its viewers, and educational television has come to play an exceedingly important role for its audiences. Over-all, ETV is second only to magazines as a carrier of art, literature, and poetry. It is second to radio as

TABLE 24.—RANKING OF DIFFERENT MEDIA BY VIEWERS AS BEING OF REAL HELP IN FIELDS OF SPECIAL INTEREST

Field	Rank	San Francisco	Lincoln	Columbus
Getting practical information	1	Magazines	Magazines	Magazines
	2	Newspaper	Newspaper	Newspaper
	3	**ETV**	**ETV**	**ETV**
	4	CTV	CTV	CTV
	5	Radio	Radio	Radio
Art, literature, poetry	1	**ETV**	Magazines	Magazines
	2	Magazines	**ETV**	**ETV**
	3	Newspaper	CTV	Radio
	4	{Radio	Newspaper	{CTV
	5	{CTV	Radio	{Newspaper
Public issues	1	Newspaper	CTV	Newspaper
	2	CTV	Newspaper	CTV
	3	**ETV**	Radio	Magazines
	4	Magazines	Magazines	**ETV**
	5	Radio	**ETV**	Radio
Serious music	1	Radio	Radio	Radio
	2	**ETV**	**ETV**	**ETV**
	3	CTV	CTV	CTV
General knowledge	1	Magazines	Magazines	**ETV**
	2	**ETV**	Newspaper	Magazines
	3	Newspaper	**ETV**	Newspaper
	4	CTV	CTV	CTV
	5	Radio	Radio	Radio

Braces indicate a tie.

a carrier of serious music. It is second only to magazines as a purveyor of general knowledge. In bringing public issues to its viewers it is rated less useful than commercial television or newspapers, and slightly less useful than magazines, but in one of the three areas it is ranked above magazines.

These results, of course, reflect to some extent the nature of the separate stations and their audiences. San Francisco's distinguished programs on the arts and on local public issues are reflected in the high rating ETV gets in San Francisco on those two services. Columbus' strong programs in general knowledge are likewise reflected in high audience ratings for this service. It would be interesting to have this same question asked in the coverage areas of the two stations where practical aid programs have been emphasized, and see whether this rating, too, does not rise among those audiences.

How do the nonviewers of ETV rate the media for their services in these areas? Full information is in Appendix C, Tables A5–6, but in general it may be said that the ratings by nonviewers follow the same order as the ratings by viewers—of course, with ETV omitted. In San Francisco, for example, where ETV is in third place and TV in fourth place among viewers, for practical information TV moves up to third place among nonviewers of ETV. It appears that ETV has not brought about the extensive reorganization among the media that commercial television brought about when it took over so many of the functions of radio. At the same time, educational television is not serving as simply an extension of the services of commercial television. It has its own strengths and weaknesses. It is clearly weaker than commercial television in its ability to cover public events and thereby to illuminate public issues. On the other hand, it has a special interest and strength in art and in general knowledge, which give it a pattern of usefulness quite different from commercial television. Thus, for example, you will notice that CTV and ETV occupy adjacent ranks in practical aid and serious music, but in public issues, in art, and general knowledge their ranks are quite different. Of course, it goes without saying that CTV is much more used as entertainment than is ETV. Therefore, in viewers' concepts of usefulness, as well as in the other qualities of the medium, we may say with some confidence that educational television is a different medium from commercial television.

What changes in ETV do viewers want?

Viewers were also asked what changes they would make in their local ETV station if they had the power. (See Appendix C, Table A17.) Responses to such a question as this should be read with caution, inasmuch as people are notoriously unable to envision changes in the media and to say specifically how they would react to new forms they have not experienced. Therefore, the fact that about half the respondents say they would make "no change" is not so significant as it might seem. On the other hand, the same viewers of ETV were much more productive in generating suggestions for changes in commercial television, as we shall see later in this chapter. And we know from other studies that highly educated persons (who are plentiful in the ETV audience) are likely to be more articulate and critical than others in speaking of television.[2] Therefore, the results would seem at least to indicate that there is no great prevailing dissatisfaction with the educational stations on the part of their viewers.

More significant than this, however, is the nature of the suggestions for change which viewers were able to make. The change most frequently suggested was to add certain programs or courses. Roughly two-thirds of all the proposed changes were of this sort. The suggestions had no central trend, except that people wanted—as might be expected—more and better. The largest number of suggestions for specific kinds of programs were for children's programs.

A number of viewers spoke of the need of more money for the station, in order to provide more professional camera work and lighting, better actors, remote coverage, and other improvements in presentation. Of the remaining one-third of the suggested changes, a little less than half were in schedule—for example, that children's programs should be put at times more convenient to the family, or that a program should be repeated when the man of the house could be home to hear it, or that week-end programs should be added, and so forth. Another 15 percent or so of the suggestions were of a very interesting kind. There were a few suggestions that the station should be less "stuffy." There were suggestions that programs should be made less difficult—for children and the uneducated, some respondents added. The problem of whether programs are too difficult is one we looked into by means of other questions, on which we shall now report.

Are ETV programs too difficult?

When respondents were asked to rate ETV programs they knew as "too hard," "too easy," or "about right," about 80 per cent of all the answers said "about right." (See Appendix C, Table A16.) The proportion of "too hard" answers varied with the audience. In San Francisco, where the educational level is higher than in some of the other audiences, only about 2 per cent of the an-

[2] For example, the Steiner study of the CTV audience found highly educated persons more critical, as did the Stanford study of Milwaukee Journal Consumer Survey data (unpublished memorandum, "Data on Broadcast Audiences in Milwaukee," Institute for Communication Research, Stanford University, 1962).

swers mentioned a program as being "too hard." In Pittsburgh, where the average education of the women is higher than that of the men, about 12 per cent of the men, 6 per cent of the women, found some program "too hard." The proportion of "too hard" responses was about 5 per cent in Columbus, 8 per cent in Lincoln, and 12 per cent of the women, 19 per cent of the men in the Alabama network audience. These are roughly proportional to the educational level of the audience. Thus, in some cases, a program rated "about right" in one area is "too hard" in another. This is what happened, for example, in the case of the "Casals Master Class" program, which was "too hard" for some members of the Alabama network audience, but was rated "about right" in San Francisco.

In the Boston study the respondents were asked to choose from a list of adjectives, which applied to WGBH. Nine per cent of the viewers called it too highbrow. That is not many, but then only 15 per cent of the nonviewers chose that label.

Respondents were also asked how far in school they felt a person needed to have gone in order to be able to enjoy the programs on the ETV channel. Considerable difference was found in responses from different station audiences, but, in general, the educational stations are considered by most of their viewers to require a high school education, not more. It is encouraging to note that the two stations in the areas with the lowest educational levels are rated by a third of their viewers as relatively unrestricted by educational level—it "doesn't matter," they say. The only stations where a sizable proportion of viewers say that a college education is needed are the two university stations. This may be a halo effect of the university affiliation, or it may be that these stations are actually demanding more than the community or school stations. Table A14, Appendix C, summarizes these judgments.

What social class does ETV serve?

There has been a great deal of speculation about the breadth of appeal of educational television. Can it serve both ends of the social spectrum? Do viewers see it as appealing mostly to the middle class, the upper class, or the lower class? We know that the audience is skewed toward the more educated, higher eco-

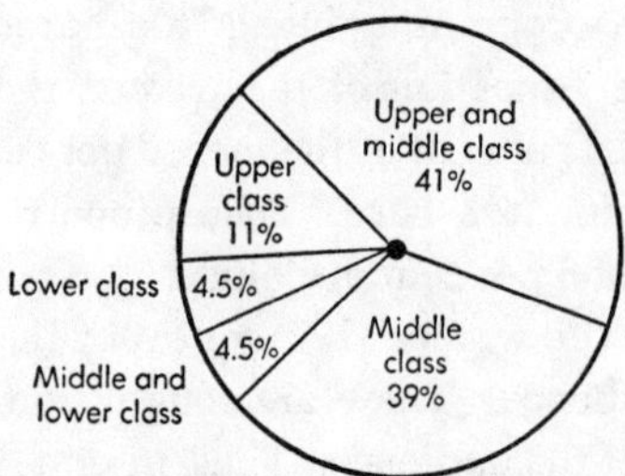

Fig. 32.—Viewers' opinions of the target audience of ETV. (About one-third of the sample said ETV appealed to "everyone" or "all classes." These respondents are not included in the figure.)

nomic, white-collar groups, but how do the viewers themselves perceive the medium? This is what we tried to find out by asking what socioeconomic class or classes the viewers saw as the target of ETV.

A detailed table of responses will be found in Appendix C, Table A15. Figure 32 indicates the general order of responses, after eliminating the 15 per cent who did not answer and the 27 per cent who made no class distinction—who answered, in effect, that educational television was for everybody.

Clearly the perception of educational television by its audience is not unlike the actual pattern of that audience—skewed toward the upper socioeconomic levels, but including all levels. There is no indication that ETV is thought of by any considerable part of its audience as exclusively an upper-social-class activity.

There is some variation between stations. The Columbus audience is the one most likely to perceive ETV as appealing to the upper half of the social spectrum, and San Francisco and Lincoln are second in this respect. On the other hand, Pittsburgh and Alabama network audiences are most likely to see their stations as appealing to the middle class and "everybody."

The answers to this question may to a considerable extent project self-image, inasmuch as the two audiences last mentioned are lowest in educational level, and the three others are highest in proportion of college people.

The qualities of ETV

Perhaps the most revealing evidence we have of people's conceptions of and attitudes toward TV is a descriptive check list of

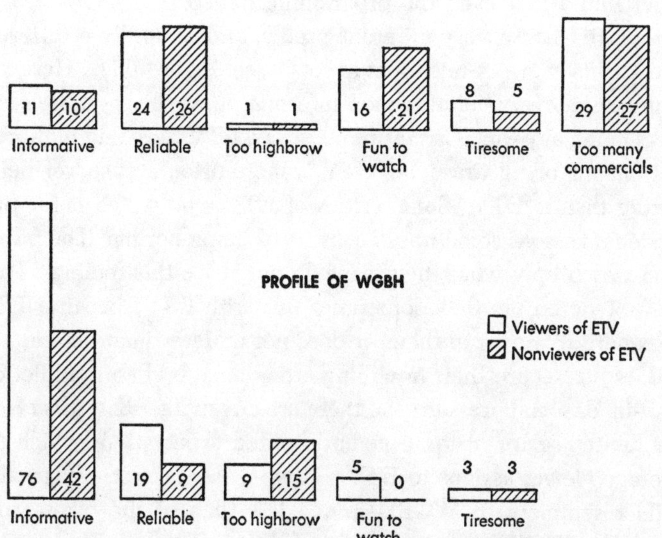

Fig. 33.–Attitudes of ETV viewers and nonviewers toward CTV and Station WGBH, Boston study. Each figure is the percentage of respondents that chose that term.

words (see Figure 33). Questions of this nature were used in both the M.I.T. and Stanford studies. In the former, a series of adjectival phrases was presented to viewers and nonviewers, who were asked to pick the phrases that best fit each channel–both the commercial channels and the educational ones.

Viewers and nonviewers alike had a remarkably similar image of the commercial channels. (We average responses for the three commercial stations.) Except for the fact that ETV viewers find CTV somewhat less fun and more often tiresome, the profiles are almost identical, demonstrating once more that both viewers and nonviewers to a large degree share common orientations toward the popular part of culture. They both saw the commercial channels as fun sources substantially more than information sources.[3] They both found that they could count upon CTV for what they

[3] But for WGBH viewers the mention of fun outpaces the mention of information by but 16 to 11, while for nonviewers the ratio is 21 to 10. The gratification ETV viewers got, even from CTV, reflects once more their eagerness for information.

expected of it, yet both complained about commercials and sometimes found that even the programing palled.

WGBH had a very different profile, and naturally a different one for its viewers and nonviewers (see Figure 33). Here the emphasis is overwhelmingly on information, with very little sense of its being any fun. Criticism focuses on ETV for being highbrow but *not* for being tiresome. CTV is more often accused of being boring than is ETV. Some critics of ETV who watch it for professional reasons sometimes accuse it of being boring. The public who watch only what they want do not share this feeling. They are not bored, as they sometimes are with CTV, because ETV does not talk down to them; it does not underestimate them; and it does not secure their unwilling attendance by habit, addiction, lead-in, or social pressure. So there are advantages that arise from the limited sector of the time and limited expectations which the average viewer assigns to ETV. There is, as a result, remarkably little resentment of WGBH—much less than of the commercial channels. WGBH is seen as a good thing even though not much fun, and the one criticism that does appear is the suggestion that the programs could be somewhat more popular.

The same suggestion, and with the same frequency, occurred in another context. Boston respondents were asked what kinds of programs they would show if they were in charge of an ETV station. Most replied by naming specific program types (e.g., science), and the distribution of these simply mirrored WGBH's actual schedule. However, 10 per cent of WGBH viewers made suggestions other than of program categories. Seven of these 10 per cent suggested such things as simpler terminology, better communication, lighter approach, and more interesting, more colorful, and less formal programs; while another 2 per cent suggested greater variety.

There is, in short, some evidence that the WGBH audience would respond happily if the station became, even more than it is now, a general cultural and informational (as distinct from instructional) station with a good deal of high-quality entertainment material. The evidence includes the fact that the audience is quite basically discontented with what they get on CTV, yet for lack of better material of its kind, they keep watching it anyhow.

Their discontent, as we have argued elsewhere, is not radical. They are not looking for a new and different kind of material from that which TV already offers. They are interested in the subjects it covers and are amused by its kinds of entertainments. But they want them better. Too often the programs offered are boring or distasteful, not enough to drive the audience away, but enough to engender malaise. A medium that met the same craving intelligently and tastefully would be welcome.

Further evidence of the ETV public's desire for high-grade but general-interest programing is contained in the few criticisms, just noted above, that they do make of WGBH. They want it to communicate more entertainingly. Evidence to the same effect arose also when we looked at the shows that they said they preferred. We found the favorites to be programs of the kind—"Open End," "Boston Symphony," and "Louis Lyons News"—that sometimes are shown on CTV and that stand out from the general run of standard television in quality rather than type.

Respondents in the eight-station study were given a list of 13 descriptive terms, each preceded by "not at all," "somewhat," "quite," and "very." The respondent was asked to describe his local educational station by checking one of the four qualifying terms for each adjective. When he had done this, he was asked to go through the list again and describe "regular commercial television" in the same way. Thus, descriptions were made available, by viewers and nonviewers, of educational television and of commercial television.

First let us look at what ETV's own viewers had to say of it. Full information is in Appendix C, Table A13. Figure 34 combines men's and women's responses for each station.

Educational television receives an overwhelming vote of confidence for being informative, useful, satisfying, and interesting. The lowest percentage to rate it quite or very informative is 78; the lowest to say that it is quite or very interesting is 69; the lowest to judge it quite or very useful is 76; the lowest to call it quite or very satisfying is 54. For each of these descriptive terms the median is in the 80's or very close to 80. In addition, between a third and a half of the viewers said that ETV was quite or very much fun, and about one-fourth said that it was hard work. As a

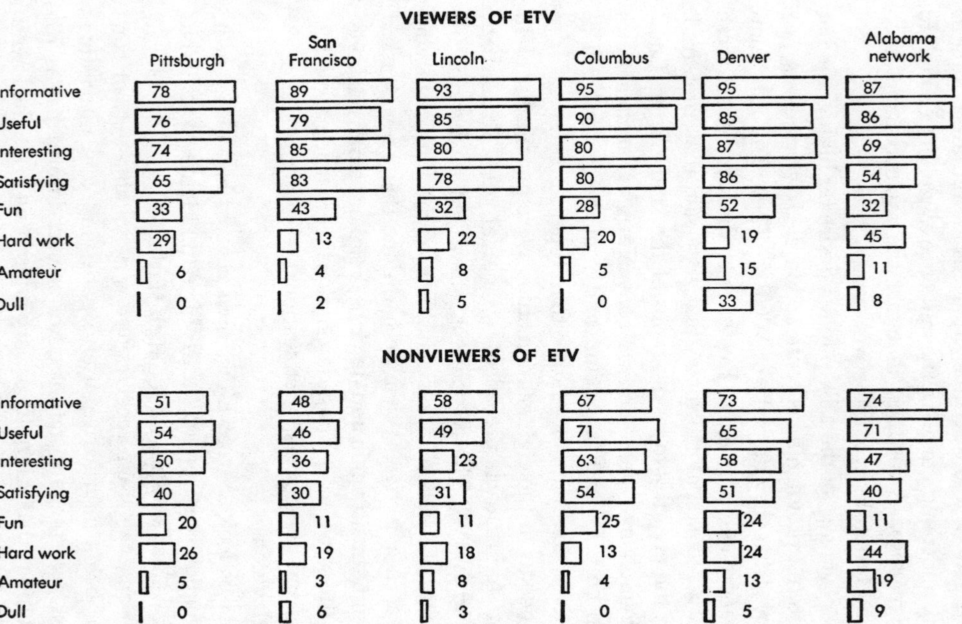

Fig. 34.—Profile of ETV. Responses, in per cent, of viewers and nonviewers to eight of the thirteen descriptive terms applied to ETV. For the remaining five terms, *snobbish, boring, violent, annoying, brutal,* the highest percentage was 7. Eight-station study.

general thing, the lowest percentages on favorable responses (such as "interesting") and the highest on unfavorable ones (such as "hard work") come from the Alabama network and Pittsburgh audiences, where the average educational level is lower than in the other audiences. But in general we can say that almost all ETV's viewers think of it as interesting, informative, useful, and satisfying. Substantial numbers consider it fun; and somewhat smaller, but still considerable, numbers find it hard work.

For comparison, let us see how nonviewers describe ETV. The result—presented in Figure 34—is somewhat surprising; for the nonviewers, if these are representative, tend to see ETV in almost the same pattern as viewers do. That is, they see it as interesting, informative, useful, and satisfying (to its viewers, doubtless), and some of them think it is fun and hard work. The only difference is that the percentages are smaller on the favorable items. Whereas about 80 per cent of the viewers describe ETV as interesting, less than 50 per cent of the nonviewers call it interesting. Whereas nearly 40 per cent of viewers think ETV is fun, only about 17 per cent of nonviewers think of it as fun. On the other hand, there are surprisingly small differences between the percentages of viewers and nonviewers who think of ETV as amateur, snobbish, boring, dull, annoying—the terms you would expect nonviewers to apply to it. More *non*viewers do describe it in those terms, but not many more. To put it into a sentence, nonviewers seem to be less attracted to ETV than its viewers are, but not strongly repelled by it.

Inasmuch as we asked both the viewers and nonviewers for their description of commercial television, we are in a position to compare each group's image of ETV with its image of CTV. The detailed information for CTV is in Appendix C, Table A12, but in Figure 35 we have summed up this comparison. We made no mention of any difference until it was at least 5 percentage points.

Look first at the left-hand columns that show the viewers' opinions. They are unanimous that ETV is more interesting, harder work, more satisfying, more informative; and that CTV is more violent, more dull, more annoying, more brutal. With only one dissent, they vote that CTV is more fun. On the other hand, with two abstentions, they vote that CTV is also more boring.

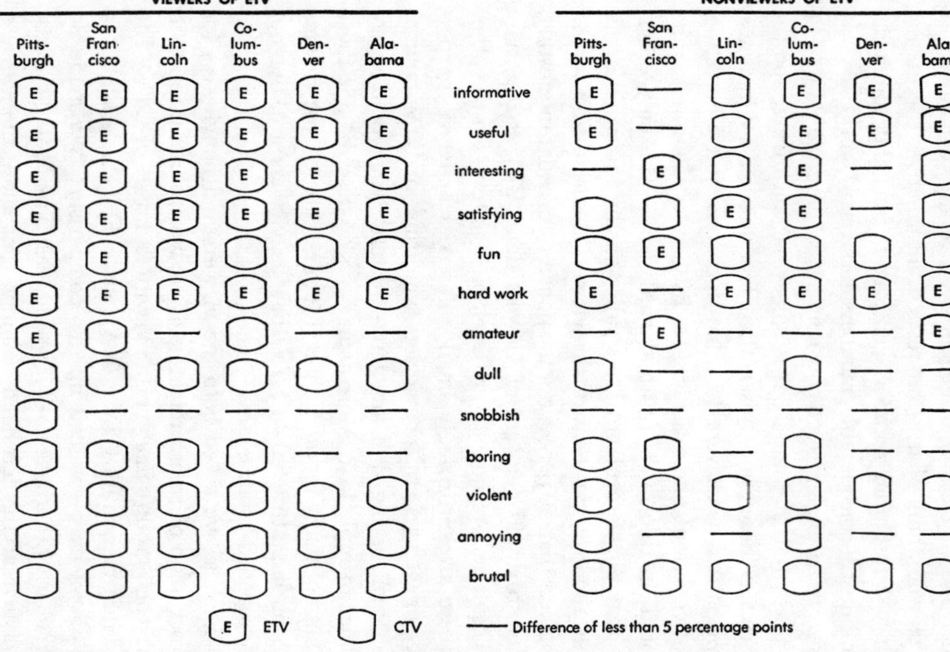

Fig. 35.—Preferences for ETV or CTV of viewers and nonviewers as recorded in response to thirteen descriptive terms, eight-station study. The upper left-hand cell should be read: "Viewers of ETV in Pittsburgh described it as more *informative* than CTV," and so forth.

Then look at the other side, where the opinions of nonviewers of ETV are represented. They agree that CTV is more violent and more brutal. With one dissent, they say that CTV is more fun. They tend to agree that ETV is harder work, more useful, and more informative, and register a majority of one for CTV being more satisfying. On the matter of which is more interesting, they are evenly divided.

Now put the two columns together. We find that

Viewers and nonviewers (in the eight-station sample) agree that educational television is harder work, commercial television is more violent and more brutal.

Viewers and nonviewers are mostly agreed that commercial television is more fun and also apt to be more boring, and educational television is likely to be more useful and more informative.

In all comparisons where there is a difference of reasonable size, commercial television is described as more annoying and more dull.

There is a real difference of opinion as to whether commercial or educational television is more satisfying, more interesting, more amateurish. The trend in all these comparisons, however, is toward ETV.

To the supporters, producers, and friends of educational television, this must seem like a good report card. But to both educational and commercial television it specifies challenges. Educational television can hardly hope to be as much *fun* as commercial television; but it certainly should try to be as interesting and as satisfying. And its program producers should not be content with having their programs thought of as "amateur." For commercial television the complaints about violence will come as no surprise, but the comments—even from nonviewers of ETV—about CTV being dull, boring, and annoying must not be pleasant to hear. It is apparently a paradox of the way CTV chooses its programs that it can be thought by the same people to be fun and exciting, dull and annoying. We have seen that there is a good reason for that paradox. TV is their only source of kinds of recreation they want, but too often it produces recreation in ways that are annoying and dull.[4] But this is a report of and from the viewers of educational, not commercial, television.

The facelessness of television?

One more point needs to be added to this report of what the people think of educational television.

Television men have sometimes been worried about the facelessness of television stations. Remembering the early years of radio, when stations had personalities of their own and were readily recognized by their call letters, television leaders have sometimes expressed regret that their medium has come to be known in terms of channels rather than call letters. Television stations, they say, have lost their identity and their faces. They have become numbers on a dial that reads from 2 to 13, and they operate essentially as pipelines from the networks. The network stars and programs are known far better than the stations.

It is not our business to study the alleged facelessness of commercial television stations, but we can report that educational television is far from faceless. In particular, the community stations in our two studies were widely known by their call letters, many of their chief programs were identified with them, and a great deal of interest and loyalty was expressed by many of their viewers. In all the nine areas the difference between educational and commercial television was known, and the presence of the educational stations seemed to be a matter of broad knowledge. The very fact that these educational stations have their center of gravity in the local area rather than in the great networks, that they sometimes must ask for funds, and that they cannot always afford high-priced talent—these factors, which are in many ways handicaps, have helped to give the stations personality and name and face in their own communities.

[4] The complaints most often recorded concerning CTV in our eight-station interviews were about violence and commercials. There were a number of suggestions that quality could be improved and that the commercial stations needed more information shows. The repetitiveness of the medium, the interruption of programs by commercials, and matters of taste were often cited as reasons for annoyance and boredom. As in Boston, so elsewhere too, the viewers of ETV were much more critical of CTV than were the persons who watched *only* CTV.

9

The Potential Audience of Educational Television

The three community stations in our sample, Boston, San Francisco, and Pittsburgh, attract to educational television approximately the same proportion of the viewers in their areas—a little over 20 per cent of the adults as regular viewers, about half the remaining adults occasionally. The other stations in our sample attract smaller proportions. Now, a question of considerable importance is the size of the *potential* audience for these stations. Have Boston, San Francisco, and Pittsburgh attracted about as many viewers as ETV can expect to reach? Are other stations—Lincoln, Denver, Alabama, Columbus—working under a potential ceiling of about 20 per cent? Or is it reasonable to expect that ETV can attract as regular viewers a much larger proportion of adults in its coverage area?

Our best information in answer to these questions comes from the Boston study. Where it is possible to use comparable data, we get the same answer from the other studies. But most of the material in this chapter comes from the study of WGBH.

Reach and frequency

The audience of WGBH can be measured in two dimensions, reach and frequency. Reach refers to the proportion of the whole population included in it, which turns out to be about one-fifth. Frequency refers to how often these people use the medium, which turns out to be fairly low, perhaps on the average of once every five days.

Awareness of the fact that there are two dimensions clarifies our thinking about the prospects of audience growth. It can grow in reach and it can grow in frequency, but these do not necessarily go together. The evidence suggests that there are prospects for both kinds of growth, but the prospects for growth in reach are small. The great opportunity is for growth in frequency.

There is some evidence that the audience was growing in reach even during the period of our study. A few persons whom the telephone interviews scored as viewers replied as nonviewers a year later, and a few who originally scored as nonviewers replied as viewers a year later. Now, most of this variation is instability of question response rather than genuine trend in behavior. But there is apparently a small difference between the directions of flow, which can be taken seriously. About 10 per cent of our viewers did not reply as viewers on reinterview, and about 14 per cent of nonviewers talked as if they were viewers when reinterviewed. The telephone survey questions and probes were not repeated in detail, so that exact equivalence cannot be established, but the suggestion is that WGBH may have gained more people than it lost during the year.

There is every reason to expect this trend to continue slowly.[1] The educational level of the population is rising. There is an ever larger proportion of the population who have the characteristics of culture, education, and occupation that distinguish the WGBH viewer.

Furthermore, tastes do develop. We have noted earlier in this study that it seems to be the case that when a person is captured into the audience by one means or another, he begins to develop an interest and a habit. This happened among males in Pittsburgh, where good sports programs captured some blue-collar men, who then began to watch other things on the station. We found the same situation in an experiment in Boston, using the "Decisions 1960" program.

[1] This same trend is seen in San Francisco, where several audience measurements have been made in the last five years. In Denver, two studies three years apart have also shown considerable audience growth.

The "Decisions" experiment

Using 2,000 of the 9,140 telephone respondents, three groups were selected. (1) A *Control Group* of 500 people, who received no stimulus to watch the program, was called only after the experiment was completed. (2) A *Mail Sample Group* of 1,000 people was sent a mailing advertising "Decisions 1960," which contained a coupon that could be checked off in one of three ways —to get a free map, to send money for a "Decisions 1960" kit, or to join a discussion group. Following the program, this group was interviewed by telephone. (3) The most highly stimulated group, the *Critics Panel*, was telephoned and the members were asked to act as critics of the "Decisions" program. They were told that after they had watched the program they would be called back to be interviewed for their opinions and suggestions.

The replies from the mailing and its effects were negligible, and we consider it no further. Few mail recipients saw the "Decisions" program.

The critics are the interesting group. Of the 265 members of our panel who promised to watch a specific program, only 94 did so. Of these, only 14 were nonviewers of WGBH and 16 were marginal cases. We received their comments by telephone within a few days.

A year later we telephoned them again without reference to the "Decisions" experiment. We simply repeated our standard telephone interview about their recent TV viewing. By that time a couple more people had moved away, or were otherwise lost. So we were finally reduced to 28 persons who had not been viewers originally, who had cooperated in watching a single "Decisions" show, and who were available a year later.

Of these 28 persons, 14 were now WGBH viewers. Of 28 controls, only five had become viewers in the meantime.[2] The numbers are very small, but the trend is extraordinary. The flattery of

[2] As one would expect, marginal cases became viewers and nonviewers became marginal cases more often than complete conversions from nonviewer to viewer occurred. Of the 14 nonviewers, six remained nonviewers, five became marginal cases, and three became viewers. Of the 14 marginal cases, 11 became viewers and one a nonviewer. The results are from a study by Bruce R. Lang.

being asked to be a critic and the experience of watching had captured some.

This same result was obtained in a small experiment within the San Francisco Bay Area.

It should be noted, however, that these persons were to some degree self-selected. Only 7 per cent of the nonviewers and 36 per cent of the marginal cases whom we asked to watch "Decisions" did so. This dismal fact spotlights the problem of extending reach. If once people can be established in the audience of ETV, a substantial proportion can be won.[3] But it is hard to get them to expose themselves in the first place unless they are so inclined already.

Perhaps it is not only hard to get nonviewers to expose themselves to ETV, but hard to the point of near-impossibility. A station manager cannot afford the kind of personal stimulation and flattery that we successfully used with a handful of people in the "Decisions" experiment. Without such audience-building efforts it may be hard to the point of impossibility to rapidly increase the reach of ETV among nonviewers because these nonviewers are such very different persons from viewers. The strongest evidence on this point is that provided by our matched samples.

The matched nonviewers: Why don't they view?

The average nonviewer, with low education, low aspirations, low cultural level, low information, is clearly not a good candidate for ETV. But are there not among the nonviewers a significant number of people who are more like the viewers? Even among the natural ETV audience—the college-educated, the professionals, etc.—ETV now gets less than half the public.

In Boston, WGBH reached 34 per cent of the respondents whose family income was over $10,000; 32 per cent of the respondents in professional families; 32 per cent of the college-educated; and 37 per cent of those with postgraduate education.

So the question arises as to whether nonviewers of high social status and education are really the same kind of people as the viewers—people who might be won to ETV but for current habits or other circumstantial matters—or does some profound difference

[3] See Himmelweit, Oppenheim, and Vince for a similar result when there was only one channel available in England.

set them apart as quite different kinds of people, who, despite their education, are not good candidates for ETV?

To test the potential for audience-building among the high-status nonviewers, we developed in Boston a matched sample of nonviewers who each resembled a viewer on major control variables.

The over-all conclusion is that the matched nonviewers are hardly more promising as clients for WGBH than the typical nonviewers. True, they have more education, but they do not have more culture. True, they have more income, but they fall short on aspirations. We matched them with the audience of WGBH as far as we could, but one does not have to look far to discover how different they are.

The samples were matched on their own occupation, but not on the occupations of their fathers or spouses. We found that matched nonviewers less often come from professional families, even though many of them have become professionals. See Figure 36, items 1–2. And those who did not become professionals have less aspiration toward so doing. We asked respondents who would have liked more education what they would have chosen to study if they had gone further. The largest number mentioned studies for a high profession such as law or medicine. The aspiration level of matched nonviewers was more like that of nonviewers (item 3).

Item	V	N	M
1. Have a "professional" as head of household	27	11	15
2. Have a "professional" father	13	4	6
3. Would have liked to study for profession	32	23	21
4. Would have liked to study for semiprofession	11	15	20
5. Live in one-family dwelling	54	35	40
6. Are Catholic	39	65	60
7. Are Jewish	20	8	6

Fig. 36.—Aspiration indicators. Per cent of viewers (V), nonviewers (N), and matched nonviewers (M) of ETV.

Many of them aspire to semiprofessional roles such as nursing or optometry (item 4).

The matching covered urban-suburban residence, but it did not cover the type of home they lived in. Nonviewers, matched and nonmatched alike, were more likely to live in a two-family dwelling than in a one-family home (item 5).

We should have matched on religion, but had not asked about that in the telephone interview. Here is a major source of the difference between our viewers and their matches. The nonviewers who are like viewers in education, occupation, income, etc., but still do not watch ETV, are likely to be Catholics (items 6–7).

And so, on each index of social aspiration that we can measure but that we did not use as a control in matching, the matched nonviewers turn out to be like other nonviewers, not like viewers.

It is the same for culture. The matched nonviewers care little for it. See items 1–12 in Figure 37. Except in radio habits and

Item	N	M	V
1. Play musical instruments	15	16	27
2. Play classical or semi-classical music	7	7	19
3. Collect classical records	17	19	34
4. Have FM radio set	21	30	37
5. Play chess or do crossword puzzles	24	31	46
6. Read cultural magazines	4	7	14
7. Have read book in past month	28	33	55
8. Are reading a difficult book	7	6	14
9. Read about their hobbies	35	46	55
10. Have taken adult courses	44	50	66
11. Have taken adult courses in academic subjects	8	13	29
12. Have participated in discussion groups	12	7	24

Fig. 37.—Culture. Per cent of viewers (V), nonviewers (N), and matched nonviewers (M) of ETV.

reading about hobbies, which are easy forms of cultural expression, the matched nonviewers are almost like any nonviewers. They play little classical music and read little serious literature.

In their interest in current news, the matched nonviewers do a little better. Culture may be beyond them, but politics and public affairs are a form of serious interest that to a limited degree they are ready to appreciate. Politics is the intellectual fare of the half-educated, and that is as true in the United States as it is in a developing country or a communist movement. The matched viewers, therefore, fall in between WGBH viewers and nonviewers in their interest in public information. They have a degree of concern which the news slots of radio, TV, and ordinary newspapers are designed to satisfy, and in which ETV also tries to play a role.

In Figure 38 we compare viewers, nonviewers, and matched nonviewers on 14 items of behavior, which represent attempts to be well informed. The matched nonviewers fall between the viewers and nonviewers on such items as reading news magazines, talking about politics, and following newspapers. Corresponding to their intermediate interest in news sources, matched nonviewers do intermediately well on the news quiz (see item 33).

An oversimple interpretation of these results would be that, if ETV is to extend its reach, it should feature public affairs broadcasting. Certainly it is in this area rather than in culture that some nonviewers have serious interests which could be tapped. But it is not clear that ETV has much chance of tapping them in competition with the excellent news coverage provided by some of commercial TV. The level of interest in information revealed by the matched nonviewers was only moderate, and it is probably well satisfied by what CTV makes available.

However, there may be one area of possible competition, namely, news and news features in prime time. CTV will not give its best hours to this interest. WGBH will, and to some extent does. Louis Lyons broadcasts the news at 6:30 P.M., and his news discussion program, "Background," at 6:45. On one typical day this was followed by the President's press conference at 7:00 P.M., a discussion of military problems at 8:00, urban politics at 8:30, and Louis Lyons again at 10:30. To the extent that some public affairs interest exists in a limited sector of the public not now part

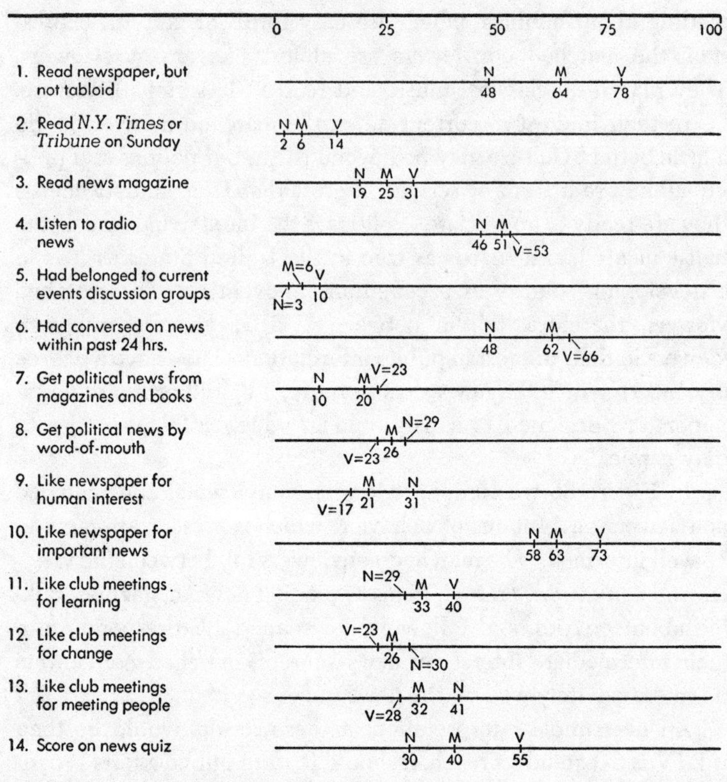

Fig. 38.—Information seeking. Per cent of viewers (V), nonviewers (N), and matched nonviewers (M) of ETV.

of the WGBH audience, which sometimes would prefer to watch the President rather than a Western, there is an opportunity for audience-building by further mixing in news with cultural features between 7:00 and 10:00 P.M.

If matched nonviewers are, as we portray them, much less aspiring than the viewers, much less interested in culture, and moderately less interested in public affairs, then we should already be able to predict a good deal about how they spend their leisure time. And indeed we can; the surprises are few. When we compared viewers with nonviewers, we found the viewers to be extremely active. Even in the mass activities of the nonviewers, such as sports and movies, they were on a par. In social and political activities the viewers participated substantially more, and in activities with a large intellectual element very much more.

Matched nonviewers are like everyone else in universal activities like sports. They are essentially like the nonviewers in intellectual activities like theater. The only surprise is how inactive they are in social and political activities. Their moderate interest in news and public affairs turns out to be a spectator interest. The same low aspiration level that is reflected in their and their fathers' career goals has kept them from trying to influence the world around them by politics.

Let us review 14 comparisons of activities of viewers and nonviewers (Figure 39) and see where the matched nonviewers fit in.

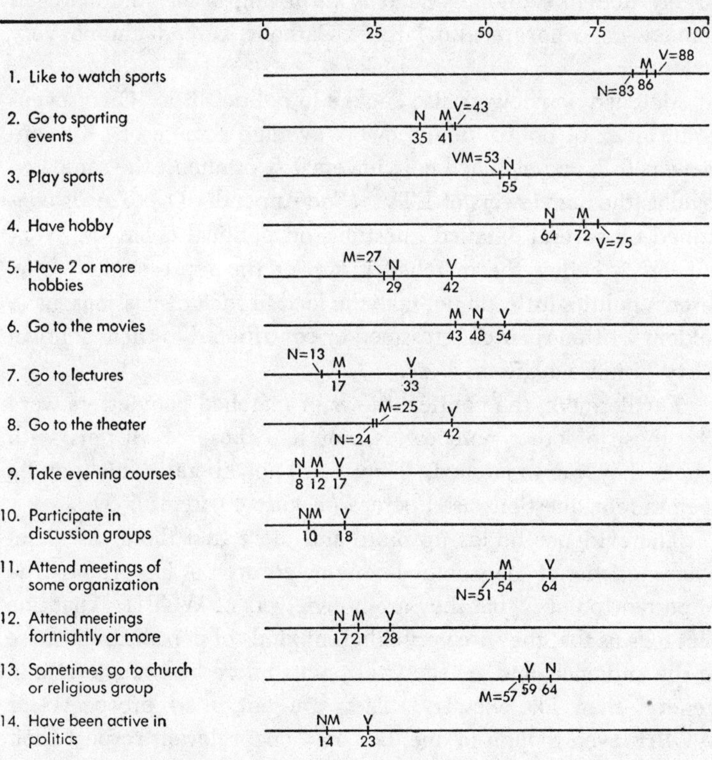

Fig. 39.—Activities. Per cent of viewers (V), nonviewers (N), and matched nonviewers (M) of ETV.

First, there are those activities in which nonviewers also participate widely (items 1–6). Matched nonviewers do not differ in any systematic way in sports or hobbies or movies. Next, there are activities with a substantial intellectual element such as lectures and theater (items 7–10). Nonviewers and matched nonviewers alike participate little in these. Finally, there is participation in social or political group activities (items 11–14). And here, to our surprise, matched nonviewers again are not much more active than nonviewers in general. The difference between viewers and nonviewers in church attendance is small and contrary to the usual direction of difference. Nonviewers are more apt to be churchgoers. But this is entirely understandable in that nonviewers are largely Roman Catholic. What is surprising is that the matched nonviewers, who are also largely Catholic, attend church very little.

Matched nonviewers also engage in politics little. On a seven-point index of politization, viewers average a score of 1.3, nonviewers 0.7, and matched nonviewers 0.8, or almost the same low level as the nonviewers of ETV. (See Appendix D.) This is confirmed by several detailed questions on political behavior. Nonviewers, whether the matched group or the representative one, discuss politics little, do not take the lead in such discussions, have seldom written their congressmen or contributed to their political party (Figure 40, items 1–4).

Furthermore, the political views of matched nonviewers were like those of other nonviewers, not like those of viewers with whom they were matched. They were not liberal. This may be seen in four questions used before (Figure 40, items 5–8).

The evidence builds up more and more that the gross social characteristics of the matched nonviewers are not important. The important point is that they are nonviewers of WGBH. That one fact tells us that they are very different kinds of persons from those in the audience, and, on the vital points, more like nonviewers in general than like viewers. They are not good prospects for WGBH, even though in one, but only one, relevant respect their TV habits are like those of its viewers. Neither ones are television addicts. That is a lower-class pattern which does diminish when we control for social variables (items 9–11). On those questions

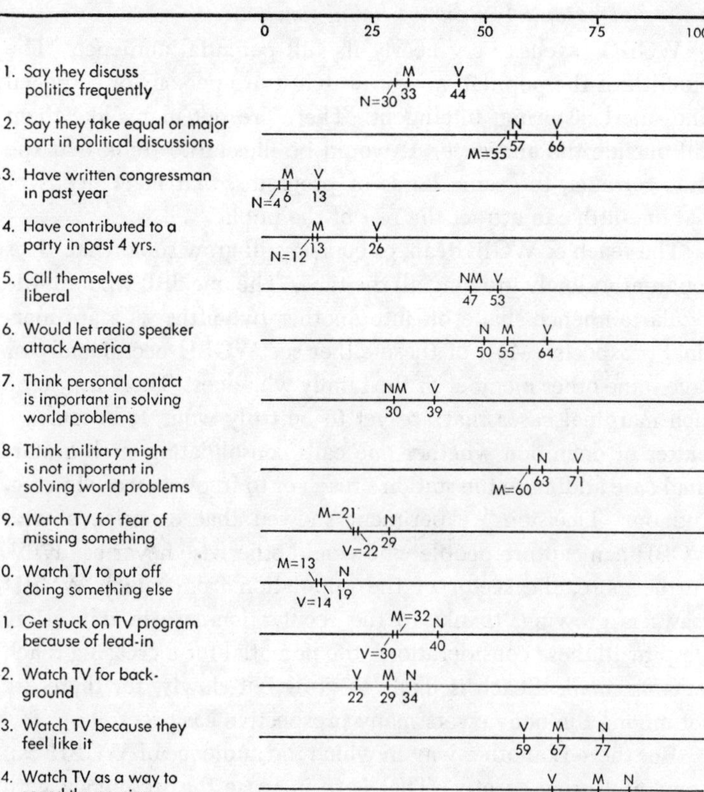

Fig. 40. – Orientations. Per cent of viewers (V), nonviewers (N), and matched nonviewers (M) of ETV.

that indicate compulsive watching of television, the matched cases respond like the viewers. And on less extreme questions indicating strong TV affinity they fall between viewers and nonviewers (items 12–14).

In other respects—in their over-all evaluation of TV, in their choices of favorite programs, in their conversations about TV—the TV-use habits of the matched nonviewers are like those of non-viewers of ETV, not like those of their matches. Once more we conclude that those members of the public who are not now watching WGBH—even those who are like the viewers in social characteristics—are not likely prospects for ETV.

Is the full potential audience being reached?

WGBH reaches very nearly its full potential audience. The one-fifth of the population who watch it are persons of a special kind—alert, aspiring, intelligent. There are not many like them still outside the audience. It would be illusion to think that the same formula, the same kinds of programs, that meet needs of that one-fifth can attract the rest of the public.

The reach of WGBH can, of course, still grow somewhat. It is apparently slowly growing all the time. The one-fifth who are the regular audience shade off into another two-fifths who are marginal prospects. Most of these either see WGBH occasionally or have some other member of the family who does. There are some such marginal cases that are yet to be truly won. It becomes a matter of definition whether one calls consolidating such a marginal case adding to the station's reach or to frequency of viewing. And our "Decisions" experiment showed that experience with WGBH can capture people who would otherwise never use ETV. Furthermore, the sector of the population from which WGBH draws is growing, thanks to the secular increase in education. Despite all these considerations, the potential for increasing reach remains small. Reach is likely to grow but slowly, for there are not among the nonviewers many prospective easy recruits.

But there is another way in which the audience of WGBH can grow, and grow greatly. That is to increase the frequency with which its own proper audience uses it. There is no reason why the forty-five minutes a week that it now commands from its viewers cannot be doubled or trebled. The WGBH viewers are devoting much more time than that to CTV, and are being dissatisfied to boot. They have tastes and interests that ETV could satisfy. The problem is to finance and produce programs that will build bridges to these people via these tastes.

What most Boston ETV viewers want is not formal schooling on the air; nor is it kinds of programs that commercial stations never provide. What WGBH viewers want is more of the intelligent, urbane fare represented by "Open End," "Boston Symphony," "Louis Lyons," or "Julius Caesar." They want better entertainment, better live news coverage, better commentary than they can get in the prime evening hours from stations that devote that time to the other four-fifths of the population.

Some ETV stations do not accept the idea that better entertainment is a proper function for them. WGBH does; it seeks to provide intelligent, artistic material. If someone does not provide such material, then that one-fifth of the public that makes up the audience for ETV will be badly served.

The people who make up the ETV audience like foreign films, for example; but where can they now get them on TV? They are interested in world-wide live coverage of the dramatic news events of the day and would like to watch them in their normal leisure time in the evenings. They also like sports, drama, comedy, and the whole of the popular culture, but they do not find satisfying the form in which these now appear on CTV. There is a function for a station that would set out to satisfy the full range of the viewing tastes of the top one-fifth of the population. WGBH has set out to be such a station. It is much more than an instructional medium. It seems to fill a large gap in the present structure of American communications.

We believe, and our information indicates, that what we have said about WGBH in Boston probably applies also to KQED in San Francisco and WQED in Pittsburgh. The other stations in our sample, not being under community ownership, may have different images of their responsibility, and of the audience they wish to serve. This probably accounts for the differences in station audiences we pointed out in Chapter 7, and may somewhat reduce the potential audience of these stations below the 20 per cent of adults that WGBH, KQED, and WQED have attained.

But always with ETV the question comes back to finances. The well-off, active one-fifth of the population that watches ETV could afford a high-quality network of channels which would give it what it wants. But how can their funds be tapped? Buying old foreign films, establishing live world-wide news coverage, putting on lively and intelligent variety-personality-commentary shows like "Open End" and "Today," capturing major cultural events like opera all cost a great deal of money, much more than does an instructional series of lectures and panels. Yet in that kind of image of the future of TV lies its great opportunity to serve the largest of the now poorly served section of the American audience.

10

The Significance of These Results

On the basis of these results, what can we say of educational television on its ninth birthday?

In nine years, has it made an impact?

Clearly, we must conclude that it has. Not so great an impact, perhaps, as its founders had dreamed of, but still a solid and significant one. A medium that supplies a part of the teaching of nearly three million school children, that attracts as regular viewers 10 to 24 per cent of all the adults in every community where it has a VHF channel, is making itself felt. It has made a significant difference in the programing available in every community where it can be seen. In communities like Boston, San Francisco, and Pittsburgh the community-owned stations have become an important interest and responsibility of the people of the area. Stations like Denver, Lincoln, and Columbus have become an important interest and responsibility of the institutions to which they belong. A network like Alabama has become a responsibility of state government, and is known to most of the people of that state.

In addition, we must record that the curve of ETV development has been upward. In the 1960's there has been a noticeable increase in plans and permits for new stations. Station KQED in San Francisco, when it was studied by the senior author of this report about four years ago, reached into about 40 per cent of the homes in its coverage area; now it reaches more than 60 per cent of those homes. Most of the widely viewed and still widely discussed programs and program series have been seen nationally only in the last few years. These include "Open End," "The Age of Kings," the nationally circulated "Boston Symphony" programs, the Khrushchev-Susskind interview, and "Ragtime Era." These are examples, but there has been a marked increase in the number of these distinguished programs in the last few years. More than anything else, this program development suggests why there has been a growth in audiences and impact.

The number of school children and college students receiving part of their teaching by ETV has risen exponentially in the last five years. In the last year, too, great progress has been made in understanding the strengths and weaknesses of teaching by television. It has been learned that the medium has a great power to attract and hold attention and interest, that it has an unequaled ability to share good teaching and excellent demonstrations (for example, permitting 100,000 students at the same time to look through a microscope, or into an atomic reactor), that good teaching on television is about as effective as classroom teaching—but that it is more effective in some kinds of teaching than in others. In particular, it is more effective when it is built into a program of class and individual activities than when it is being used to carry the entire burden of a class.

In nine years, has ETV succeeded in attracting a significant audience?

The regular ETV audience is only a minority of all the television audience; for any given program it is likely to consist of a small minority of sets in use at the time. But its viewers include a high proportion of the better-educated people in the community (although there are some poorly educated ones, too). The ETV audience includes an abnormally high proportion of the people with professional, managerial, and other white-collar jobs (although it includes also a number of blue-collar people). Its viewers are more likely than others to be active in the cultural and civic affairs of the community—to go to concerts, lectures, civic meetings, discussion groups. They are more likely than others to discuss politics and to be asked for their advice on public questions. They are more likely to read books and serious magazines. They are more likely to be on the way up. In other words, in every respect except size, the audience for educational television is the kind broadcasters dream about—the best-educated, most articulate, best-informed, most upward-mobile, culturally and civically most active persons in the community.

It must be acknowledged, however, that ETV has never quite fulfilled the dream that some of its founders had for it—that it would become the school and the university of people who had little opportunity for education. Its audiences are highly skewed toward the people who *have* had opportunity for education. It is an open question whether ETV can do both jobs—serve both the little educated and the much educated. However, we found a considerable number of upward-mobile blue-collar people for whom ETV was performing a real service. Literacy-aiming programs that have been presented by television in Memphis, Philadelphia, and elsewhere are obviously successful with the little educated. And when one gets to the years of high school and junior college, there is no doubt about ETV's potency in filling in for many of the experiences of classroom and campus. The City of Chicago, in putting its entire junior college curriculum on television, has made thousands of persons eligible for professions, business, and industry that require that level of education. But despite these accomplishments, it is clear that the chief impact of ETV, up to the present time, has been with the educational upper half, rather than the lower half, of the community.

In nine years, has it found a distinctive place for itself among the mass media?

One of the significant findings of this study is that educational television has really performed a separate function from commercial television; it has carved out a distinctive place for itself. There is certainly overlap; for example, the program "Open End" has appeared on both educational and commercial stations. But television, as we have tried to indicate, is both a great entertainment and a great educational medium. Commercial television has specialized in the entertainment end of the spectrum; educational television in the other end. It is clear that the behavior of watching educational television is more like the behavior of reading books and other serious print. It is what we have called "deferred gratification" rather than "immediate gratification" behavior, and this is why it is more likely to be engaged in by the upper parts of society where that norm is strong, or by members of the lower parts of society who are moving upward toward the levels where such a norm is strong. Some of the more interesting charts in this study demonstrated that use of educational television usually goes with high use of print rather than with high over-all use of television.[1]

Educational television as it functions today is very little competition for commercial television in furnishing an entertainment service, in swift handling of news, or in expensive coverage of public events. Its special place, so far, is in the area of providing cultural programs, intellectual challenge and stimulation, information other than spot news, and educational opportunities. More than commercial television, it has the advantage of being able to use the full strengths of the medium for education. More than print, it has the advantage of being able to offer sound and visual representation, as well as words. It does not stand still, like print, to be a source of reference or to have its difficult parts repeated, but, on the other hand, it can breathe motion and sound and life into the performing arts, into discussions, demonstrations, and lectures.

A characteristic of the mass media is that they do not have sharp and uncrossable borders. Ordinarily, one function will be shared by several media, each contributing in its own way. This is the case with educational television. Many of its most popular programs could well be on CTV, and some of them have been. There is no sharp break between ETV and CTV; there is only a

[1] The Steiner report and other surveys supported by the commercial television industry have found that persons who are critical of the standards of commercial television nevertheless choose to watch commercial entertainment programs of the kind they criticize even though an informational or cultural program is available at the same hour. We have no doubt of this, but tend to interpret it otherwise than simply as human inconsistency. Our observation is that a person who is seeking intellectual stimulation is likely to learn to seek it elsewhere than on commercial television. While he continues to use the medium for its entertainment and its coverage of events and sports, he goes to printed sources for his intellectual stimulation, or, if there is ETV available, to ETV.

difference in emphasis on different sides of the border. Perhaps some of the best opportunities for both ETV and CTV lie in the border area between entertainment and education. But that is for the future. The remarkable thing is that, in nine years, ETV has been able to develop so much individuality and to serve such specific purposes.

In nine years, what has it come to mean to its viewers?

As we saw in Chapters 7 and 8, educational television has come to mean many things, but basically it is depended upon for cultural programs, for intellectual stimulation, for serious information, and for educational opportunities. In some places more than others it has come to mean a source of practical aid—how to do it, and so forth. In none of the places we studied, either among or outside the viewers, has it come to mean to very many people "egghead" behavior, or snobbishness, or an upper-class activity.

As a matter of fact, ETV got a very good report card both from its viewers and from the persons who know it only from the outside. By a large majority of its viewers it was called informative, useful, interesting, and satisfying. More than a third called it "fun," and about one-fourth of the viewers called it "hard work." Among the nonviewers all the favorable percentages were smaller, but the trend was the same. Viewers and nonviewers agreed that ETV is not so much fun as commercial television, but they differed as to which medium is the more satisfying, the more interesting, and the more amateurish. Strangely enough, they tended to agree that commercial television often is duller and more boring (chiefly because of the monotony of theme, plot, and tone) than ETV, and also more annoying (chiefly because of the commercials and, some said, because of the violence). Both the viewers and the nonviewers of ETV spent most of their television hours on CTV. And after a dozen or more hours a week its clichéd fare began to pall. They tuned to ETV, on the other hand, only when it offered something they really desired to see. Thus ETV was exciting to them, seldom boring.

The loyalty that many ETV viewers feel toward the educational station, the fact that it had a personality for them and an importance, was clearly evident. In the same tone, however, many of the viewers wished that the station had more money to hire needed personnel of high quality; to maintain professional standards of production; to keep on the air longer; to broadcast programs that would be sometimes a little more "fun," a little more "interesting," a little more "challenging." This is both a good and a bad signal to ETV. Audience concern and involvement are good. But the audience will not continue indefinitely unless some of their wishes for the station come true. Unlike watching CTV, which is a habit, they will watch ETV only if it offers what they like.

In the light of that danger of the audience vanishing, we take note of the answers in Boston when each respondent was given a chance to say which was his favorite among the four Boston TV channels. Sixteen per cent of the WGBH viewers chose WGBH. Eighty-four per cent divided their choices among the three commercial channels, none of which fell as low as 16. Somehow, educational television is not fully meeting the cravings of its audience. That may be because it is playing a specialized role which fulfills only one part of their wants. The man who enjoys a program on Japanese brush painting does not necessarily want classes all the time. He may also enjoy spending part of his evenings collapsed in a chair watching "Gunsmoke." Perhaps educational television is destined to play a subordinate and supplementary role even for its own audience, filling in what alert, intelligent, educated people cannot get from commercial TV.

But if that charitable interpretation of the low preference and viewing scores achieved by WGBH in competition with the commercial stations were to be accepted, then the members of the WGBH audience should be satisfied with television as a whole. Their need for a little pepper and spice added to a basic diet of standard TV fare would be adequately met in Boston by the present arrangement of one very strong ETV channel along with three commercial ones. But they are not satisfied.

One of the questions asked was: "There has been a lot of talk about TV lately. Of these two points of view which would you agree with more? (*a*) The programs on TV are generally pretty good and should not be changed too much. (*b*) The programs on TV are not very good and need a lot of improvement." Note that this is a question not about educational television, but about television in general.

On the question thus formulated, the majority of the population turned its thumbs down on the present state of TV. This is a result quite at variance with that reported by many other studies, and the reason lies in a difference in question wording. The usual question form, with variation in detail, is to ask whether TV is very good, good, fair, or poor. A response set that every pollster is familiar with leads people to pick an upper-middle level of approval, such as "good." With a three-or-more-positioned range of choice, people prefer to pick the middle rather than an extreme, and when offered only the choice of using pleasant or pejorative terms, they choose the former. The etiquette of our culture, which carries over to the survey situation, requires that our over-all judgments always be expressed on the positive side even if the object described is then cut to pieces in detail. It is rare to find an efficiency rating or book review where the over-all rating is less than "good," no matter what follows in the text. We know of one market research study where the "excellent, very good, good, fair, poor" categories were used in which the answer "good" was predictive of least use of the product.

Aware of these response sets that guarantee an endorsement of present television if the usual question is used, we framed our question differently. In the first place, we excluded the chance for a middle choice, by posing a forced choice between two alternatives. In the second place, we avoided making either alternative a flat negative word. The negative judgment was linked to the prospect of improvement, while the positive judgment required a vote in favor of leaving things as they were.

With this question form, 61 per cent of our cross-section sample of the Boston population said the programs were not very good. Among nonviewers, that percentage fell only to 58 per cent. Among WGBH viewers the negative judgments rose to 70 per cent.

And so we cannot avoid the conclusion that something is lacking in the present TV situation, especially for the ETV viewers. Commercial television gives them some things they want; witness their choices of commercial programs as favorites, their extensive watching of CTV, and their common knowledge of and interest in the popular culture of the nation, whether in entertainment, games, or sports. ETV also gives them some of the things they want, as we have made abundantly clear in the preceding pages. But there is still something missing. The fare available to them, whether from CTV or ETV, is not all they want.

After nine years, what seems to be the destiny of educational television?

It is clear that educational television, in the years immediately ahead, is going to reach far more people than ever before. School use has been greatly increasing. The advent of the New York station will considerably increase the audience, and if Los Angeles too comes on the air with ETV, the national audience may be doubled in the course of a year or two. A number of other stations are in various stages of planning, and if there is a move toward the UHF band or a notable increase in the number of sets equipped to receive UHF, it is possible to envisage a large part of the population getting some service from educational television.

The real question is whether, by nature, educational television is condemned forever to program ratings of 1, to minority audiences heavily skewed toward high education and high social status, and to viewers who come purposefully to ETV for one program and then turn off the set.

It hardly needs pointing out that if a viewer of ETV could be induced to stay for two programs rather than one, the station audience would be doubled. This would require a very skillful kind of block programing. One strength of educational programing, of course, is that it is not necessary to program constantly in such a way as to maximize the audience; rather, it is desirable to program so that the maximum number of different educational and cultural interests and needs in the audience are met in the course of a day or a week. To combine these two elements—to program in such a way as to meet a variety of needs and at the same time to appeal with consecutive programs to a viewer who has liked one program—is not easy, but it is not impossible. Furthermore, it should be possible to gain some viewer-time by better promotion. Only about one-sixth of all the viewers of the eight-station sample said that they received their chief information about programs from the station's program guide. If this number could be increased, and if the station itself could be used to better advantage to promote its future programs, then it is reasonable to think that more viewers would find out about programs they would not want to miss.

So much for present viewers. Can the station be made attractive to a broader spectrum of users? Is there any reason why a university station or a state network should attract only 9 or 10 per cent of the adults in its community as regular viewers, or why a school-board station should attract only 13 per cent? And is the 24 per cent attracted as regular viewers by Pittsburgh and San Francisco about as many as ETV can hope for?

Certainly the 24 per cent is a very respectable figure. We have said in the preceding chapter that it may not be easy to go over it. But few ETV stations attract an audience so large. We know that the audience of San Francisco has increased in the last few years, and this can be attributed in no small degree to "wide-band" programs like "Open End," which attract wide segments of the social spectrum. The destiny of educational television will depend in part on whether it can develop more such programs with intellectual challenge and broad appeal, in addition to other programs, of undoubted excellence but more specialized appeal, like "Casals Master Class."

A useful result of this study was the finding that, even among educational programs, there is a great difference in the kinds of people attracted to a given program. A program like "Ragtime Era," for example, would attract many viewers who would be unlikely to view "Open End" or "Heritage." A program like "The World of Music" had a much larger part of its appeal among the less educated groups than did a program like "The Greeks Had a Word for It." The more we know about the kinds of people who select a particular kind of program, the easier it should become to devise and combine programs so as to appeal to different segments of the potential audience, and thus gradually to widen the station's coverage.

The import of this study is that, in nine years, educational television has won a beachhead. It has 75 stations, a central program service which operates like a network by mail, a small but loyal and important audience, and enough good programing to whet the appetites of the viewers. This is a significant accomplishment. Now, does it rest with this, or does it go ahead? If it rests, the chances are that it will become increasingly a channel for school broadcasts rather than for community broadcasts. If it goes ahead, then it must have more and better programing, and to have more and better programing it must have more adequate financing.

The struggle to buy equipment, to house the station, to meet the weekly payroll, and to keep the station on the air has been so demanding that a lion's share of educational television's attention has had to go to it, rather than to the making and circulating of programs that are the only unique contribution of ETV. This has been the case both in community broadcasts and in classroom broadcasts. For example, the great technical achievement of Airborne Television (MPATI) in laying down a signal over a radius of 200 miles from an airplane has not been matched by any similar achievement in the making of classroom programs to be broadcast over this huge area. Here, as elsewhere, the basic technical demands have absorbed the money that might have gone into making programs. At the present time the National Educational Television and Radio Center is operating at an annual rate of about $3.5 million, as compared with a commercial network expenditure of several hundred million dollars. More money would enable NETRC to furnish more programs so that stations could upgrade the average quality of their community service and stay on the air longer. More money would enable NETRC to develop or hire more talent for such programs and to rent live lines to serve the stations for at least part of the day, so that the network could cover timely events and furnish up-to-date public affairs programs. More money would help in the new effort of the educational stations to function as a fourth network, rather than as a loose federation of stations sharing some of their programs through videotape and the U.S. post office.

Therefore, the most easily visible sign of the destiny of educational television will be the amount of financing it is able to put behind its programing in the next five years. But this is not the only determinant.

Over and beyond the question of what can be financed is the question of what skill, imagination, and talent can be found. Admittedly, proper financing will make those qualities easier to find. But we have said that educational television is a different medium from any other. Many able people in commercial television, in the printed media, in films, in education have great skills that would be highly useful and usable on ETV. But ultimately ETV must provide its own talent, its own writers, its own producers, skilled in and concerned with the unique task of ETV. Films, radio, commercial television, each emerged in full strength and unique qualities only when the first great directors, writers, and performers emerged. It will be so with educational television. Its destiny will ride on its programing, and its programing will ride on its financing. But just as financing will make it easier to find and develop talent for distinguished programs, so will an infusion of talent, skill, and imagination make it easier to obtain financing. This is the destiny that beckons to educational television if it can muster the strength to go beyond its beachhead.

APPENDIXES

APPENDIX A

NONCOMMERCIAL TELEVISION STATIONS, MARCH 1963

Channel	Station	
ALABAMA		
26	WAIQ	Montgomery
10	WBIQ	Birmingham
7	WCIQ	Munford
2	WDIQ	Dozier
		Alabama Educational Television Commission
ARIZONA		
8	KAET	Temple, Arizona State University
6	KUAT	Tucson, University of Arizona
CALIFORNIA		
6	KVIE	Sacramento, Central California Educational Television, Inc.
24	KVCR-TV	San Bernardino Valley Joint Union Junior College
9	KQED	San Francisco, Bay Area Educational Television Association
COLORADO		
6	KRMA-TV	Denver, Denver Public Schools
CONNECTICUT		
24	WEDH	Hartford, Hartford Educational Television
DISTRICT OF COLUMBIA		
26	WETA-TV	Washington, Greater Washington Educational Television Association, Inc.
FLORIDA		
5	WUFT	Gainesville, University of Florida
7	WJCT	Jacksonville, Community Television, Inc.
17	WSEC-TV	Miami, Dade County Board of Public Instruction
2	WTHS-TV	Miami, Dade County Board of Public Instruction
11	WFSU-TV	Tallahassee, Florida State University
3	WEDU	Tampa, Florida West Coast Educational Television, Inc.
GEORGIA		
8	WGTV	Athens, Univ. of Georgia (Center for Continuing Education)
30	WETV	Atlanta, Board of Education of the City of Atlanta
8	WXGA-TV	Waycross, Georgia State Board of Education
ILLINOIS		
8	WSIU-TV	Carbondale, Southern Illinois University
11	WTTW	Chicago, Chicago Educational Television Association
12	WILL-TV	Urbana, University of Illinois
IOWA		
11	KDPS-TV	Des Moines Independent Community School District

Channel	Station	
KENTUCKY		
15	WFPK-TV	Louisville, Louisville Free Public Library
LOUISIANA		
13	KLSE	Monroe, State Department of Education
8	WYES-TV	The Greater New Orleans ETV Foundation
MAINE		
10	WCBB	Augusta, Colby, Bates, Bowdoin Educational Telecasting Corporation
MASSACHUSETTS		
2	WGBH-TV	Boston, WGBH Educational Foundation
MICHIGAN		
56	WTVS	Detroit, Detroit Educational Television Foundation
10	WMSB	East Lansing, Michigan State University
MINNESOTA		
2	KTCA-TV	Minneapolis–St. Paul, Twin City Area Educational Television Corporation
MISSOURI		
19	KCSD-TV	Kansas City, School District of Kansas City
9	KETA	St. Louis, St. Louis Educational Television Commission
NEBRASKA		
12	KUON-TV	Lincoln, University of Nebraska
NEW HAMPSHIRE		
11	WENH-TV	Durham, University of New Hampshire
NEW MEXICO		
5	KNME-TV	Albuquerque, University of New Mexico and Albuquerque Board of Education
NEW YORK		
17	WNED-TV	Buffalo, Western New York Educational Television Association, Inc.
13	WDNT	New York, Educational Television for the Metropolitan Area
31	WNYC-TV	New York, City of New York
17	WMHT	Schenectady, Mohawk Hudson Council of Education
NORTH CAROLINA		
4	WUNC-TV	Chapel Hill, Consolidated University of North Carolina
OHIO		
20	WOUB-TV	Athens, Ohio University
48	WCET	Cincinnati, Greater Cincinnati Television Educational Foundation
34	WOSU	Columbus, Ohio State University
28	WGSF	Newark, Newark Public School District
14	WMUB-TV	Oxford, Miami University
30	WGTE-TV	Toledo, The Greater Toledo Educational Television Foundation
OKLAHOMA		
13	KETA-TV	Oklahoma City, statutory corporation established by Oklahoma State Legislature

Channel	Station	
25	KOKH-TV	Oklahoma City, Independent School District No. 89 of Oklahoma County
11	KOED-TV	Tulsa, statutory corporation established by Oklahoma State Legislature
OREGON		
7	KOAC-TV	Corvallis, State Board of Higher Education
10	KOAP-TV	Portland, State Board of Higher Education
PENNSYLVANIA		
35	WHYY-TV	Philadelphia, nonprofit corporation composed of educational, cultural, and public service interests in Pennsylvania, New Jersey, and Delaware area surrounding Philadelphia
13	WQED	Metropolitan Pittsburgh Educational Television Station
16	WQEX	Pittsburgh, same
PUERTO RICO		
3	WIPM-TV	Mayaguez, Department of Education of Puerto Rico
6	WIPR-TV	San Juan, Department of Education of Puerto Rico
SOUTH DAKOTA		
2	KUSD-TV	Vermillion, University of South Dakota
TENNESSEE		
10	WKNO-TV	Memphis, Memphis Community Television Foundation
2	WDCN-TV	Nashville, Davidson County Board of Education
TEXAS		
9	KLRN	Austin, San Antonio, Southwest Texas Educational Television Council
13	KERA-TV	Dallas, Area Educational Television Foundation
8	KUHT	Houston, University of Houston
5	KTXT-TV	Lubbock, Texas Technological College
23	KRET-TV	Richardson, Richardson Independent School District
UTAH		
9	KOET	Ogden, Ogden City Board of Education
18	KWCS-TV	Ogden, Weber County School District
7	KUED-TV	Salt Lake City, University of Utah
VIRGINIA		
15	WHRO-TV	Norfolk, Hampton Roads Educational Television Association
WASHINGTON		
56	KEPC-TV	Lakewood Center, Clover Park School District No. 400
10	KWSC-TV	Pullman, Washington State University
9	KCTS-TV	Seattle, University of Washington
62	KTPS-TV	Tacoma, Tacoma School District No. 10
47	KYVE-TV	Yakima, Yakima School District No. 7
WISCONSIN		
21	WHA-TV	Madison, University of Wisconsin
10	WMVS-TV	Milwaukee, Board of Vocational and Adult Education
36	WMVT-TV	Milwaukee, Board of Vocational and Adult Education

APPENDIX B

The Interview Samples

Respondents	Boston	Pitts-burgh	San Fran-cisco	Lin-coln	Colum-bus	Denver	Alabama Network
*Telephone calls completed with owners of TV sets**							
Regular viewers.......	1,810	419	1,004	310	50	446	501
Occasional viewers	2,707	698	1,574	1,217	217	1,053	1,365
Nonviewers	4,149	632	1,609	1,763	1,721	1,781	2,907
GRAND TOTAL......	8,666	1,749	4,187	3,290	1,988	3,280	4,773
Detailed interviews completed by telephone (Subsample of total calls completed)							
Regular viewers:							
Men	—	136	228	121	17	144	153
Women	—	200	317	238	29	292	307
Total	—	336	545	359	46	436	460
Occasional viewers:							
Men	—	285	49	354	86	361	544
Women	—	403	44	441	121	683	801
Total	—	688	93	795	207	1,044	1,345
Nonviewers:							
Men	—	198	148	191	86	130	414
Women	—	365	212	262	137	231	713
Total	—	563	360	453	223	361	1,127
GRAND TOTAL......	—	1,587	998	1,607	476	1,841	2,932

* More than 30,000 calls had to be made in order to complete these 19,267 interviews. The majority of the additional calls were no answers or busy signals; three callbacks was the rule adopted in such cases. A few persons were noncooperative. Between 5 and 10 per cent reported they did not have television sets. All Boston phone calls used the same interview schedule.

Respondents	Boston	Pitts-burgh	San Fran-cisco	Lin-coln	Colum-bus	Denver	Alabama Network
***Home interviews completed* (*Subsample of telephone interviews*)**							
Regular viewers:							
Men	106	40	86	No breakdown by sex		26	78
Women	116	53	92			28	251
Total	222	93	178	218	40	54	329
Occasional viewers:*							
Men	36	41				36	
Women	47	45				68	
Total	83	86			145	104	
Nonviewers:							
Men	94	32	35	No breakdown by sex		9	22
Women	112	47	33			11	63
Total	206	79	68	88	24	20	85
GRAND TOTAL	511	258	246	306	209	178	414

* In San Francisco, Lincoln, and Alabama, no occasional viewers were interviewed at home. In Columbus, the occasional viewers were not divided by sex.

APPENDIX C

Tables from the Stanford Studies

TABLE A1.—BASIC FIGURES ON ETV AUDIENCES

Area	Regular Viewers		Occasional Viewers		Nonviewers	
	Male	Female	Male	Female	Male	Female
Median number of hours estimated "average weekly watching of ETV"						
Pittsburgh	1:13	1:59	:43	:39	—	—
San Francisco	1:49	1:73	:34	:39	—	—
Lincoln	1:39	1:39	:28	:24	—	—
Columbus	2:59	3:15	:34	:37	—	—
Denver	—	—	—	—	—	—
Alabama network	1:07	1:20	:20	:21	—	—
Median age						
Pittsburgh	49	44	46	45	44	44
San Francisco	41	44	43	43	49	46
Lincoln	42	44	40	44	42	40
Columbus	45	39	47	43	40	41
Denver	42	41	44	39	43	38
Alabama network	41	45	44	45	49	45
Per cent who have less than high school diploma						
Pittsburgh	45.3	24.6	30.1	35.0	41.2	42.0
San Francisco	10.5	6.3	10.2	18.2	36.4	28.3
Lincoln	11.5	11.4	18.0	15.0	22.0	22.9
Columbus	11.8	—	15.1	11.7	24.4	27.0
Denver	15.3	12.7	22.7	19.8	33.1	31.1
Alabama network	19.0	14.7	38.9	40.5	52.4	56.2
Per cent who have some college education						
Pittsburgh	22.1	37.3	35.3	20.5	24.0	12.7
San Francisco	63.6	63.7	44.9	40.9	28.3	20.2
Lincoln	65.3	58.0	50.2	45.4	38.2	27.0
Columbus	70.5	55.2	48.7	50.4	32.7	27.7
Denver	52.8	49.6	41.2	36.2	20.0	20.3
Alabama network	49.6	60.8	31.9	26.0	16.0	13.5

TABLE A1 (*continued*)

Area	Regular Viewers Male	Regular Viewers Female	Occasional Viewers Male	Occasional Viewers Female	Nonviewers Male	Nonviewers Female
Per cent having no children						
Pittsburgh	52.3	44.0	46.6	48.5	45.6	51.3
San Francisco	38.1	45.4	40.8	38.6	45.3	53.8
Lincoln	31.4	44.1	35.6	46.0	43.5	44.7
Columbus	47.1	41.5	37.2	40.6	37.2	36.4
Denver	36.1	29.1	39.0	34.6	34.6	37.2
Alabama network	35.3	37.1	36.7	41.0	47.8	45.4
Mean number of children						
Pittsburgh	1.1	1.4	1.1	1.2	1.3	1.1
San Francisco	1.5	1.3	1.3	1.4	1.1	.8
Lincoln	1.8	1.5	1.6	1.5	1.4	1.4
Columbus	1.2	1.4	1.6	1.6	1.3	1.4
Denver	1.5	1.7	1.2	1.4	1.3	1.3
Alabama network	1.4	1.4	1.3	1.3	1.0	1.1
Per cent having preschool-age children						
Pittsburgh	16.3	24.0	17.3	19.1	22.9	25.2
San Francisco	29.4	24.0	24.5	29.5	14.2	15.6
Lincoln	51.2	45.9	45.6	42.4	55.6	51.7
Columbus	5.9	24.1	33.7	24.0	25.6	23.4
Denver	25.7	29.8	24.9	27.5	23.8	32.9
Alabama network	30.1	27.7	26.2	24.6	19.9	19.4
Per cent having elementary-school-age children						
Pittsburgh	19.8	30.7	26.6	25.2	27.4	22.9
San Francisco	29.4	27.8	26.5	20.4	25.0	21.2
Lincoln	43.9	49.6	44.3	47.0	36.1	42.8
Columbus	23.5	27.6	25.6	33.1	23.2	29.9
Denver	36.1	35.3	27.7	31.5	26.9	23.4
Alabama network	37.9	30.3	25.4	27.4	21.5	23.9
Per cent having junior-high-school-age children						
Pittsburgh	22.1	18.7	14.2	16.1	19.4	16.7
San Francisco	17.5	13.2	14.3	15.9	14.2	8.0
Lincoln	31.7	33.1	29.4	31.5	23.1	23.4
Columbus	11.8	13.8	9.3	16.5	10.5	16.1
Denver	20.1	23.2	16.9	16.1	12.3	10.8
Alabama network	19.6	16.0	20.0	20.5	19.6	20.1
Per cent having high-school-age children						
Pittsburgh	18.7	17.3	17.0	13.5	12.0	10.5
San Francisco	11.7	12.0	14.3	9.1	14.2	10.4
Lincoln	20.8	20.3	26.3	26.0	18.5	21.4
Columbus	11.8	13.8	5.8	14.9	11.6	12.4
Denver	11.8	13.0	11.9	13.9	13.1	9.5
Alabama network	11.8	19.5	17.6	18.1	10.4	15.9

TABLE A1 (*continued*)

Area	Regular Viewers Male	Regular Viewers Female	Occasional Viewers Male	Occasional Viewers Female	Nonviewers Male	Nonviewers Female
Per cent whose children watch ETV						
Pittsburgh	22.1	25.3	15.9	24.7	—	—
San Francisco	27.6	31.5	26.5	20.4	—	—
Lincoln	22.3	25.6	18.4	17.0	—	—
Columbus	29.2	41.4	26.9	31.4	—	—
Denver	42.4	47.2	27.4	33.7	—	—
Alabama network	39.9	41.7	29.1	37.8	—	—
Per cent whose spouse watches ETV						
Pittsburgh	29.1	20.0	26.0	12.3	—	—
San Francisco	61.5	40.7	46.9	27.3	—	—
Lincoln	55.4	40.3	36.1	22.4	—	—
Columbus	64.6	68.9	43.0	47.1	—	—
Denver	50.7	40.4	41.6	22.2	—	—
Alabama network	47.0	23.4	35.8	18.1	—	—
Per cent where no one else in household watches ETV						
Pittsburgh	36.0	31.3	41.9	49.9	—	—
San Francisco	19.7	29.0	30.6	47.7	—	—
Lincoln	21.5	25.6	31.9	42.4	—	—
Columbus	17.6	10.3	32.6	26.4	—	—
Denver	15.3	25.0	32.4	42.4	—	—
Alabama network	22.2	29.0	36.8	41.3	—	—
Median number of books read "since last summer"						
Pittsburgh	2.3	3.8	2.5	.6	.4	0
San Francisco	5.6	9+	3.6	4.5	2.0	2.3
Lincoln	5.7	4.4	2.5	2.6	1.7	1.3
Columbus	5.0	9+	3.1	4.7	2.1	2.0
Denver	2.9	3.9	2.3	2.7	.4	.4
Alabama network	5.1	3.8	1.7	1.6	0	0
Median number of magazines "read regularly"						
Pittsburgh	2.3	2.7	2.1	1.8	1.7	1.5
San Francisco	3.3	3.2	2.9	2.6	.6	.9
Lincoln	4.0	3.9	2.9	3.4	2.6	2.6
Columbus	5.0	4.3	3.2	3.8	2.3	2.9
Denver	3.1	3.1	2.8	2.8	1.9	1.6
Alabama network	3.5	3.3	2.3	2.5	1.6	1.5
Per cent who have attended concerts, etc.						
Pittsburgh	9.3	30.0	11.8	12.3	7.4	9.2
San Francisco	27.6	30.9	20.4	20.5	13.5	10.4
Lincoln	28.1	34.5	17.2	22.4	8.9	9.9
Columbus	47.1	27.6	23.2	29.8	8.3	8.8
Denver	20.1	25.0	15.5	19.2	6.2	8.2
Alabama network	17.6	20.2	13.3	12.2	7.7	10.5

TABLE A1 (*concluded*)

Area	Regular Viewers Male	Regular Viewers Female	Occasional Viewers Male	Occasional Viewers Female	Nonviewers Male	Nonviewers Female
Per cent who have attended lectures						
Pittsburgh	12.8	19.3	17.3	11.9	9.7	4.8
San Francisco	33.8	32.8	22.5	18.2	15.5	12.3
Lincoln	41.3	26.9	18.4	16.3	13.1	8.8
Columbus	47.1	24.1	17.4	24.8	7.0	15.3
Denver	22.9	19.9	14.9	10.2	2.3	7.4
Alabama network	34.0	25.7	20.9	13.3	8.3	9.3
Per cent who have attended discussion group or evening course						
Pittsburgh	11.6	24.7	13.4	11.3	12.0	7.6
San Francisco	28.5	30.9	16.4	27.3	10.8	9.9
Lincoln	28.1	29.4	18.4	17.5	11.5	8.0
Columbus	17.6	27.6	18.6	15.7	13.9	13.1
Denver	22.2	20.2	13.8	13.0	10.8	9.5
Alabama network	30.1	26.4	20.6	16.9	11.7	9.4
Per cent who have attended civic meetings						
Pittsburgh	32.6	36.0	32.6	28.6	25.7	21.0
San Francisco	34.2	39.7	22.5	15.9	24.3	18.9
Lincoln	39.7	43.7	28.0	28.8	21.5	18.7
Columbus	47.1	55.3	32.5	46.3	31.4	32.8
Denver	27.8	21.6	17.4	17.0	9.2	10.0
Alabama network	56.2	49.8	40.2	41.8	33.8	32.2
Per cent of husbands having white-collar jobs						
Pittsburgh	15.1	11.1	21.4	16.4	16.6	9.2
San Francisco	43.8	34.7	32.6	18.2	18.3	12.7
Lincoln	61.1	40.8	42.9	33.1	37.5	26.0
Columbus	11.8	34.5	25.6	23.9	27.9	22.7
Denver	—	—	—	—	—	—
Alabama network	33.0	25.7	19.9	19.2	12.8	10.6

TABLE A2.—RELATIVE PROPORTION OF DIFFERENT AGE GROUPS WHO ARE REGULAR VIEWERS OF ETV

(*Per cent; N in parentheses; based on age 20–29 as 100 per cent*)

Area	Age 20–29	Age 30–39	Age 40–49	Age 50–59	Age 60+
Pittsburgh	100 (*249*)	141 (*355*)	133 (*407*)	118 (*299*)	154 (*279*)
San Francisco	100 (*136*)	110 (*230*)	101 (*259*)	85 (*178*)	90 (*155*)
Lincoln	100 (*340*)	147 (*357*)	149 (*336*)	131 (*237*)	175 (*270*)
Columbus	100 (*108*)	92 (*141*)	117 (*125*)	85 (*71*)	116 (*83*)
Denver	100 (*346*)	151 (*498*)	161 (*377*)	146 (*257*)	161 (*281*)
Alabama network	100 (*383*)	115 (*688*)	112 (*723*)	126 (*531*)	109 (*542*)

TABLE A3.—USE OF FIVE TYPES OF ETV PROGRAMS IN FOUR AREAS

Total ETV Time Claimed	San Francisco		Lincoln	Denver		Alabama Network
	Men	Women		Men	Women	
Formal educational programs (courses)						
None	57%	69%	—	70%	64%	27%
50% or more......	9	2	—	12	16	44
Practical aid programs						
None	14	65	44%	86	68	59
50% or more......	4	1	25	9	19	8
Cultural programs (art, music, drama)						
None	42	30	30	62	70	55
50% or more......	15	22	35	8	6	14
Information, public affairs programs						
None	29	40	35	34	62	71
50% or more......	50	36	21	52	29	5
Children's programs (all types)						
None	81	79	100	88	83	78
50% or more......	4	6	—	6	6	9

TABLE A4.—COMPARISON OF TYPES OF AUDIENCE THAT DIFFERENT ETV PROGRAMS ATTRACT IN SAN FRANCISCO

Audience	Audience Interested in: Instruction ($N = 20$)*	Culture ($N = 37$)	Information ($N = 85$)
Comparative index of ETV time	107	110	100
Rationale for viewing ETV:			
Practical aid	40%	0%	21%
Keep better informed	45	62	64
Continue education	45	27	28
More satisfying than CTV	55	51	52
Cultural programs	70	67	66
Something one should do	15	8	8
Example for children	15	—	9
Intellectual stimulation	75	67	64
Fills cultural void	40	32	31
Age:			
Under 40	36	46	40
40–49	21	22	32
50 and over	37	27	27
Have no children	47	41	38
Highest educational level:			
High school only	26	27	29
Some college	42	49	39
B.A. degree	10	11	18
Graduate work	21	14	11
"Quite" or "very" interested in:			
Practical information	65	32	44
The arts	55	67	51
Public issues	75	76	88
Serious music	60	65	59
General knowledge	80	67	66
Attend:			
Concerts or plays	53	38	35
Lectures	63	32	36
Discussion groups or courses	42	27	28
Civic affairs meetings	32	60	39

* In some rows, $N = 19$.

TABLE A5.—VIEWERS AND NONVIEWERS OF ETV IN SAN FRANCISCO CITING DIFFERENT MEDIA AS BEING OF REAL HELP

Sex and Number	Intensely, or Very, Interested	Paper	Magazines	Radio	CTV	ETV	Other
Practical information							
Male viewers (32).........	37%	33%	66%	17%	9%	33%	6%
Female viewers (46).......	50	59	67	6	22	30	9
Male nonviewers (13)......	37	46	69	15	15	8	—
Female nonviewers (26)....	33	50	46	12	19	12	—
Art, literature, poetry							
Male viewers (29).........	34	10	38	17	17	69	21
Female viewers (55).......	60	16	54	6	6	47	33
Public issues							
Male viewers (75).........	86	50	34	22	61	35	1
Female viewers (78).......	85	83	35	20	53	39	1
Male nonviewers (27)......	77	74	19	15	22	—	—
Female nonviewers (27)....	82	67	4	15	52	—	4
Serious music							
Male viewers (37).........	43	5	5	68	27	43	24
Female viewers (55)	60	4	6	66	24	40	27
General knowledge							
Male viewers (54).........	63	37	52	15	24	48	22
Female viewers (54).......	59	48	52	13	33	43	24
Male nonviewers (16)......	46	25	38	19	19	—	6
Female nonviewers (14)....	42	43	36	—	36	15	15

TABLE A6.—VIEWERS AND NONVIEWERS OF ETV IN LINCOLN CITING DIFFERENT MEDIA AS BEING OF REAL HELP

Number	Intensely, or Very, Interested	Paper	Magazines	Radio	CTV	ETV	Other
Practical information							
Viewers (111)	51%	34%	47%	9%	15%	18%	2%
Nonviewers (31)	35	45	48	2	39	3	—
Art, literature, poetry							
Viewers (78)	36	5	44	3	6	38	31
Nonviewers (20)	21	5	50	5	15	—	45
Public issues							
Viewers (187)	86	59	18	19	61	10	1
Nonviewers (67)	76	57	15	13	63	1	—
Serious music							
Viewers (101)	46	—	1	44	25	39	29
Nonviewers (19)	22	—	—	63	16	10	37
General knowledge							
Viewers (90)	41	33	34	3	30	33	20
Nonviewers (16)	18	44	31	—	19	—	19

TABLE A7.—REGULAR AND OCCASIONAL VIEWERS AND NONVIEWERS OF ETV IN COLUMBUS CITING DIFFERENT MEDIA AS BEING OF REAL HELP

Number	Intensely, or Very, Interested	Paper	Magazines	Radio	CTV	ETV	Other
Practical information							
Reg. viewers (20)	50%	40%	65%	15%	5%	30%	—
Occ. viewers (64)	44	41	53	11	23	16	6%
Art, literature, poetry							
Reg. viewers (12)	30	8	58	17	8	33	17
Occ. viewers (43)	23	19	51	7	7	30	21
Public issues							
Reg. viewers (39)	98	67	31	13	59	18	—
Occ. viewers (125)	86	66	23	22	56	10	1
Nonviewers (18)	75	39	17	11	78	—	—
Serious music							
Reg. viewers (14)	35	—	—	50	14	43	7
Occ. viewers (55)	38	2	—	64	34	33	18
General knowledge							
Reg. viewers (22)	55	23	32	18	23	41	18
Occ. viewers (66)	46	48	39	12	41	21	17

TABLE A8.—REASONS GIVEN FOR WATCHING A STATION: FIVE MAJOR RESPONSE CATEGORIES*

Area	Educational Value	Specific Programs	Relief from CTV	Entertainment	Meets Personal Interest
Alabama network					
Men	37%	17%	13%	14%	11%
Women	30	14	16	12	4
Lincoln	19	18	18	22	10
Denver					
Men	32	32	20	8	16
Women	42	19	8	19	19

* The question was: "What would you say are the main reasons you watch Station YYYY?"

TABLE A9.—PROPORTION OF VIEWERS IN HIGH AND LOW SOCIOECONOMIC STATUS GROUPS CITING EACH OF THE NINE RATIONALES FOR VIEWING ETV

Rationale	Columbus SES		Pittsburgh SES		San Francisco SES		Denver SES	
	Low	High	Low	High	Low	High	Low	High
Practical aid	20%	9%	27%	15%	24%	24%	12%	39%
To be informed	70	65	46	80	42	61	33	51
Continue education	30	26	27	30	24	20	25	26
More satisfying	40	35	41	25	24	52	33	26
Cultural programs	50	68	36	70	40	78	25	67
Should do	20	3	5	20	12	6	42	13
Example for children	20	6	41	15	10	13	42	20
Intellectual stimulation	70	50	27	63	36	65	42	75
Fills cultural void	10	21	14	20	32	26	50	28

TABLE A10.—CORRELATION MATRIX FOR THE NINE RATIONALES

Values in the matrix are phi coefficients based on a number of 1,247

	1	2	3	4	5	6	7	8	9
1. Practical aid	—	.10	.22	.07	.07	.21	.16	.09	.04
2. To keep better informed	.10	—	.27	.16	.28	.16	.12	.23	.19
3. To continue my education	.22	.27	—	.10	.17	.15	.15	.20	.26
4. More satisfying than CTV	.07	.16	.10	—	.28	.09	.15	.33	.30
5. Cultural programs	.07	.28	.17	.28	—	.05	.13	.37	.25
6. Something I should do.	.21	.16	.15	.09	.05	—	.17	.14	.17
7. Example for children. .	.16	.12	.15	.15	.13	.17	—	.09	.18
8. Intellectual stimulation.	.09	.23	.20	.33	.37	.14	.09	—	.31
9. Fills cultural void.	.04	.19	.26	.30	.25	.17	.18	.31	—

TABLE A11.—PER CENT CITING INDIVIDUAL RATIONALES AS BEING ESPECIALLY WELL FULFILLED BY THEIR LOCAL ETV STATION

Area	Practical Aid	To Be Better Informed	Help Continue Education	More Satisfying Than CTV	Providing Cultural Programs	Example for Children	Intellectual Stimulation	Filling Cultural Void	None
Pittsburgh									
Men	10%	25%	28%	15%	38%	12%	15%	10%	23%
Women	13	34	30	11	45	23	32	26	21
San Francisco									
Men	9	22	13	10	37	9	36	14	16
Women	20	28	32	18	41	13	44	23	11
Lincoln	9	18	21	8	40	9	23	17	16
Columbus	18	25	32	15	50	5	38	15	14
Denver									
Men	43	35	24	13	—	20	33	18	11
Women	34	20	10	8	—	20	25	17	11
Alabama network									
Men	17	27	31	10	28	17	12	4	12
Women	23	36	25	9	39	20	23	16	5

TABLE A12.—PROPORTION OF ETV VIEWERS AND NONVIEWERS CHECKING "QUITE" OR "VERY" FOR EACH TERM IN DESCRIBING COMMERCIAL TELEVISION

Term	Pittsburgh		San Francisco		Lin-coln	Colum-bus	Denver		Alabama Network	
	Men	Women	Men	Women			Men	Women	Men	Women
Informative										
Viewers	35%	42%	23%	27%	52%	38%	39%	27%	39%	46%
Nonviewers	41	32	28	58	70	47	48	47	47	46
Useful										
Viewers	35	30	19	20	39	35	24	20	27	48
Nonviewers	31	36	44	45	59	42	45	42	53	44
Interesting										
Viewers	32	42	35	39	50	40	54	36	39	52
Nonviewers	50	51	63	67	74	42	56	72	63	60
Satisfying										
Viewers	35	40	24	23	42	35	32	25	34	36
Nonviewers	34	55	42	61	65	33	64	50	47	52
Fun										
Viewers	38	47	34	32	51	42	25	45	39	58
Nonviewers	34	42	66	64	63	38	72	60	58	52
Hard work										
Viewers	15	15	8	7	11	10	8	12	20	21
Nonviewers	28	32	17	12	8	12	4	12	26	26
Dull										
Viewers	12	11	28	20	13	10	13	10	5	9
Nonviewers	6	6	6	15	4	12	3	—	5	8
Boring										
Viewers	15	23	27	24	15	12	20	12	8	10
Nonviewers	12	11	14	12	2	21	8	7	11	6
Violent										
Viewers	45	40	71	60	57	52	52	47	49	48
Nonviewers	41	28	43	24	56	33	36	29	42	42
Annoying										
Viewers	8	23	38	33	19	25	20	14	3	13
Nonviewers	22	13	32	15	7	17	11	3	10	4
Brutal										
Viewers	35	43	57	56	47	45	47	40	34	42
Nonviewers	31	19	46	33	41	29	27	15	21	36

TABLE A13.—PROPORTION OF ETV VIEWERS AND NONVIEWERS CHECKING "QUITE" OR "VERY" FOR EACH OF THE DESCRIPTIVE TERMS IN DESCRIBING THE LOCAL ETV STATION

Term Checked	Pittsburgh		San Francisco		Lin-coln	Colum-bus	Denver		Alabama Network	
	Men	Women	Men	Women			Men	Women	Men	Women
Informative										
Viewers	75%	81%	84%	93%	93%	95%	95%	95%	90%	85%
Nonviewers	50	51	40	55	58	67	73	74	74	74
Useful										
Viewers	78	74	73	85	85	90	82	88	87	85
Nonviewers	53	55	40	52	49	71	63	72	74	70
Interesting										
Viewers	78	70	78	89	80	80	93	82	62	76
Nonviewers	47	53	32	39	23	63	43	74	—	—
Satisfying										
Viewers	58	70	79	87	78	80	88	84	46	61
Nonviewers	34	45	23	36	31	54	48	53	32	48
Fun										
Viewers	38	28	45	41	32	28	57	47	29	33
Nonviewers	19	21	—	21	49	25	23	28	5	16
Hard work										
Viewers	30	28	13	13	22	20	25	13	40	49
Nonviewers	31	21	26	12	18	13	22	26	53	36
Amateur										
Viewers	10	2	5	3	8	5	10	12	14	13
Nonviewers	—	4	6	—	8	4	8	14	21	18
Dull										
Viewers	—	—	1	2	5	—	4	3	9	8
Nonviewers	—	—	6	6	3	—	1	8	11	8
Snobbish										
Viewers	2	—	2	2	3	—	6	—	5	5
Nonviewers	—	2	6	3	5	—	1	3	11	4
Boring										
Viewers	—	—	1	1	2	—	6	—	3	3
Nonviewers	—	2	9	3	5	—	1	8	5	6
Violent										
Viewers	—	—	—	1	3	—	12	—	1	6
Nonviewers	—	—	3	—	1	—	0	3	5	2
Annoying										
Viewers	—	2	—	1	2	5	—	1	1	8
Nonviewers	—	4	6	—	6	—	1	9	11	0
Brutal										
Viewers	—	—	—	1	2	—	5	—	3	5
Nonviewers	—	—	—	—	1	—	1	3	5	2

TABLE A14.—EDUCATIONAL LEVEL SPECIFIED AS NEEDED TO ENJOY PROGRAMS ON ETV CHANNEL

Area	Some College	High School	Elementary Only	Doesn't Matter	Don't Know
Pittsburgh					
Men	5%	42%	12%	30%	11%
Women	4	24	15	34	23
San Francisco					
Men	6	54	9	21	10
Women	4	51	9	20	16
Lincoln	15	53	13	13	6
Columbus	25	57	5	5	8
Alabama network					
Men	5	32	19	31	13
Women	6	40	14	32	8

TABLE A15.—SOCIOECONOMIC STATUS LEVEL SPECIFIED AS TARGET AUDIENCE OF ETV CHANNEL

Area	Upper Class	Upper and Middle Classes	Middle Class	Middle and Lower Classes	Lower Class	Every-body	Don't Know
Pittsburgh							
Men	5%	12%	12%	2%	5%	45%	19%
Women	2	9	23	0	9	38	19
San Francisco							
Men	5	21	35	1	0	16	22
Women	6	21	22	1	0	35	15
Lincoln	8	22	21	2	2	35	10
Columbus	12	45	10	0	0	25	8
Alabama network							
Men	0	17	33	4	1	37	8
Women	4	13	26	3	1	45	8

TABLE A16.—RATING OF LEVEL OF ETV PROGRAMS BY VIEWERS

	Pittsburgh		San Francisco				Alabama Network	
Rate ETV as	Men	Women	Men	Women	Lincoln	Columbus	Men	Women
Too hard	12%	6%	2%	2%	8%	5%	19%	12%
About right	75	68	79	85	88	82	72	77
Too easy	5	4	2	1	1	2	1	1

TABLE A17.—MOST FREQUENTLY SUGGESTED CHANGES TO BE MADE IN LOCAL ETV STATION OPERATION

Area	Add Certain Programs	Add Certain Courses	Make Easier, Less Stuffy	Schedule Changes	No Change
San Francisco					
Men	9%	6%	9%	3%	48%
Women	20	4	10	2	39
Lincoln	32	2	8	5	42
Denver					
Men	24	12	4	—	44
Women	19	4	8	15	44
Alabama network					
Men	16	7	16	7	35
Women	16	4	7	5	53

TABLE A18.—COMPARATIVE PER CENTS OF VIEWERS AND NONVIEWERS OF ETV CITING SPECIFIED COMPLAINTS ABOUT COMMERCIAL TELEVISION

Area	Reduce Commercials	Reduce Violence	Improve Quality	More Information Shows
Pittsburgh				
Men viewers	53%	48%	52%	35%
Men nonviewers	31	13	28	22
Women viewers	40	36	45	23
Women nonviewers	51	28	19	13
San Francisco				
Men viewers	38	14	23	5
Men nonviewers	23	17	28	0
Women viewers	32	26	14	14
Women nonviewers	24	12	12	0
Lincoln				
Viewers	36	29	23	10
Nonviewers	32	20	32	5
Columbus				
Viewers	53	18	22	25
Nonviewers	58	21	8	4
Denver				
Men viewers	35	58	23	35
Men nonviewers	21	21	11	11
Women viewers	29	71	32	68
Women nonviewers	27	55	0	55
Alabama network				
Men viewers	36	47	54	22
Men nonviewers	41	23	36	19
Women viewers	38	50	55	14
Women nonviewers	33	49	49	12

APPENDIX D

Tables from the Boston Study

TABLE A19.—TOTAL FAMILY INCOME

Family Income	Total Number Interviewed (9,140)	Confirmed Viewers (1,810)	Nonviewers (4,149)	Marginal Cases (2,707)	No TV in Household (474)
Under $5,000	27%	21%	31%	22%	35%
$5,000–$7,000	24	25	23	27	18
$7,000–$10,000	11	17	7	13	7
Over $10,000	8	13	4	9	7
Refusal, don't know, no answer	30	24	35	29	33

TABLE A20.—EDUCATION

Education	Total Number (9,140)	Con-Viewers (1,810)	Nonviewers (4,149)	Marginal Cases (2,707)	No TV in Household (474)
Grade school					
Incomplete	3%	1%	4%	2%	2%
Complete	6	3	9	4	5
High school					
Incomplete	11	6	15	10	5
Complete	31	26	33	33	11
Vocational or commercial school					
Incomplete	3	3	3	3	1
Complete	10	13	9	11	6
College					
Incomplete	7	9	5	7	14
Complete	12	22	7	14	19
Postgraduate	5	9	2	4	18
No answer	12	8	13	12	20

TABLE A21.—PER CENT OF CONFIRMED VIEWERS AT DIFFERENT EDUCATIONAL AND FAMILY INCOME LEVELS
(*Per cent; N in parentheses*)

Family Income	Grade School	High School	Vocational School	College	Post-graduate
Under $5,000	9% (*404*)	12% (*1,241*)	24% (*341*)	24% (*290*)	33% (*87*)
$5,000–$7,000	11 (*114*)	16 (*1,111*)	21 (*376*)	32 (*453*)	28 (*106*)
$7,000–$10,000	22 (*23*)	19 (*308*)	31 (*181*)	36 (*363*)	51 (*94*)
Over $10,000	18 (*11*)	26 (*121*)	32 (*72*)	37 (*344*)	39 (*123*)

TABLE A22.—LOCALITY

Urbanization	Total (9,140)	Confirmed Viewers (1,810)	Non-viewers (4,149)	Marginal Cases (2,707)	No TV in House-hold (474)
Highly urbanized	41%	35%	43%	37%	68%
All other towns........	59	65	57	63	32

Table A23.—Spare Time Activities Participated in by Respondent

Activities	Total (9,140)	Confirmed Viewers (1,810)	Non-Viewers (4,149)	Marginal Cases (2,707)	No TV in Household (474)
Attend a sporting event?					
No	58%	55%	62%	53%	57%
Yes	39	43	35	43	35
Within last week	10	12	10	11	7
No answer	3	2	3	4	8
Go to a lecture?					
No	74	65	83	72	45
Yes	22	33	13	23	47
Within last week	5	7	3	5	19
No answer	4	2	4	5	8
Take an evening course?					
No	84	80	88	82	74
Yes	12	17	8	13	17
Within last week	5	8	4	6	8
No answer	4	3	4	5	9
Go to the movies?					
No	46	44	48	46	32
Yes	50	54	48	49	61
Within last week	10	10	9	8	18
No answer	4	2	4	5	7
Go to the theater?					
No	63	54	72	61	40
Yes	32	42	24	34	52
Within last week	2	4	1	2	6
No answer	5	4	4	5	8
Take part in a discussion group?					
No	80	77	85	78	71
Yes	14	18	10	16	18
Within last week	5	6	3	5	10
No answer	6	5	5	6	11

Table A24.—Reasons Given by Nonviewers for Not Viewing WGBH

Reason	Per Cent
Cannot receive it*	21
Poor reception*	25
No interest	19
No time	4
For children	4
Unaware of existence of WGBH	0
No interest in TV	2
No reason given	19

* Poor reception and even nonreception should not be taken at face value. Appropriate orientation of the antenna is generally what is needed. Where the motivation exists, this is apt to be done.

INDEXES

Receptivity to information on television

Questions:

Now let's talk . . . about reasons for watching television. Here is a list of possible reasons. . . . How often does each of these reason apply to you?

Are there people with whom you discuss TV? What did you talk about?

Apart from the news, can you tell me anything in particular that you have learned from a TV program?

In general, do you feel you learn things from watching TV, or not?

Results (coefficient of reproducibility, .90):

Scale Score	Viewers	Nonviewers	Matched Nonviewers
0	5%	10%	10%
1	8	16	20
2	22	29	25
3	13	19	20
4	27	13	11
5	16	10	12
6	9	3	3

Receptivity to information: interest in news

Questions:

Did you talk to anyone in the last 24 hours . . . about something in the news?

What [radio] programs do you usually listen to?

Which of these [radio] stations do you listen to most often?

Which newspapers do you usually read on Sundays?

About how much time do you spend reading the newspapers?

What would you say you like most about the newspapers?

Results (coefficient of reproducibility, .88):

Scale Score	Viewers	Nonviewers	Matched Nonviewers
0	1%	8%	8%
1	14	24	15
2	27	33	31
3	31	26	26
4	23	9	18
5	4	1	1
6	0	0	0

Receptivity to information: performance on quiz

Question:

Identify: Fidel Castro, Ralph Bunche, Mao Tse-tung, Robert Frost, Nigeria, J. Robert Oppenheimer.

Results (coefficient of reproducibility, .92):

Scale Score	Viewers	Nonviewers	Matched Nonviewers
0	5%	12%	13%
1	15	42	31
2	14	20	15
3	17	15	14
4	15	4	10
5	14	3	6
6	19	4	12

Receptivity to information in classes and discussions

Questions:

Have you ever taken classes since you finished with school, like evening classes . . . ?

Have you ever belonged to a discussion group?

What do you like most about the meetings you attend?

Do you read about your hobbies in magazines, newspapers, or books?

Results (coefficient of reproducibility, .90):

Scale Score	Viewers	Nonviewers	Matched Nonviewers
0	13%	29%	27%
1	23	40	34
2	41	23	27
3	19	7	9
4	4	0	3

Receptivity to information: composite scale of four scales

Results (coefficient of reproducibility, .91):

Scale Score	Viewers	Nonviewers	Matched Nonviewers
0	21%	58%	46%
1	29	30	31
2	32	12	16
3	16	0	6
4	2	0	1

Cultural level in music

Questions:

Do you play a musical instrument?
What instrument?
What kind of music do you play most?
Do you have a record collection?
What kinds of records do you usually listen to?

Results (coefficient of reproducibility, .95):

Scale Score	Viewers	Nonviewers	Matched Nonviewers
0	32%	43%	42%
1	13	18	15
2	13	12	19
3	26	17	17
4	3	4	2
5	4	4	5
6	11	1	1

Cultural level of activities

Questions:

Which of the following activities do you take part in: attend a sporting event, go to a lecture, take an evening course, go to the movies, go to the theater, take part in a discussion group?

Results (coefficient of reproducibility, .91):

Scale Score	Viewers	Nonviewers	Matched Nonviewers
0	8%	7%	7%
1	43	46	44
2	31	36	33
3	14	10	14
4	4	1	3
5	—	0	0
6	0	0	0

Cultural level of reading and discussion

Questions:

Do you happen to have read any books in the past month?
What were they?
What is your favorite magazine?
Do you read about your hobbies in magazines, newspapers, or books?
[If you ever belonged to a discussion group] what was the subject?
[If you ever took adult education class] what was the subject?

Results (coefficient of reproducibility, .93):

Scale Score	Viewers	Nonviewers	Matched Nonviewers
0	24%	57%	51%
1	17	15	14
2	22	17	22
3	21	7	10
4	9	4	2
5	5	0	2
6	1	0	0

Cultural level of radio listening

Questions:

Do you have an FM radio?
Which . . . station do you listen to most often?
What [radio] programs do you usually listen to?

Results (coefficient of reproducibility, .93):

Scale Score	Viewers	Nonviewers	Matched Nonviewers
0	39%	66%	60%
1	37	28	25
2	17	6	10
3	7	0	5

Cultural level of favorite TV programs

Question:

What are your favorite programs on television?

Results (coefficient of reproducibility, .95):

Scale Score	Viewers	Nonviewers	Matched Nonviewers
0	6%	16%	14%
1	51	69	61
2	31	12	15
3	11	2	8
4	1	1	1
5	—	0	1

Cultural level: attitude toward TV

Questions:

Are TV programs "pretty good" or "not very good"?

Here is a list of possible reasons [for watching TV]. . . . When you watch TV, how often does each of these reasons apply to you?

Apart from the news, can you tell me anything in particular that you have learned from a TV program?

Results (coefficient of reproducibility, .90):

Scale Score	Viewers	Nonviewers	Matched Nonviewers
0	12%	20%	21%
1	34	48	45
2	39	26	27
3	15	6	6

Cultural level: composite scale of six scales

Results (coefficient of reproducibility, .87):

Scale Score	Viewers	Nonviewers	Matched Nonviewers
0	10%	20%	24%
1	22	42	33
2	20	25	22
3	20	11	12
4	14	1	3
5	11	1	6
6	3	0	1

Liberalism

Questions:

Which [do] you feel is most important: keeping taxes down, improving our schools, strengthening the free world by aiding our allies?

If you were in charge of a radio station and someone gave a speech on it attacking America, would you cut him off the air, or would you let him say whatever he thought?

How would you rate yourself in politics: liberal or conservative?

Results (coefficient of reproducibility, .88):

Scale Score	Viewers	Nonviewers	Matched Nonviewers
0	9%	15%	10%
1	25	34	27
2	37	33	43
3	29	18	20

Politization

Questions:

How often do you discuss political issues?
Have you contributed money to a party or candidate in the past four years?
Have you ever been active in politics?
When was that?
Have you written to a Congressman or other public official . . . during the past year?
What are your favorite programs on television?

Results (coefficient of reproducibility, .93):

Scale Score	Viewers	Nonviewers	Matched Nonviewers
0	30%	52%	50%
1	35	35	32
2	21	9	8
3	7	3	7
4	4	1	3
5	1	0	0
6	1	0	0

Cosmopolitanism

Questions:

About how many trips, overnight or longer, do you take in a year?
Have you ever been outside of the United States?
How often do you think about living abroad for a while?
Do you like foreign movies?

Results (coefficient of reproducibility, .91):

Scale Score	Viewers	Nonviewers	Matched Nonviewers
0	9%	16%	16%
1	30	42	38
2	30	29	25
3	25	11	18
4	6	1	3

Bibliography

Carter, Roy E., Jr. "Summary of Educational Television Inquiry in Minneapolis–St. Paul" (mimeo.). Minneapolis: University of Minnesota, 1961.

Carter, Roy E., Jr., and Verling C. Troldahl. "The Size and Composition of the Adult Evening Audience for Educational Television in the Twin Cities," Report No. 3, Studies of the Adult Evening Audience for Educational Television in the Twin Cities (mimeo.). Minneapolis: Communication Research Division, School of Journalism, University of Minnesota, April 1961.

———. "Some Responses of Evening Viewers to Educational Television in the Twin Cities," Report No. 4, Studies of the Adult Evening Audience for Educational Television in the Twin Cities (mimeo.). Minneapolis: Communication Research Division, School of Journalism, University of Minnesota, May 1961.

Educational Television: The Next Ten Years. Stanford, Calif.: Institute for Communication Research, Stanford University, 1962.

Geiger, K., and R. Sokol. "Social Norms in Television Watching," *American Journal of Sociology,* LXV, 1959.

Himmelweit, Hilde, A. N. Oppenheim, and P. Vince. *Television and the Child.* London: Oxford University Press, 1958.

McClelland, David. *The Achievement Motive.* New York: Appleton-Century-Crofts, 1953.

Maccoby, Eleanor. "Why Do Children Watch Television?" *Public Opinion Quarterly,* XVIII, 1954.

O'Dea, Thomas F. *American Catholic Dilemma: An Inquiry into the Intellectual Life.* New York: Sheed and Ward, Inc., 1958.

"One Week of Educational Television, May 21–27, 1961; A Study of Structure and Content in Educational Television and Programming" (monograph). Waltham, Mass.: Communications Research Center, Brandeis University, 1961.

Parker, Edwin B. "The Audience for Educational Television in Champaign-Urbana" (mimeo.). 1961.

Pool, Ithiel de Sola, and Barbara Adler. "Educational Television: Is Anybody Watching?" *Journal of Social Issues,* XVIII, 1962, No. 2.

Powell, John W. *Channels of Learning.* Washington, D.C.: Public Affairs Press, 1962.

Schneider, L., and S. Lysgaard. "The Deferred Gratification Pattern," *American Sociological Review,* XVIII, 1953.

Schramm, Wilbur (ed.). *The Impact of Educational Television.* Urbana, Ill.: University of Illinois Press, 1960.

Schramm, Wilbur, Jack Lyle, and Edwin B. Parker. *Television in the Lives of Our Children.* Stanford, Calif.: Stanford University Press, 1961.

Steiner, Gary A. *The People Look at Television: A Study of Attitudes.* New York: Alfred A. Knopf, 1963.

Index

Adams, Arthur, 5
Adler, Barbara, 54
Adult courses, audience for, 107–8
Age and ETV viewing, 60
"Age of Kings," 93
Air time of ETV stations, 36–39
Airborne television, 10, 173
American Association of School Administrators, 6
American Council on Education, 6
"Animals of the Seashore," 93, 94
Arness, Jim, 72, 73
Asch, Nathan, 16
"Ask the Candidate," 96, 97
Audience of ETV: building of, 109, 152–63; compared with nonviewers, 72–75, 142–50, 169–71; composition of, 59–89, 100–109, 122–29, 132, 141–42, 165–66, 182–85, 187, 194, 196–98; deviant patterns of composition, 63–64, 84–88, 106–7; education of, 60–65, 140–41, 182–85, 194, 196; favorite programs of, 92–100; motivations for viewing ETV, 65, 70–75, 110–33, 190–91; satisfaction with ETV, 134–41, 168–71; size of, 47–58, 91–95; socioeconomic status of, 60–65, 132, 141–42, 194; time spent viewing ETV, 36, 51–54. *See also* Educational television

"Backyard Farmer," 93, 94, 100
"Band Concert," 94
Bardot, Brigitte, 72, 73
Berelson, Bernard, 112
Bessie, Alvah, 16
Bevis, Howard, 5
Blue-collar viewers, 63–64, 84–88
"Boston Symphony," 96, 97, 162
Building ETV audience. *See* Audience of ETV, building of
Bunche, Ralph, 72

"Capstone Concert," 93, 94
Carter, Roy E., Jr., 36, 49
"Casals Master Class," 93, 94, 102, 172
Castro, Fidel, 72
Channels, allocation of, to ETV, 6
"Children's Corner," 94
"Civil War," 93, 94
Clark, Walter Van Tilburg, 15
Closed-circuit ETV, 10
Commercial TV: related to ETV viewing, 46, 65; opinions of, compared with ETV, 147–49; Tables, 192, 193, 195
Commercials, 72
Community ETV stations and broadcasts, 8ff., 40
Composition of ETV audience. *See* Audience of ETV, composition of
"Concert Hall," 94
"Conference on World Tensions," 94
"Continental Classroom," 2
Cost of ETV, 6–11
Council of Chief State School Officers, 6
Curtis, Tony, 72, 73

Debates, Kennedy-Nixon, 2
"Decision," 94
Delayed gratification, 65
Dunham, Franklin, 5

Educational television: characteristics of, 142–50; costs of, 7–8, 10–13,

60, 162–63; future of, 171–74; impact of, 164ff.; opinions of, 134–50, 168–71, 188–89, 192–95; origins of, 3ff.; problems and methods of research on, 19–30, 151–52, 180–81; for schools, 10ff., 37, 42, 55; use of, related to use of other media, 66, 68, 70–71, 137–38; viewers and nonviewers compared, 72–75, 142–50, 169–71. *See also* Audience of ETV; Programs on ETV; Stations, ETV
Educational Television: The Next Ten Years, 3, 18
"Elementary Science," 94
"Eliot Norton Reviews," 96, 97
"ETV behavior," characteristics of, 46–47
"Evening Prelude," 94

"Face the People," 94, 104–5, 107
"Facelessness" of television, 150
"Family Challenge," 94
Family viewing of ETV, 78–79
"Famous Features," 94, 104–5, 107
"Farm Facts," 94
Federal Communications Commission, 3–6
Financing ETV, problems of, 60, 162–63
Fletcher, C. Scott, 6
Ford Foundation, 6, 10
Frost, Robert, 72
Fund for Adult Education, 6
Furness, Betty, 72, 73

Geiger, K., 65
Gitlin, Irving, 16
"Grass Roots Voters," 96, 97
"Great Plains Trilogy," 94
"Greeks Had a Word for It," 94, 104, 105, 106, 107, 131, 172
Growth, rate of, of ETV, 9–10, 164–65

Hennock, Frieda, 4
"Heritage," 93, 94
Himmelweit, Hilde, 95, 154
Holder, Geoffrey, 15
"House and Home," 94
Hudson, Robert B., 5
Hull, Richard B., 5

Impact of ETV, 164ff.
"Income Tax Guide," 94
Indexes (Boston study), 199–204
"Inquiring Mind," 94
"Invitation to Art," 94
Iowa State College station, 3

Jansky, C. M., 6
Johns, Augustus, 16
Joint Council on Educational Television, 6
"Julius Caesar," 96, 97, 162

"Kaleidoscope," 94
KQED (San Francisco), 21, 33, and *passim*; auction, 12
KRMA (Denver), 21, 33–34, 52, and *passim*
KTHE (Los Angeles), 8–9
KUHT (Houston), 8
KUON (Lincoln), 21, 34, and *passim*

Lang, Bruce R., 153
Lavallade, Carmen de, 15
"Layman's Guide to Modern Art," 94
"Legally Speaking," 94, 104–5
"Let's Learn More," 94
"Living Arts and Crafts," 94
Lyle, J., 52, 78
Lyons, Louis, 96, 97, 99, 145, 157, 162

Maccoby, E., 67
Magazines, related to ETV use, 70–71, 137–38
"Make Believe Clubhouse," 96, 97
Mannes, Marya, 16
Mao Tse-tung, 72
McClelland, David, 65
Marks, Melvin, 6
Merrill, I. R., 50
Midwest Program on Airborne Television Instruction (MPATI), 10
Minow, Newton N., 15–16
"Moon, Planets, Stars," 93, 94
Motivations for viewing ETV. *See* Audience of ETV, motivations
"Music Box," 94

National Association of Educational Broadcasters, 6
National Education Association, 6
National Educational Television and Radio Center, 9–10, 11, 38–39, 173
Newspapers, related to ETV use, 70, 137–38

Nigeria, 72
"Noncommercial," "nonprofit," and educational TV, 2, 4–5

O'Dea, Thomas F., 68
One Week of Educational Television, 38, 40, 42
"Open End," 16, 92, 94, 102–3, 105, 106, 107, 131–32, 145, 162–63, 165, 172
Opinions of ETV. *See* Educational Television, characteristics of
Oppenheimer, J. Robert, 72
Osgood, Charles, 30

Parker, Edwin B., 36, 50, 52, 78
"Performance," 96, 97
Pool, I. de S., 54, 112
"Pittsburgh Roundtable," 94
"Portrait in Music," 94
Powell, John W., 7
"President's Press Conference," 96, 97
Probst, George, 5
"Profile Bay Area," 93, 94
Programs on ETV: choice of, 79–81, 100–106; favorite, 92–100; ratings, 91–93; time on air, 36–39; type, 13–17, 39–45, 186. *See also individual program names*
Public figures, information on, of viewers and nonviewers, 72–75

Radio, related to ETV use, 70, 137–38
"Ragtime Era," 93, 94, 105, 106, 107, 117, 132, 165, 172
Reading, related to ETV use, 66, 68
"Redman's America," 93, 94
"Religions of Man," 94
Research, design of, for these studies, 21–30
"Robert Herridge Theater," 93, 94
Roosevelt, Eleanor, 15

Samples, 22–23, 180–81
Satisfaction with television, of viewers and nonviewers of ETV, 169–71
Schneider, L., 65
Schools, ETV broadcasts for, 10ff., 37, 42, 55
Schramm, W., 50, 52, 66–67, 78, 83
"Science Reporter," 94, 96, 97
"Scotch Gardener," 94
"Semantic differential," 30, 89
"Shakespeare," 94
Siegel, Seymour, 5
Sokol, R., 66
"Spanish," 94
State network ETV stations, 9ff.
State Universities Association, 6
Stations, ETV, 3, 8–9, 12, 21, 31–45; complete list of, 177–79; earliest, 6–9; growth rate, 9–10, 164–65; "personalities" of, 43; university, school-system, and state-network stations, 3, 8–11, 31–45 *passim. See also individual station names (call letters)*
Steiner, Gary A., 66, 167
Stoddard, George D., 5
"Stones and Bones," 94
Suburban living and ETV viewing, 61, 197
Susskind, David, 16

Tastes, building of, 99–109
Taylor, Telford, 5
Television in the Lives of Our Children, 52, 78, 84
"This Week in Science," 94
"Time to Grow," 94
Tyler, I. Keith, 5

UHF, 6
"UN Review," 94
University ETV stations, 8ff.
"University News," 94

VHF, 6
Viewing time. *See* Audience of ETV, time spent viewing

WAIQ, WBIQ, WCIQ (Alabama), 21, 35, and *passim*
WGBH (Boston), 21, 31–32, and *passim*
WHA (Madison, Wisc.), 3
White, John F., 16
"World of Music," 131
"World Press Review," 94
WOSU (Columbus), 21, 34–35, and *passim*
WQED (Pittsburgh), 21, 32, and *passim*
WTHS (Miami), 9

"Your Unicameral," 94